Repression in the Digital Age

DISRUPTIVE TECHNOLOGY AND INTERNATIONAL SECURITY

Series Editors

BENJAMIN JENSEN

Marine Corps University and Center for Strategic and International Studies

JACQUELYN SCHNEIDER

Hoover Institution, Stanford University

BRANDON VALERIANO

Marine Corps University

OTHER BOOK IN THE SERIES

**Leveraging Latency: How the Weak Compel the Strong with
Nuclear Technology**
Tristan A. Volpe

Repression in the Digital Age

Surveillance, Censorship, and the Dynamics of State Violence

ANITA R. GOHDES

OXFORD
UNIVERSITY PRESS

Oxford University Press is a department of the University of Oxford.
It furthers the University's objective of excellence in research, scholarship,
and education by publishing worldwide. Oxford is a registered trade mark of
Oxford University Press in the UK and in certain other countries.

Published in the United States of America by Oxford University Press
198 Madison Avenue, New York, NY 10016, United States of America.

© Oxford University Press 2024

All rights reserved. No part of this publication may be reproduced, stored in a retrieval system,
or transmitted, in any form or by any means, without the prior permission in writing of Oxford
University Press, or as expressly permitted by law, by license or under terms agreed with the
appropriate reprographics rights organization. Inquiries concerning reproduction outside the scope
of the above should be sent to the Rights Department, Oxford University Press, at the address above.

You must not circulate this work in any other form and you must impose this same condition on any acquirer

CIP data is on file at the Library of Congress.

ISBN 978–0–19–774357–7 (hbk.)
ISBN 978–0–19–777261–4 (pbk.)

DOI: 10.1093/oso/9780197743577.001.0001
DOI: 10.1093/oso/9780197772614.001.0001

Contents

Acknowledgments	vii
List of Figures	ix
List of Tables	xi

1. Introduction	1
1.1 Argument	5
1.2 Evidence	9
1.3 Plan of the book	15
2. What are online controls, and how do they work?	18
2.1 Connecting to the Internet	18
2.2 Censorship	20
2.3 Monitoring content and people	34
3. Theory	40
3.1 The role of information in repression	41
3.2 The logic of online surveillance	46
3.3 The logic of online censorship	51
4. Online controls and repression in Syria	60
4.1 Information control for regime stability	60
4.2 Digital politics pre-conflict	62
4.3 2011 uprising and repression	64
4.4 Digital politics following the uprising	67
4.5 Studying repression in Syria: data and measurement	70
5. Nationwide shutdowns and government offensives	78
5.1 Understanding full shutdowns	81
5.2 Internet shutdowns and documented violence	87
5.3 Underreporting during shutdowns	94
6. Internet accessibility and targeted violence	98
6.1 When is online surveillance useful?	98
6.2 Regional Internet accessibility in Syria	100
6.3 Measuring the regime's violent strategy	102
6.4 Subnational evidence	105
7. Online controls and the protest-repression nexus in Iran	113
7.1 Elections and protest in 2009	114

vi CONTENTS

7.2 Ramping up online controls after 2009   115
7.3 Protests and Internet shutdown, November 2019   120

8. Global evidence   130
    8.1 How to measure Internet outages   131
    8.2 Internet outages and political institutions   134
    8.3 Internet outages and state repression   135

9. Conclusion   141
    9.1 Summary of findings   141
    9.2 The implications of tech-supported repression   143
    9.3 Resistance to online repression   147
    9.4 Beyond state control: the role of private companies   149

Notes   151
Bibliography   155
Index   177

Acknowledgments

This book would not have been written without the intellectual and emotional support of many friends, collaborators, and colleagues.

I am deeply grateful to Sabine Carey who expertly guided my work on this topic from the very first day. I have been lucky to move from working under her guidance as a PhD student to becoming co-authors and trusted colleagues. Her generous mentorship taught me that it is not enough to just be a good researcher: we need to keep working on making the academy a place where more of us can thrive. I intend to pay it forward.

Over the years, many brilliant colleagues and mentors provided detailed comments and suggestions that helped shape this book. Pablo Barberá, Kanisha Bond, Jessica Maves Braithwaite, Mike Colaresi, Kathleen Cunningham, Christian Davenport, Ron Deibert, Chris Fariss, Tina Freyburg, Lisa Garbe, Christian Glaessel, Kelly Greenhill, Stathis Kalyvas, Roxani Krystalli, Will Lowe, Jason Lyall, Nikolay Marinov, Will Moore, Rich Nielsen, Sarah Parkinson, Mascha Rauschenbach, Molly Roberts, Espen Rød, Adam Scharpf, Livia Schubiger, Nils Weidmann, and Yuri Zhukov all contributed to the development of the ideas presented here, and I thank them for their generosity. A special thank you goes to Erica Chenoweth, Cassy Dorff, Kristine Eck, and Josh Kertzer for encouraging me to not give up when I was stuck. Thank you to Dara Kay Cohen for providing a wonderful intellectual home during my post-doctoral fellowship.

My HRDAG family, Patrick Ball, Megan Price, Kristian Lum, Tarak Shah, Maria Gargiulo, with whom I have been fortunate to work for over a decade: thank you for teaching me how to think critically about the quantification of violence, how to strive for scientific rigor in the name of accountability and justice, and for teaching me technical skills I use every day. Our years of collaboration allowed me to investigate many of the questions in this book with sound empirical footing. In 2020 I was fortunate to work with and learn from Sophie Dyer, Sam Dubberly, Likhita Banerji, Matt Mahmoudi, Raha Bahreini, and Mahsa Alimardani: thank you for all your insights. Thank you to Rama Padmanabhan and Alberto Dainotti for helping me work with the IODA data on Internet shutdowns, and to Allison Koh for the excellent research assistance. Thank you to Dayna Sadow for proof-reading.

viii ACKNOWLEDGMENTS

I am grateful to the series editors Brandon Valeriano, Jackie Schneider, and Ben Jensen, as well as to Angela Chnapko at OUP for making the publication process so smooth. Earlier versions of parts of Chapters 5 and 6 draw, with permission, from previously published work. This includes Anita R. Gohdes (2020) "Repression Technology: Internet Accessibility and State Violence," *American Journal of Political Science* 64(3): 488–503, and Anita R. Gohdes (2015) "Pulling the Plug: Network Disruptions and Violence in Civil Conflict," *Journal of Peace Research*: 52(3): 352–367.

Katha, Tarik, Anja, Amina, Peter, Shira, Moritz, Domi, Basti, Kristian, Sam, Nina, Zara, and Gabi: I am indebted to you for putting up with me talking about this project over the many years it took me to complete it. Thank you for your friendship, care, and gentle patience. Thank you to Zara Rahman for the joyful days spent co-working as I finished this manuscript. And to Sarah, Marci, and Eddie for keeping me going. I am immeasurably grateful to and for Lukas: thank you for everything, and more.

This book is dedicated to my parents Catherine and Rolf Gohdes, to whom I owe so much. Thank you for the unconditional love and support.

List of Figures

1.1 Average number of individuals using the Internet, by regime type 1990–2017.   2

1.2 Development of Internet penetration in Syria and Iran.   11

4.1 Individual sources, and integrated data, over time, Syria, March 2011–April 2015.   74

4.2 Density of reported killings, by governorate, Syria, March 2011–April 2015.   74

5.1 Nationwide Internet shutdowns and change in average number of killings, by governorate.   89

5.2 Average daily number of documented killings in Syria in the days leading up to a nationwide Internet shutdown, as well as the days following a shutdown.   90

5.3 Expected change in daily documented regime killings during a shutdown.   92

5.4 Time-shifted placebo test, nationwide shutdown.   93

5.5 Reporting patterns of violence in the three days before, during, and three days after each shutdown.   95

6.1 Network (mobile phones, 3G, and 2G) accessibility by Syrian governorate, June 2013–April 2015.   101

6.2 Targeted and untargeted violence, observed and estimated counts, over time.   103

6.3 Armed group presence in Syria—community level, January 2014 and 2015.   107

6.4 Percentage of violence that is targeted, by type of control.   108

6.5 Expected proportion of targeted killings, given Internet accessibility and different levels of government control.   109

6.6 Expected proportion of targeted killings, given Internet accessibility and whether a region is inhabited by the Alawi minority.   111

7.1 Normalized Internet traffic in Iran, November 15–25, 2019.   122

7.2 Average number of daily concurrent Tor users.   127

X LIST OF FIGURES

7.3 Boxplots, daily concurrent Tor users before and after the shutdown   128

8.1 Percent of countries where at least one nationwide Internet outage was measured   134

8.2 Marginal effect of nationwide Internet outages and repression, global analysis.   139

List of Tables

2.1	Conceptualizing censorship.	21
4.1	Summary of empirical approach to study cyber controls and repression in the Syrian conflict.	77
5.1	Expected effects for network disruptions and violence.	86
5.2	Nationwide Internet shutdowns and documented regime violence.	91
6.1	Internet accessibility (3G) and violent repression.	106
8.1	Network disruptions and state repression.	138

1

Introduction

If the past two decades of worldwide digital expansion have taught us anything, it is that Internet access is deeply political. Few countries have been left untouched by the digital revolution, and many have seen contentious political processes overturned by mass adoption of the Internet. Unsurprisingly, policy-makers, researchers, and pundits alike have made far-reaching claims about the role cyberspace plays in either promoting or endangering the pursuit of democratic politics. In 2009, the US State Department perceived the role of social media platforms in the fight for democracy to be so crucial that it requested Twitter to reschedule planned maintenance work in order to provide full accessibility to Iranians rallying in post-election protests (Landler and Stelter, 2009). When civilian uprisings spread like wildfire across the Arab world at the start of the 2010s, some observers declared "the revolution will be tweeted" (Hounshell, 2011; Lotan et al., 2011; Else, 2012). In recent years, the optimism of the early days of mass Internet usage has significantly dampened. Online information operations aimed at interfering with democratic elections are becoming commonplace (Benkler, Faris, and Roberts, 2018), and the growing number of digital hate campaigns aimed at stoking ethnic tensions are casting a light on the ways in which online access may amplify societal contention (Stevenson, 2018).

Amidst evolving debates around the Internet's impact on politics, the percentage of individuals with fixed or mobile access to the Internet has exploded. Figure 1.1 provides us with the average share of individuals using the Internet between 1990 and 2017, depending on the degree to which the country is governed through democratic institutions. What is striking is that although liberal democracies were the earliest adopters of the Internet, autocratic countries have been making strides in catching up. In the early 2010s, liberal democracies had more than twice as many individuals using the Internet than any other type of political regime. Initially, some autocratic leaders were quite skeptical of introducing mass access to the Internet, as this would create challenges in regulating unwanted content (Deibert et al.,

---

Repression in the Digital Age: Surveillance, Censorship, and the Dynamics of State Violence. Anita R. Gohdes,
Oxford University Press. © Oxford University Press 2024. DOI: 10.1093/oso/9780197743577.003.0001

2 REPRESSION IN THE DIGITAL AGE

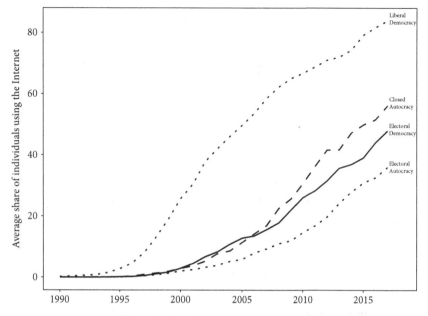

Fig. 1.1 Average number of individuals using the Internet, by regime type 1990–2017. Regime type data is from the V-Dem Regimes of the World Measure (Coppedge et al., 2021). Country-level Internet penetration data is collected by the International Telecommunication Union (ITU, 2022).

2008: 361). But over the past decade, non- and semi-democratic countries across the world have worked hard to close this gap, and some are now easily outpacing their democratic counterparts. In 2019, Bahrain, Kuwait, and Qatar reported that more than 99% of their population were online, numbers that only a very small number of liberal democracies (such as Iceland, Denmark, or Norway) can compete with.

Throughout this time, governments have maintained substantial decision-making power over their country's digital development. If Internet access, and in particular social media, offers a form of empowerment to non-state actors that can help start revolutions and sow tensions, then what explains this continued worldwide digital expansion? Prospects of increased economic prosperity are certainly part of the story (World Bank, 2016). But these developments also point to an increasing realization that network accessibility could provide previously unseen opportunities for political control. Governments across the world have been working hard to expand Internet access for their own people, and many have simultaneously

INTRODUCTION 3

invested in and refined a whole arsenal of tools to control the digital flow of information in the realm of their authority (see Kalathil and Boas, 2003; Deibert et al., 2011; Feldstein, 2021). Recent scholarship has shown that higher levels of Internet access in autocracies favor governments by reducing the likelihood of mass protests, but that those protests that do get off the ground are more likely to continue where digital access is higher (Weidmann and Rød, 2019). And the pervasive use of online restrictions implemented by—for the most part—illiberal governments when encountering domestic challenges suggests that leaders must perceive the free access to and exchange of information online as a threat to their political stability.

As a result, there is hardly a week that passes without reports of political protests being accompanied by accusations of state-ordered tampering with citizens' access to the Internet. The sophistication, context, length, coverage, and location of such controls varies (Gohdes, 2016; Taye, 2019). For example, in India, the Internet is frequently restricted in Jammu and Kashmir, but can be accessed regularly in other parts of the country (Rydzak, 2019). Following the military coup in 2021, Myanmar implemented nightly digital curfews to prevent citizens from going online after work (Padmanabhan et al., 2021). In 2014, Turkey's prime minister Erdoğan blocked access to Twitter amidst leaks shared on the platform that allegedly document government corruption (Rawlinson, 2014). And in January 2022, the Kazach authorities shut down the Internet amidst mass protests against the government's decision to lift price caps on liquid natural gas (Hu, 2022).

These examples indicate that control of the Internet is now part and parcel of states' strategies aimed at maintaining and increasing their authority. They also show that visible forms of online restrictions tend to be relatively short. Full shutdowns are mostly limited to a few days, specific regions, or times of day. Specific apps or social media websites may be blocked for longer, but usually not without significant pushback (Tufekci, 2014; Hobbs and Roberts, 2018; Akbari and Gabdulhakov, 2019). What this suggests is that digital controls are most useful when they are updated and adjusted according to the level of political tensions felt by the government. Work by Molly Roberts offers important insights into the adaptive logic and sophistication of online censorship strategies in China. Her exploration of the Chinese censorship model shows how digital controls are most likely to be successful in supporting political stability when they are based on the *management* of sensitive content, not on the outright and overall *ban* thereof (Roberts, 2018). For example, China's social media censors have been found to be

4 REPRESSION IN THE DIGITAL AGE

most active during collective action events, and are more lax about general criticism directed at the state (King, Pan, and Roberts, 2013).

Just because online controls are not always visible does not mean that they are not being used, nor does it mean they are ineffective. The types of disruptive restrictions just described have been complemented by an ever growing sector of monitoring and surveillance technology, often in the name of fighting crime and preventing terror (Andrejevic and Gates, 2014; Choudry, 2019; Hegghammer, 2021). Such surveillance technology is by now ubiquitous, having developed from home-grown, crude pieces of software to encompassing a booming market for off-the-shelf and custom-made software leveraging cutting-edge technology aimed at intercepting and analyzing individual and mass behavior. The Pegasus program sold by the NSO group to dozens of countries across the world is only a more recent example of governments investing in software that allows the invisible surveillance of digital devices (Marczak et al., 2018; Kirchgaessner et al., 2021).

Control of domestic cyberspace has been most heavily studied in large authoritarian countries, notably China and Russia (e.g. MacKinnon, 2011; Gunitsky, 2015; Kerr, 2016). But recent work has highlighted that digital controls are becoming increasingly attractive tools for leaders who seek popular legitimacy through elections that are at least somewhat competitive. In his recent book, Feldstein (2021) provides an overview of different Internet controls and the pervasiveness with which they are used across the world. His findings suggest that autocracies most heavily engage in online censorship, surveillance, and media manipulation. But they are not the only ones: democratic countries and those that combine elements of democratic rule with authoritarian methods are also actively engaged in these practices, and interest in improving their capacities to engage in digital control has only grown over the past decades.

Taken together, these findings suggest that digital controls such as online surveillance and censorship are both attractive and powerful tools that have the potential to help governments prevent and manage political dissent. They also point to the fact that few countries engage in consistent or rigid controls. Digital responses are instead adjusted to political developments, including elections, protests, or other forms of political tensions (Freyburg and Garbe, 2018; Lutscher et al., 2019; Stukal et al., 2022). The pervasiveness and dynamic adaptation of these digital tools raises important questions regarding states' overall responses to popular threats. What is the relationship between online controls and more traditional methods of state control? What role do we expect censorship and surveillance to take on in a state's broader repressive strategy? Research on violent state repression has consistently shown that domestic threats in the form of dissent, protest, and insurgency are the best predictors for violent state repression (Davenport, 2007a; Hill and Jones, 2014; Chenoweth, Perkoski, and Kang, 2017). Have online controls affected the nature of traditional coercive state behavior in the face of domestic political contention, and if so how? The relationship between modes of online control and states' strategies of violent repression is the subject of this book.

1.1 Argument

I argue that cyber controls present themselves as natural additions to governments' arsenal of tactics aimed at supporting the repression of challenges to state authority. I use the terms online controls and cyber controls interchangeably, and conceptualize them as activities undertaken by or on behalf of state authorities with the aim of either monitoring, filtering, or blocking communication and information on the Internet. I distinguish between controls that are primarily intended to suppress information, and those that are primarily intended to gather information. While we might assume that cyber controls are employed in non-random ways by governments, it is not immediately clear in what way they would be connected to violent forms of repression. To understand their role in states' repressive strategies it is necessary to study how they have changed the mechanisms of access and control to information—for both state and non-state actors. I then show how the infrastructure of online surveillance and censorship has transformed traditional forms of gathering and controlling information for the purpose of raising the costs of collective mobilization.

Traditional forms of in-person *surveillance* rely on single-purpose infrastructure that is extremely resource-intensive and requires long-term investment to yield high-quality and actionable intelligence for state security forces. Online surveillance relies on multi-purpose infrastructure by exploiting the mass adoption of the Internet as a means of obtaining access to new domains and types of information on potential threats. The drawbacks of relying on the Internet for information gathering are twofold. While the infiltration, interception, and ultimate control of online communication and content has transformed and enhanced the surveillance capabilities of many security services, the infrastructure it makes use of also *democratizes* information access, thereby inadvertently benefiting non-state actors. Second, filtering or blocking access to the Internet can directly affect online surveillance efforts. Online surveillance requires a certain level of Internet access so that individuals can exchange their ideas and plans online, which state actors can then monitor and analyze.

Important differences are also apparent when comparing traditional censorship to online censorship. Traditional media censorship usually involves shutting down, regulating, and restaffing newspapers and other media outlets (Van Belle, 1997). An established method to stop individual dissidents from speaking out against the government has been deterrence through repression and intimidation. While both of these strategies continue to be popular, online censorship has added a more centralized, low-cost, and responsive form of controlling information. I discuss how various forms of filtering and blocking Internet access have provided governments with a method to simultaneously censor media outlets and individuals in a responsive manner.

Mass access to the Internet thus presents governments who fear for their political survival with a set of response options. When faced with a political threat, they can either temporarily restrict or block online access in an attempt to diminish opposition groups' mobilization and outreach capabilities or they can opt to continue or expand mass access to online information and monitor it to their own advantage. While censorship and surveillance are not always mutually exclusive, censorship weakens a state's ability to obtain high-quality information through online surveillance. I argue that the type of online control states choose to implement is inevitably linked to their capacity to act in other areas, one being the exertion of violence.

The theoretical argument I present in this book shows how the choice of Internet control is linked to the *type* and *scale* of state-sanctioned violence used against perceived domestic threats. Choosing either censorship or surveillance as a form of digital control limits the use of some forms of violence and enables the use of other forms. Where states have chosen to respond to critical domestic threats through a demonstration of visible control in the form of censorship, they will also be more likely to visibly demonstrate their authority through a heightened use of violent repression. Censorship severely limits the choices for violent action on the side of the government by censoring its own access to high-quality intelligence on precise targets. During periods of censorship, state-sanctioned violence is likely to affect the domestic population indiscriminately.

In constrast, online surveillance is likely to support targeted acts of localized violence against those identified as critical to the future success of opposition movements. Repressive governments are keenly interested in understanding which individuals and groups they should fear the most, whether the threat they face is increasing, and to what extent their challengers have been able to organize dissent successfully. The availability of high-quality information regarding the intentions and location of opposition leaders enables states to use targeted violence. Digital surveillance measures are likely to be linked to the use of targeted, individualized state-sanctioned violence.

A number of observable implications can be formulated based on this distinction. When and where censorship is low and the predominant form of online control is surveillance, we should expect to see more individualized campaigns of violence, such as targeted instances of arrest and torture, or the targeted assassination of individuals deemed threatening to the government. I therefore expect that state forces will be more likely to employ *targeted campaigns of violent repression* in areas where they grant citizens unhindered access to the Internet. Shutdowns, blocking of applications, and increased filtering of specific web content are likely to go hand in hand with increases in indiscriminate repression. Where the government is heavily censoring both access and content of the Internet, we should therefore expect to see *more intense and frequent use of violence* by state forces.

Scope conditions

This book focuses on the relationship between domestic online controls and violent state repression. The arguments presented here provide insights into understanding broader trends involving cyber controls and contentious politics. There are, however, a number of scope conditions that apply to both my theoretical argument and subsequent analyses.

The first scope condition is that I expect my theoretical argument to most directly apply to countries with non-democratic forms of government. I build on insights from a number of different fields, including research on authoritarian survival, state repression and human rights, the logic of violence in civil conflict, and Internet censorship. Traditionally, much of this research has focused on non- or semi-democratic institutional contexts where leaders are more likely to opt for violent strategies of control. Non-democratic states are more likely to violate human rights (Davenport, 2007*b*; Carey, 2010) and engage in traditional and digital forms of censorship (Whitten-Woodring, 2009; Stier, 2015; Hellmeier, 2016; Bak, Sriyai, and Meserve, 2018). At the same time, growing evidence in the field of state repression and in the study of domestic cyber controls suggests both modes of control are also being used in democratic countries. Recent work on digital repression has highlighted how countries that combine elements of democratic and autocratic institutions also engage in censorship, manipulation, and surveillance of their domestic cyberspace (Feldstein, 2021). Democratic countries have also been found to more actively employ violent repression when and where they can deny their wrongdoing and evade accountability (Conrad, Hill, and Moore, 2018; Carey and Gohdes, 2021). Even though the primary focus is on autocratic countries, I expect that certain insights from my theoretical argument can be generalized in order to also explain dynamics of control and repression in countries that at least allow for minimum levels of political contestation and participation (Dahl, 1971).

In my analysis of a state's perceived threats, I primarily focus on popular challenges to central government authority, which is the second scope condition. In her work on understanding states' coercive institutions, Greitens (2016: 19) distinguishes between external and internal threats to a regime's stability. States that face internal threats may deal with secessionist claims, or may be confronted with challenges to the central government's authority. Challengers attempting to attack the central government's authority may be based within the elite and operate through the means of a coup, or they could be based in the broader population and be mobilized in a popular revolt or an insurgency. Governments are usually confronted with multiple threats, and their strategies of maintaining control are likely to reflect that. The argument I present in this book focuses on the ways in which cyber controls can advance a government's power over their population's information infrastructure by either withholding said infrastructure, or providing it for monitoring purposes. As a consequence, my theoretical expectations are more likely to apply in instances where governments are intent on defending themselves against internal, mass-based threats.

The argument I advance focuses on how the state-ordered monitoring and disruption of online information are associated with coercive strategies. I do not explore questions related to the production and manipulation of information. A growing number of studies highlight important ways in which governments, in particular semi-democratic governments, make use of social media for propaganda, disinformation, and harassment campaigns against journalists and opposition members (Pearce, 2015; Nyst and Monaco, 2018; Sinpeng, 2020; Lu and Pan, 2021). The relationship between these forms of media manipulation and violent state coercion is an important topic for future research.

1.2 Evidence

This book seeks to document the prevalence of cyber controls and their role in states' repressive strategies by providing both descriptive and multivariate evidence from a range of contexts. The toolbox of cyber controls has evolved over the years, and the ease with which some of these methods can be applied has also changed. In Chapter 2, I present an overview of some of the most popular and widely used forms of cyber controls for limiting and gathering information. Evidence in Chapters 4–6 examines the Syrian government's use of cyber controls and violent coercion in the context of the civil conflict that commenced in 2011. Chapter 7 shifts the focus to Iran to trace the role the Internet shutdown played in the repressive response to nationwide protests in late 2019. Syria and Iran share similarities in their desire to maintain and expand control of their digital infrastructure. While Iran's government has repeatedly faced mass political protest, the level of domestic upheaval and the degree to which the regime's political authority was challenged throughout the decade of the 2010s fundamentally differs from Syria.

Moving beyond individual cases, I conclude the empirical section of the book with a global comparative analysis of the relationship between Internet shutdowns and state repression. The global comparative investigation of Internet shutdowns and repression allows me to test some of the theoretical expectations beyond individual cases, thereby contributing to the external validity of my argument.

Repression technology in Syria

The Syrian government has weaponized its digital infrastructure for population control since the introduction of the Internet for the general public in 2000. The Baathist state formed by the current president's father has been described as an authoritarian-populist (Hinnebusch, 1993: 246) and highly personalized regime that has justified its repressive control over society through the constant invocation of external and domestic threats, most notably the threats posed by Israel and political Islam (Wedeen, 1999, 2019).

Syria's repressive strategy is instructive for studying the interplay between online and offline repression as it was arguably the first to employ a full arsenal of digital controls in conjunction with mass repression in the context of a large-scale civil conflict. In the early years of the conflict, it was frequently referred to as "the most socially mediated civil conflict in history" (Lynch, Freelon, and Aday, 2014: 5), with events painstakingly captured, documented, and communicated via the Internet. From the earliest days of the Syrian uprising, activists within and outside the country used countless social media accounts to inform each other about military operations and massacres and to help organize and coordinate the revolution (Shehabat, 2012; Poulsen, 2013; Pearlman, 2020). Citizen journalists have recorded hundreds of thousands of YouTube videos of people killed and injured in morgues, hospitals, and market places (Miller and Sienkiewicz, 2012). The amount of user-generated content is so vast that more hours of digital material now exist on documenting the conflict than the conflict has been long (Deutch and Habal, 2018: 50). The Assad regime has used an array of methods to spy on the country's population, such as the use of commercial spyware, DDoS attacks by the Syrian Electronic Army, and even detaining individuals in order to obtain Facebook and Twitter passwords. It has also fully or partially shut down Internet access on a frequent basis, thereby cutting millions of people's access to communication.

Since the start of the Syrian conflict more than a decade ago the role of digital technology in warfare has only grown, and strategic communication by conflict actors on various social media sites has become the norm. Interested observers are now accustomed to following kinetic warfare through social media and other online spaces from anywhere in the world. Militaries and insurgents alike have become aware of the importance of digital imageries and story-telling in keeping both their domestic and international audiences engaged and (dis)informed. Studying one of the earliest instances of domestic conflict where both state and non-state actors were heavily engaged in online activity while fighting offline is instructive for our understanding of the ways in which states can weaponize their control over digital infrastructure. Understanding the motivation behind network manipulations instituted by regimes fearful of their political demise will become an indispensable tool for our theoretical and practical understanding of conflict dynamics. Learning from current cases such as Syria is an important place to start.

Internet infrastructure and usage in Syria and Iran

In the early years of the Internet, Syria and Iran had similarly slow growth trajectories, as is evidenced by the depiction in Figure 1.2 of the percentage of each country's population that has access to the Internet. This trend changed in 2013 when Iran overtook Syria, and by the end of the decade its penetration levels were double those of Syria. In both countries foreign social media and messenger apps such as Skype, WhatsApp, Telegram, and Twitter have been popular among young and tech-savvy users (Abadpour and Anderson, 2013; Brownlee, 2018). Alongside control of the digital infrastructure and implementation of wide-reaching web filters the regimes in both countries have actively built and expanded their ability to engage in targeted and mass surveillance.

Syria and Iran both fall into the category of countries that exhibit high levels of centralization when it comes to their domestic Internet infrastructure. In 2012, Renesys[1] estimated that 132 countries worldwide were at severe or significant risk of experiencing Internet shutdowns (Cowie, 2012) due to the

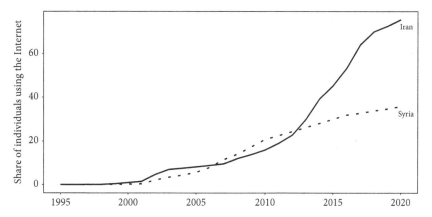

Fig. 1.2 Development of Internet penetration in Syria and Iran. Country-level Internet penetration data is collected by the International Telecommunication Union (ITU, 2022).

low diversity in their telecommunications sector. In both Syria and Iran the telecom sector is centralized in ways that puts the control of access to the Internet into the hands of a few decision-makers (Cowie, 2012).

In 2011, the year of the civilian uprising in Syria and the implementation of its first nationwide shutdown, Syrian access to the Internet primarily depended on one provider, the state-owned Syrian Telecommunications Establishment (STE) (Cowie, 2011b). In the same year, 71 countries were estimated to have fewer than ten service providers, which included Iran. Iran's domestic Internet infrastructure has significantly developed over the past decade, yet despite these developments and the growing influence the country has achieved through network provision in the region, its access to the global Internet remains dependent on two entities that essentially serve as chokepoints to the digital outside world (Madory, 2019).

Methodological approach

Investigating cyber controls and repressive state behavior is a complicated endeavor. Some cyber controls require relative secrecy to be effective while others are meant to be observed and feared. Likewise, state violence can be overtly used against public protesters, or it can be clandestine, such as when dissidents are quietly arrested in their homes in the middle of the night. State actors have incentives to hide, obfuscate, outright deny, or even overstate their repressive intentions and actions.

The evidence I present in this book draws on qualitative and quantitative data from a variety of sources. It might have been useful to interview senior members of government, of the security services, the secret service, and the telecom sector and it would most certainly have been helpful get access to archival material on the procurement of censorship and surveillance software as well as on military strategy. However, senior figures in authoritarian countries are generally not available for comment on their repressive strategies, and while I was able to draw on some documentation on IT procurement, archival materials are either limited or tend to only become available with regime change. The evidence in this book builds on the collection and analysis of a multitude of sources, such as information collected by human rights documentation groups, media sources, and network measurement data.

To measure state repression in the Syrian conflict, I draw on individual-level reports of killings from multiple Syrian documentation groups and make use of recent innovations in quantitive text analysis to classify them as targeted or untargeted violence. This distinction allows me to study changes in the type of violence that go beyond merely measuring scale, thereby contributing towards a more differentiated understanding of repression (see Hoover Green, 2019; Bagozzi, Berliner, and Welch, 2021). Post-sampling estimation in the form of multi-recapture estimation helps account for violence that went unreported in the chaos of war. When investigating changes in the nature of repression used by the Iranian authorities during the protests in November 2019 I draw on quantitative and qualitative accounts of violence as they were reported by Iranian and international human rights groups, as well as in international media reports. The global comparative analysis in Chapter 8 draws on network measurement data to classify Internet shutdowns, and on the Political Terror Scale, a standards-based measure of repression that codes how widespread state repression is in a given country in any given year.

This book presents evidence on the relationship between cyber controls and repression at varying observational units. In Chapter 5, the investigation of the Syrian conflict traces Internet shutdowns and daily changes in violence at the national and regional (governorate) level. In Chapter 6, I analyze bi-weekly levels of Internet accessibility and strategies of state violence at the regional level. To understand the qualitative shifts in repression in Iran, I investigate changes before and during the nationwide shutdown in November 2019. This chapter also looks at changes in online behaviors by comparing usage of a popular censorship circumvention tools before and after the shutdown. Finally, in Chapter 8, I leave the subnational level and construct yearly indicators of Internet shutdowns using network measurement data, and study its co-occurrence with state repression across countries.

The investigation of Internet controls and violent coercion relies on observational data, which comes with challenges to making causal claims. Experimental approaches have been successful in studying public opinion towards digital controls and exposure to state repression, but experimentally manipulating or eliciting information about repressive state behavior is, in most cases, either unfeasible or unethical. I aim to provide insights into this understudied area of state behavior by empirically approaching the research question from a multi-method perspective that tests aspects of the

14 REPRESSION IN THE DIGITAL AGE

theoretical argument at different levels of aggregation for multiple cases using a multitude of data sources using a variety of statistical techniques to account for possible confounders in measurement and estimation.

Context and approach to researching this topic

It is worth briefly reflecting on the way in which my background and training frame the focus of my work. My approach to this topic is formed by the fact that I was trained and have worked in European and US-American institutions that have prioritized positivist research methods, which has heavily influenced the way I have collected, analyzed, and structured the evidence I present in this book. This book focuses on the behavior and activities of state and state-affiliated authorities. There are important reasons to criticize this approach: it de-centers victims and the agency of those who are oppressed, and it glosses over individual stories and the lived experiences of communities who have suffered at the hands of pro-government perpetrators. It is also fraught with challenges related to obtaining reliable information on the workings of repressive state apparatuses. Yet as Noelle Brigden and I have written about elsewhere, it is no coincidence that undertaking "[r]esearch that makes the state legible to everyday people, rather than everyday people legible to the state, can be more difficult" (Brigden and Gohdes, 2020: 254), precisely because of power asymmetries that lead to differing access and permissibility (Mountz, 2007). With this book, I hope to shed light on the logic of states' repressive machineries against the backdrop of digital expansion.

As a social scientist who has predominately observed the issues studied in this book from afar I come to this research from the perspective of an outsider. My academic work has been informed by collaborations with the non-profit organization Human Rights Data Analysis Group (HRDAG),[2] as well with Amnesty International. In consulting for HRDAG I have had the privilege of working with fearless Syrian human rights documentation groups (see Section 4.5) who have actively kept a record of lethal violence committed by Syrian regime forces since the start of the Syrian uprising and subsequent conflict, and have done so at great personal cost. Starting as early as 2012 the Human Rights Data Analysis Group worked with Syrian documentation groups to establish documented death tolls of Syrians killed by the Assad regime. Much of this work was motivated by the need to honor every victim of state violence, as well as the assumption that rigorous evidence of the scale of these atrocities would bring with it the promise of accountability. Our work at HRDAG was focused on providing the scientific support required to clean, canonicalize, link, and analyze the data collected by our Syrian partners (see e.g. Price, Gohdes, and Ball, 2014). In 2020, colleagues at Amnesty International asked me to join a project on uncovering and understanding the role of the 2019 Internet shutdown in Iran (Amnesty International, 2020a). I joined as an outsider and non-expert on Iranian politics. My role was to provide expertise on both Internet shutdowns and the challenges of working with incomplete evidence on violence.

These collaborations with teams that comprised individuals who were both local and foreign to the specific contexts we studied permitted me to draw on information that is largely the result of primary data collection of "insiders." As Malejacq and Mukhopadhyay (2016: 1020) have noted, this process can inevitably build distance between myself as a researcher and the "field" I am studying. And so while this study makes use of a range of statistical tools to help address biases in conflict data (Bell-Martin and Marston, 2019), it is important to acknowledge its limitations in terms of providing a more subtle, contextual picture of individual cases (Fujii, 2015; Bond, 2018).

1.3 Plan of the book

Under what conditions can a digitally connected society actually facilitate effective state repression? Why do some governments restrict Internet access in times of political unrest while others do not? Why do different forms of Internet control go hand in hand with different forms of state violence, and how has Internet accessibility become a tool in the weapons arsenal that states use in civil conflict? In the following chapters, this book will provide an introduction to Internet controls, provide a theory to link them to state violence, and offer comparative and subnational case evidence to unravel and answer these questions.

Understanding what online controls are and how they can be employed by governments is an important precondition to the analysis of their relationship with repressive violence. For this reason, Chapter 2 provides a nontechnical overview of what online controls are, how they work, and how they affect the flow and gathering of information in a state's domestic cyberspace. It focuses on the resulting outcome of censorship methods and surveillance tactics as well as insights from previous research on the dynamics and logic of online controls.

Chapter 3 sets out the theoretical framework, linking the logic of online controls to the use of violent state repression. The infrastructure and innovation of online information controls are discussed and analyzed with respect to their costs and benefits for repressive states. The chapter then formulates the observable implications of the theoretical argument.

Chapter 4 provides an overview of digital politics and repression in Syria. It commences with pre-conflict digital politics and then briefly recounts the conflict's initial trajectory, paying special attention to the unprecedented role social media has played in mediating and amplifying the dynamics of violence. The chapter includes a discussion of the data and methodological approach that form the basis of studying online controls and regime violence in Syria.

Chapter 5 studies the logic and dynamics of Internet shutdowns as they were implemented in Syria between 2011 and 2014. It discusses central motives for implementing nationwide shutdowns in the context of an armed internal conflict, namely shutting down the Internet as part of a concerted repressive effort or as a reputation-saving measure. It then deducts testable implications to account for these different motives. The results of the analysis of network outages and daily conflict fatalities in Syria suggest that the government implemented large-scale disruptions selectively and purposely in conjunction with repressive offensives against the opposition. In a second step, I estimate levels of undocumented violence before and during Internet shutdowns and show that the shutdowns did not systematically affect the reporting of violence.

Chapter 6 zooms in on the relationship between Internet accessibility and the state's ability to use targeted repression. Focusing on within-case variation in online controls, it asks under what conditions online surveillance is likely to be particularly useful for repressive governments. The chapter presents findings using an integrated database on the incidences of state-perpetrated killings in Syria between 2013 and 2015, as well as disaggregated measures of Internet accessibility. With the help of supervised machine-learning, I analyze over 60,000 records of killings and classify them according to their event circumstances to distinguish between targeted and indiscriminate acts of repression. Capture-recapture models are then used to estimate the total number of killings in both categories for each governorate and time period in the dataset on network restrictions. The results reveal that when and where the Syrian government provides Internet access and surveils its population, repression tends to be highly targeted. Where Internet is throttled or shut down, more indiscriminate campaigns of violence are carried out. This relationship is mediated by local conditions that determine whether the regime is able to rely on more traditional forms of intelligence or whether digital surveillance will enhance their ability to target those deemed threatening to their political survival.

In Chapter 7, I seek to understand the strategy and impact of Internet shutdowns in an authoritarian context outside of armed conflict. I study the mass protests that spread across Iran in November 2019 to investigate how Iranian security forces engaged in violent repression during the regime-ordered nationwide shutdown of the Internet. I combine insights from NGO and news reports, network measurement data on the Internet shutdown, and data on censorship circumvention to show how the Internet shutdown was accompanied by mass repression intended to cover up violence by security forces and motivate witnesses and bystanders to self-censor, even once the Internet was turned back on.

Chapter 8 presents a global comparative analysis of the relationship between Internet outages and state repression. Due to the clandestine nature of digital surveillance, the global analysis focuses on Internet shutdowns as the observable implication that can most reliably be measured across different countries and time. Taking into account the most important determinants for violent state repression, the results show that nationwide disruptions of the Internet are associated with higher levels of state-ordered repression.

In Chapter 9, I discuss the central findings and reflect on the implications they hold for our understanding of domestic cyber controls, for future research, and for activists faced with the consequences of online controls in their everyday life.

2

What are online controls, and how do they work?

What are popular forms of online controls, and how do they work? In the following chapter I offer an overview of some of the most frequently used techniques for curbing and monitoring online information flows. Some of these techniques require little technical expertise, while others require the active involvement of specialists. The aim of this chapter is to provide an overview of the logic and outcome of various online controls and to understand how it is possible for states to vary the scope and depth of their management of the Internet. The next section gives a simplified introduction into how accessing information on the Internet works. This will make clear at what points in the process online controls can be integrated. I then distinguish between controls that are aimed at censoring and those that are aimed at surveilling information. This distinction is conceptually useful for trying to understand when and why states choose one form of control over the other. In practical terms, however, we will see that software exists which is designed to both monitor and filter online content.

2.1 Connecting to the Internet

Let's imagine that a person wants to access their favorite blog called *FancyBlog*. They know the address of the blog by heart, which is www.fancyblog.net, and type it into the web browser. Once they hit enter, the browser sends out a request for a copy of the website. Websites, such as the blog they have just requested, have two different types of addresses. The address this person has memorized is called the "Uniform Resource Locator" (or URL). The other one is called the IP or "Internet Protocol" address, which is the real address used to locate the website.[1] Because IP addresses are hard to remember for humans, domain names were invented to make surfing the web easier.[2] Therefore, their browser first has to figure

Repression in the Digital Age: Surveillance, Censorship, and the Dynamics of State Violence. Anita R. Gohdes,
Oxford University Press. © Oxford University Press 2024. DOI: 10.1093/oso/9780197743577.003.0002

WHAT ARE ONLINE CONTROLS, AND HOW DO THEY WORK? 19

out what the associated IP address is. This is done by contacting a domain name system (DNS) server that looks up the IP address(es) associated with the domain name. This key feature of how the Internet works—through the translation of domain names to IP addresses—is an important entry point for many different forms of digital censorship.

Most ISPs have their own DNS server that uses a local database to translate domain names into IP addresses.[3] Once the correct IP address has been found, the browser's request travels through the connection provided the ISP, which is connected to the larger backbone of the Internet, and is comprised of many other Internet Service Providers of various sizes. If the server with the requested IP address (corresponding to www.fancyblog.net) is available, it sends back an "ok" to the browser request and then starts transferring the requested content in small chunks or "packets" of data that are then reassembled in the browser to show up as *FancyBlog*'s website. This simplified depiction of what happens when we call up a website may seem like an awful lot of work for one person just to see one website, but it illustrates how many different steps are involved in accessing and sharing content through the Internet. To add another layer of complexity, let's imagine that fancyblog.net is hosted on a server that is located in a different country than the person requesting to see it. The blog they want to look at may have to traverse through many different ISPs and at some point cross international borders. While there are Internet Service Providers that operate across different countries, their activities and licenses still tend to be bound by national legal restrictions and regulations. For example, Vodafone has its headquarters in the UK but offers services across Europe, Africa, and the Asia-Pacific region. During the major Internet shutdown in Egypt in 2011, Vodafone Egypt issued a statement (BBC News, 2011*a*) that they had been instructed by the Egyptian government to suspend services.

Internet Service Providers play an important role in the maintenance of the network, for example by running tests and monitoring the functioning of processes. Through their central role within the current Internet infrastructure, ISPs are also able to implement various forms of filters that can pre-select what types of requests get sent out, and what type of information is returned. Thus, a provider may check whether the data requested from fancyblog.net includes any known malware or viruses. If they were to find potentially dangerous code, they may opt to block the data. Instead of sending the requested information to the browser, a different webpage warning the user of malicious software embedded in their favorite blog's data may show up instead. Or they may just see an error message. In either case, the provider has opted to block the user from seeing the content they originally requested.

Because providers are in the powerful position to block and manipulate content requested by Internet users and at the same time are subject to domestic regulations and orders, governments can order them to control what information users in their jurisdictions get to access, and what not. ISPs oftentimes face the challenge of trying to provide fast and reliable Internet access to their customers in order to keep them happy, and also of complying with government mandated controls that may directly jeopardize both their customers' satisfaction and privacy.

2.2 Censorship

Online censorship can take on many different forms, and consequently its impact can differ profoundly (Marchant and Stremlau, 2020). Between 2012 and 2020, SFLC.in (2021) documented 507 regional Internet shutdowns across India. During widespread protests in Iran in 2017, Telegram was repeatedly inaccessible across the country. Websites affiliated with the opposition in Myanmar were repeatedly targeted, with Distributed Denial of Service attacks essentially shutting them down throughout the summer of 2008.

In conceptualizing censorship I focus on *what* information is being censored and *who* is affected by said information being unavailable. These two dimensions can help us identify strategic considerations made by governments.[4] Table 2.1 offers an overview of the different types of censorship strategies that focuses on the pervasiveness of censorship along these two dimensions. Some forms of censorship affect users everywhere, regardless of where in the world they are located. Global censorship can be extremely costly and difficult to maintain. More frequent are censorship techniques that affect a subset of users, such as those based in a certain country, region, or those serviced by a specific provider. When it comes to *what* is targeted, I define *top-level* censorship as targeting all forms of online communications and content, *domain-level* censorship as aimed at specific websites or services, and *content-level* censorship aimed at specific content published online.

WHAT ARE ONLINE CONTROLS, AND HOW DO THEY WORK? 21

Table 2.1 Conceptualizing censorship: pervasiveness of *what* is censored online and *who* is affected by it.

	Global users affected	Subset of users affected
Top-level	• Attacking global infrastructure	• Shutdowns (national, regional) • Neglecting digital infrastructure • Bandwidth throttling

Domain-level	• Hacking websites
	  • denying access
	  • manipulating content
		• Blocking websites/apps
		• Domain-level throttling

Content-level	• Requests/orders for removal • Manipulating content removal policies • Harassement & threats • Distraction & drowning out	• Requests/orders for removal

Top-level censorship

Top-level censorship is aimed at impeding access to all online content. Few governments attempt to prevent access to the Internet at a global level. The closest thing governments have managed to do is attack large swathes of the worldwide web by targeting global infrastructure providers. These types of attacks are seldom successful, and when they are, their success is usually cut short, as global providers quickly patch up insecurities and reroute traffic through unaffected channels. An example of a large and somewhat successful DDoS attack occurred in October 2016, when Dyn, a large DNS provider, experienced a massive attack against its services, involving tens of millions of IP addresses. The attack was reportedly carried out through the use of a botnet, where millions of Internet of Things devices, such as digital baby monitors, printers, and fridges, were hijacked with malicious software to send DNS requests to Dyn's systems. The attack led to some of the largest Internet platforms being temporarily unavailable in parts of the world (York, 2016).

Shutdowns

A full shutdown of Internet access can occur either nationwide or in specific parts of a country. Full shutdowns target all forms of content, so that any user trying to access any type of information online will be affected. As such, indiscriminate access denial for all forms of information present the most extreme form of online control. No talking to family and friends online, no checking work emails, no reading the news, no online banking, and the list goes on. When the Internet is only shut down in a specific part of the country, anyone using a device located in that region will be faced with the same issue.

There are a few different ways such blackouts can be implemented. The most damaging way to do this is to cut the cables that connect the country to the web's international gateways. A country's network access is usually routed through submarine or terrestrial cables that connect it to rest of the Internet. Physically attacking these entry points may be quite effective but also leads to a more permanent loss of access that requires extensive repairing before being reinstated. A less damaging method involves manipulating the protocol that manages access to the domestic networks, which is called the Border Gateway Protocol. By manipulating the entry points, they can essentially block international access. Network specialists suggest that this is what happened when Egypt shut down the Internet in January 2011 in the midst of massive anti-government protests (Cowie, 2011a). When servers outside of Egypt tried to send data to Egyptian IP addresses, they suddenly were no longer able to find these addresses. This meant that the Egyptian network had virtually dropped off the Internet.[5] With the international network cut off, communication between computers connected through local ISPs within the country would technically still have been possible. To counteract this, the authorities also shut down the main Egyptian Domain Name System. With the DNS, which functions as an address book for the Internet, shut down, every request that uses conventional URLs could not be translated into a correct IP address, thereby preventing users from accessing the web services they were requesting.

Shutting down access to the Internet for an entire country, and making a country essentially vanish from the international network is no small technical task. Governments have to rely on the compliance of all Internet Service Providers to follow suit (Freyburg and Garbe, 2018). Compliance is easier to enforce in countries where ISPs are controlled by forces close to the government than in countries with a multitude of competing providers. Top executives and senior management of telecommunications companies have reportedly been heavily pressured to comply with shutdown orders (Mare, 2020). More important than the technical difficulties associated with a full shutdown are the domestic and international consequences governments have to deal with once the Internet has been shut down. Country-wide shutdowns were met with intense international outrage and in both Syria and

WHAT ARE ONLINE CONTROLS, AND HOW DO THEY WORK? 23

Egypt during the Arab Spring, even though these country-wide shutdowns were limited to a few days. In addition to the negative international media coverage these incidences provoked, the countries' economies suffered from not being able to go about their day-to-day business (Kathuria et al., 2018). Governments therefore usually opt for what Deibert et al. (2010) call "just in time" censoring that is restricted to short periods.

Longer shutdowns tend to be restricted to smaller localities, or limited to certain times of the day. During its post-election crisis in 2016, Gabon implemented Internet "curfews." Access was cut every evening until the following morning in the hope of allowing businesses to go about their work, but preventing election-related anti-government activities from being planned and documented online in the evening hours. In the aftermath of Myanmar's military coup in February 2021, the Internet was also virtually shut down every night (Padmanabhan et al., 2021). Other countries have opted for longer shutdowns but restricted them to specific parts of the country. Examples of longer regional shutdowns include Xinjiang province in China in 2009, the Tigray region in Ethiopia in 2020, and repeated shutdowns in Kashmir.

In contrast to "just in time" shutdowns, governments also pursue more long-term strategies of digital exclusion by failing to provide, build, and expand Internet infrastructure in areas populated by groups that are deemed threatening. Weaponizing the longer-term availability and expansion of infrastructure has long been found to be part of punishment and reward mechanisms implemented by authoritarian governments. For example, Blaydes (2010: ch. 4) shows how the Mubarak government in Egypt systematically withheld investment into public infrastructure in areas displaying lower levels of electoral support for the incumbent. Work by Weidmann et al. (2016) demonstrates these longer-term patterns by showing that, globally speaking, areas inhabited by politically excluded ethnic groups are likely to have lower levels of access to the Internet than other parts of the country. These findings underline that infrastructure is highly political, and availability, or lack thereof, is likely to be intentional. As I discuss in the next chapter, this strategy presents a double-edged sword for leaders attempting to expand (digital) control over a hard-to-reach population.

Despite the fact that Internet shutdowns draw a lot of attention, impact all forms of content, and affect large numbers of users, digital rights organizations have been documenting an increasing number of such shutdowns

24 REPRESSION IN THE DIGITAL AGE

across the world (Taye, 2021). According to Howard, Agarwal, and Hussain (2011), the majority of Internet shutdowns between 1995 and 2010 were conducted under the guise of national security concerns, which cited terrorist threats and preventing the spread of state secrets as the main reasons for implementing such a move (Howard, Agarwal, and Hussain, 2011: 226). In recent years, governments have been quick to justify the shutdown of domestic network services under a new pretense, citing the fight against spreading "fake news," rumors, and inflammatory content as the reason to cut communication access. While inflammatory content aimed at inciting violence has been shared on social media platforms, such as Facebook's Messenger service in the case of Myanmar, the fight against fake news has also given governments a new acceptable reason for censoring all forms of communication and content.

Slowing down access
An increasingly popular form of broadly censoring online content is making access painfully slow. The bandwidth of an Internet connection tells us how fast information is being transmitted to our computer or phone. A common way to limit access is to intentionally lower the speed of an Internet connection, a practice that is also known as throttling. ISPs may throttle access to all online content for individuals when they have exceeded the amount of data they paid for. In some countries subscriptions allow users to use unlimited data on certain domains (such as Facebook), so that ISPs will only throttle access to other websites. During large demonstrations, however, reports have mounted of networks slowing data access significantly. Computer scientists examined the network performance in Iran in 2011 and 2012 and have provided digital evidence suggesting Iranian ISPs throttled Internet access during periods of political unrest at this time (Anderson, 2013).

Like full shutdowns, throttling can be implemented nationwide or at the regional or ISP-level, depending on the government's censorship goals. But from the perspective of governments, bandwidth throttling offers a number of advantages over shutdowns. The reduction of bandwidth is more subtle and provides opportunities for plausible deniability to both government and service providers. Ample research on the logic of state repression demonstrates the conditions under which governments will choose repressive strategies that make it hard for outsiders to establish who is responsible for them. Events attended by large numbers of people can naturally lead to an overloaded network, making it difficult for attendees to distinguish between

WHAT ARE ONLINE CONTROLS, AND HOW DO THEY WORK?   25

intentional and non-intentional speed reductions. And even though content may still be available, albeit slowly, previous work has shown that merely creating a little friction will lead users to reduce their activity and their motivation to access information online (Roberts, 2018: 57–58).[6] This has the potential of being particularly disruptive for opposition members who aim to spread awareness and information about their resistance activities through photos, videos, and maps. Bandwidth throttling has the potential to affect all online content, but the biggest problems tend to arise for services that are data intensive, including platforms that share large amounts of multimedia content.

Creating friction for users wanting to access the Internet can be a long-term and a short-term censorship tactic. Next to throttling, governments can also create friction by de facto pricing out large proportions of the population from using the Internet by making data plans prohibitively expensive.

Domain-level censorship

Because shutdowns are so imprecise with regards to the content and the users they target, a popular form of digital censorship is blocking or throttling access to individual websites or applications (Aryan, Aryan, and Halderman, 2013). Examples include Twitter in Turkey in 2014, Signal in Egypt in 2016, Facebook in Iran in 2009, or Instagram in China in 2014. Bandwidth throttling can also be implemented at the domain-level. As we will see in Chapter 7, Iran has limited bandwidth to Telegram and other messenger apps in an attempt to encourage users to switch to domestic mobile apps.

Blocking global access to individual domains

On the morning of Thursday, March 26, 2015, data scientists across the world found their work grinding to a halt. GitHub, the most popular repository for code, was suddenly no longer accessible. On March 27, the monitoring account @githubstatus tweeted "We've been under continuous DDoS attack for 24+ hours [...]" The biggest code repository in the world had been targeted by a distributed denial of service (DDoS) attack so powerful that it shut down access to its servers for more than five days. Why would anyone target a code repository platform? It turns out that the attack was aimed at two GitHub URLs, namely /greatfire/ and /cn-nytimes/ (Anthony, 2015). The first URL leads to the repository of greatfire.org, a project that provides tools to circumvent online censorship in China, while the second hosts access to replicas of the Chinese edition of the *New York Times*.

A key difference between DoS attacks and the types of website blocking previously described is that DoS attacks are effective at denying access for *all* potential users, globally. When governments implement bans in cooperation with domestic ISPs, they may be able to effectively and durably shut down access within their own jurisdictions. But for those browsing the Internet in other countries—and those skilled in circumventing domestic access restrictions—banned websites remain accessible. When a website is flooded with requests it becomes impossible for anyone to visit it. A popular way to do this is to overwhelm the hosting server(s) with data requests. As we saw above, the normal way for users to access content on the web is to have their browser send a request to see a webpage located on some server. If an unusually large number of requests are sent out at the same time, the server may be overwhelmed. The targeted server then responds to requests with reduced speed, meaning that a website will load very slowly in the user's browser, and eventually may not be able to respond to new requests. Nowadays, denial of service attacks usually involve simultaneous requests sent from hundreds of thousands of different machines, hence the name distributed denial of service attack (DDoS). The extent to which websites will be vulnerable to such attacks depends on their size and maintenance. In the case of GitHub, Swedish researchers were able to identify that millions of Chinese Internet users who were accessing the popular Chinese search engine Baidu were not aware that a small piece of code had been injected into their online traffic, which caused their browsers to send endless requests to the two URLs mentioned above (Goodin, 2015). Just a very small percentage of all Baidu visitors unknowingly sending requests to these GitHub pages created a distributed denial of service attack large enough to briefly take down GitHub.

Websites that aren't accessed by millions of users everyday from across the world can usually be taken down with less effort. Dissident newspapers, opposition websites, and websites written in languages of threatened minorities are often hosted by smaller providers, although evidence from Venezuela shows that commercial DoS protection is becoming more popular among independent websites (Lutscher, 2021). Nevertheless, the smaller and less well maintained a website is, the more likely it is going to be vulnerable to DoS attacks. Attacks on opposition websites are nothing new; as early as 2005, the Open Net initiative reported DDoS attacks against servers hosting media, NGO, and political party websites in Kyrgyzstan (OpenNet Initiative, 2005) during election campaigns, effectively shutting down access to opposition media. The attacks against Mexican opposition parties in 2018 demonstrate that the strategy is still being used. What has changed since the attacks in the early 2000s is that many independent media and activist sites have adapted their dissemination strategy by duplicating information and moving much of their content to larger social networking platforms in the hope of maintaining a more visible presence during times of unrest. Building on the larger and more protected infrastructure of multinational companies allows smaller organizations and groups to mitigate the risk of cyber attacks. However, the hacking of opposition accounts on social media websites and blogging services such as blogger show how the methods used by pro-government attackers have co-evolved.

DoS attacks offer states considerably higher plausible deniability than conventional website bans. No official involvement by Internet Service Providers is required, and the attackers themselves can be based in a different country (or multiple countries) and be directly or indirectly hired by a government or their supporters (Lutscher et al., 2019). While attacks can often be traced back to their origins, the attackers frequently act as mercenaries. In early June 2018, the websites belonging to Mexico's National Action opposition party were targeted with DDoS attacks. Reports claimed that they had been hacked by an unusual amount of traffic coming from both Russia and China (Solomon, 2018). While involvement from either of these country's governments cannot be ruled out, computer specialists point out that the attacks may have been carried out by Russian or Chinese hackers on behalf of other actors looking to censor the opposition's online presence. Denial of service attacks thus allow those ordering them to dodge responsibility and plausibly deny involvement. Attacks may also be implemented by groups that are loyal to the government but aren't directly under their command. As with pro-government militias, pro-government hackers can be useful to do the dirty work, but hard to rein in when they go overboard.

Instead of just making a website unavailable, attackers can hack into a website and manipulate content so that when users request the webpage, they are made aware that the website has been compromised. In 2015, the pro-regime Syrian Electronic Army hacked into the official website of the US Army and added a popup message reading "Your commanders admit they are training the people they have sent you to die fighting," supposedly in protest of further US military involvement in the Syrian conflict. Instead of defacing a website, attackers can meddle directly with the domain naming system by changing the IP address to which a name is mapped. And in 2009, the Iranian Cyber Army managed to alter Twitter's DNS records so that Twitter users were redirected to a different webpage reading "this site has been hacked by the Iranian Cyber Army" (Arrington, 2009). The same was done to a website that was campaigning against the re-election of Mahmoud Ahmadinejad, the president at the time. Altering DNS records is a relatively simple way to redirect website traffic without having to hack the actual webpage.[7] In summary, hacking solutions bring with them a number of benefits for governments wanting to block content, but targeting the servers of powerful companies, such as those of GitHub or Twitter, is expensive and time intensive with a small probability of success. Less well-resourced targets, such as the webpages supporting activists or opposition groups, are likely to be far more vulnerable to denial of service attacks. The attacks by the Iranian Cyber Army in 2009 were mitigated by Twitter in a matter of hours, whereas the opposition website was redirected to the attackers webpage for far longer and was reportedly offline for more than six weeks following the initial attack (Zuckerman, 2010).

Blocking domestic access to individual domains

Application or website blocks are considerably less disruptive than full shutdowns and are therefore widely used. Individual websites that host politically sensitive content can quietly be blocked without raising too much attention. Many countries have blanket bans on websites that cover certain topics. Russia, Iran, Saudia Arabia, Malaysia, UAE, and Indonesia regularly block access to websites with LGBTQ+ content (Dalek et al., 2021). Germany blocks access to websites that deny the Holocaust, among other things, and many countries across the world block access to websites that include child pornography. Different ISPs within one country may implement different solutions for blocking websites (Deibert et al., 2008). Governments will give ISPs a blacklist of full URLs to be blocked, or they can specify words included in website requests that should be prohibited. Users trying to access such content may see an error page or a specifically designed blockpage that informs them about the block (known as block-pages), or redirects them to another website. Filtering based on content provided on individual webpages may be done using software, human review, or a combination of the two. Many ISPs use off-the-shelf software that allows them to preselect certain types of content to be caught in their filters.

When the Russian government introduced a new law in 2012, it forced Russian ISPs to shut down or block websites that are included on a blacklist created and maintained by *Roskomnadzor*, the Federal Service tasked with supervising communications and media affairs in Russia. Since then, "approximately 20 new laws have been passed further restricting Internet content, permitting increased levels of mass surveillance, and enforcing legal penalties on Internet users and service providers" (Kerr, 2016: 1). As of August 2021, almost half a million sites have been blocked.[8]

A frequently used method is called DNS blocking or redirection, where requests of specific websites are not forwarded to the actual IP address. Governments may determine one or more unwanted websites and share this list with the Internet Service Providers. The ISP in turn can institute new rules for these websites, such as forwarding their requests to a new webpage that warns the user that the requested page cannot be accessed. DNS blocks can be relatively easy to circumvent, for example if users know what IP address can be used to access the website directly, or if the website creators change their URL to something more innocuous. In contrast, so-called IP-blocks, blocks where requests to access a certain group of IP addresses are ignored, are harder to circumvent.

If governments want to move beyond a fixed blacklist or the keyword filtering of a website's URL, deep packet inspection (DPI) software can be used to inspect and intercept the content of websites as well. DPI technology helps identify data packets that include certain content, which allows ISPs to detect words or terms that have been blacklisted and block data, thereby expanding the censorship possibilities (see e.g. Sevom, 2012). DPI is not only used for the interception and censorship of content deemed politically sensitive by governments but is also employed to trace cybercrime, block spam, or to detect computer viruses (Porcedda, 2013). It can also allow the intercepter to modify content, for example by injecting malicious code. Governments don't always order the blocking of sensitive content, but instead task ISPs with intercepting and collecting information on the browsing patterns of the users in question. The surveillance implications of DPI will be discussed in the following section.

Website blocking requires cooperation and compliance by the ISPs, and in countries with functioning levels of rule of law, such specific bans may also require specific executive orders or legislation, which can prove tricky to uphold. In Turkey, two weeks after Twitter was banned in 2014, the country's constitutional court ruled that the ban violated Turkish citizens'

30 REPRESSION IN THE DIGITAL AGE

fundamental freedom of expression, and the ban had to be lifted. While such official bans may prove to be effective in blocking websites and especially applications powered by large international companies, they can be complicated to coordinate and uphold. They also make it hard for governments to plausibly deny their involvement.

Where governments are keen to maintain a moderate level of plausible deniability, pro-government hackers can directly attack individual websites without having to go through ISPs. Prior research has demonstrated that governments outsource the use of repression to pro-government militias when they fear high audience costs from the international community (Carey and Mitchell, 2017). Delegating dirty work, such as hacking websites, allows states to either claim ignorance or incompetence in trying to control the perpetrators. It should therefore come as no surprise that blocking techniques requiring no official involvement of governments and Internet Service Providers are so popular.

Hacking large social media websites is considerably harder than attacking more obscure opposition sites. Large technology corporations have a financial interest in seeing their platform being used without interruption and tend to invest heavily in smooth service provision. However, the relative monopoly status that certain social media platforms now enjoy in many countries, such as WhatsApp in Brazil, means that if a government wants to ban online discourse and has the technical capabilities to do so, it can target a single application and thereby shut down online exchanges of millions of users within their country (Santos, Saldaña, and Rosenberg, 2020). But while domain-level censorship continues to be popular, shutting down people's access to parts of the Internet has the potential to backfire (Hobbs and Roberts, 2018; Rydzak, 2019) and signal desperation on the side of the government. For this reason, governments increasingly target specific *content* posted online.

Content-level censorship

Content-level censorship requires governments to have a clear understanding of the type of information that should be made unavailable online. State-controlled social media platforms allow governments to censor individual posts or keywords directly, making them globally inaccessible (King, Pan, and Roberts, 2013; Ng, 2013). When content is hosted on websites or social media that are not controlled by the state, global removal of individual content is very difficult to achieve. Governments or courts will frequently request companies to have content removed, hidden, banned, or removed from search results.[9] Compliance with such requests, even if limited to domestic cyberspace, has traditionally been low and likely depends on companies' interests in local markets (Gohdes, 2018c). State actors have therefore become increasingly creative in their attempts to remove specific content, such as manipulating social media websites' posting rules to get content removed (Youmans and York, 2012). For example, pro-government groups in Sudan reportedly infiltrated anti-government pages on Facebook and flooded them with pornography, only to then flag them for violating Facebook's community guidelines (Boswell, 2011).

Harassment and threats

Instead of preventing users outright from seeing content, governments are increasingly engaging in aggressive tactics aimed at threatening and harassing the producers of unwanted content (Nyst and Monaco, 2018; Kargar and Rauchfleisch, 2019), as well as discrediting and contesting their reputation and work, oftentimes through disinformation campaigns (Deibert et al., 2011). In addition to sowing mistrust and doubt about the content in question, threats and harassment campaigns are meant to encourage self-censorship. While early research on social media usage highlighted the ways in which online spaces afforded new freedoms for users to express their true political attitudes, recent work on autocratic stabilization has argued that online self-censorship is higher than previously expected (Robinson and Tannenberg, 2019), and rising (Moore-Gilbert and Abdul-Nabi, 2021).

Offline repression, or the threat thereof, is also frequently employed in an attempt to deter activists and other critical voices from posting online. Arresting, threatening, and even killing activists, bloggers, and journalists is aimed at silencing critical voices and discouraging others to rise up in their place (Pan and Siegel, 2020; Carey and Gohdes, 2021). National security concerns have long been used as a guise to ban content, and increasingly, countries such as Malaysia, Singapore, and Cambodia have introduced laws targeting content under the premise of preventing the spread of "fake news" (Morgenbesser, 2020; Neo, 2020; Sinpeng, 2020). In 2018, the Tanzanian government passed the "Electronic and Postal Communications (Online Content) Regulations" law which formulated such restrictive and ambiguous policies for online content creators that many users have essentially ceased sharing political content online (Parks and Thompson, 2020: 4294).

Distraction and drowning out content

Online information can also be hidden by creating sufficient noise to drown out any other content. Instead of overwhelming websites with requests, social media ecosystems may be overwhelmed with certain types of content. State-affiliated actors can write hundreds of thousands of comments and posts that take up space online, thereby either burying critical content completely or, at a minimum, acting as a distraction. To achieve the volume of content needed, states use both human or automated social media accounts. Scholars have documented a range of strategies that can be demobilizing (Munger et al., 2019), can include content aimed at becoming popular clickbait (Lu and Pan, 2021), can focus on controlling the political agenda (Stukal et al., 2019), or be aimed at flooding online spaces with content that cheerleads the government (Roberts, 2018).

Requesting or ordering content removal

Next to domain-level blocks of websites, governments frequently force website maintainers to moderate content posted by third parties to their services. For example, social media platforms, such as Twitter or Sina Weibo, may be obliged to delete posts by their users. According to Twitter's rules and policies, the content of certain tweets, as well as entire accounts, may be censored in individual countries. Twitter regularly publishes the number of requests for deletion it received, as well as the platform's level of compliance with said requests. In 2017, the majority of removal requests were submitted by Turkey and Russia.[10] In China, employees of Sina Weibo's censorship department regularly receive updated instructions that detail the type of content to focus upon, and then either delete or make them invisible.[11] Chinese censorship strategies include many highly sophisticated and nuanced forms of content moderation and deletion. For example, content need not always be deleted, but can also be subject to search filtering, a process that omits specific topics or content from "trending topics," and excludes certain words from users' search results (Roberts, 2018: 108).

Social media platforms from China to the US are making increasing use of computer-assisted methods to censor content deemed politically, socially, or culturally sensitive. In China, social media posts are generally pre-screened by computer algorithms designed to pick up content that is considered sensitive (Wang, 2016), before human censors then review them individually. In June 2017, Google (of which YouTube is a part) announced plans to fight terrorism online, which included ramping up the use of machine learning methods to detect and remove extremist and terrorism-related content (Walker, 2017). While there are many important issues and problems that arise when large corporations take censorship of digital content into their own hands (O'Flaherty, 2018), we will focus here on censorship that is either state sponsored, state motivated, or executed at the interest of the government.

Constrained choices

The degree to which governments are able to choose between these types of censorship depends on their ability to exercise control over the Internet at the top, domain, or content-level. The fewer international entry points connect a country to the international network, the less difficult it is to control and manipulate the routing protocols and the border gateways for censoring content at the top- or domain-level. IT experts have long argued that countries with fewer access points to the global Internet, with lower numbers of Internet Service Providers, and with a higher proportion of providers that are state-owned will have an easier time shutting down parts or all of the Internet (e.g. Cowie, 2012; Musiani et al., 2016). The choice between domain and content level censoring is oftentimes influenced by a state's ability to gain access to the content-level.

Few countries have the ability to engage in censorship at the content-level in the way Chinese authorities are able to directly manage what posts get seen on Chinese social media platforms. Chinese tech companies dominate the domestic market and are therefore able to provide the type of nuanced access to content that would not be possible with foreign companies (Pan, 2017). In countries where the most popular social media sites are foreign companies governments have to apply for content removal, and oftentimes find themselves being ignored by tech companies (Gohdes, 2018b). In such situations authorities frequently turn to domain-level censorship.

2.3 Monitoring content and people

As more and more content and communication has been relegated online, online surveillance has exploded in popularity (Deibert, 2003). In July 2021, a consortium of journalists, researchers, and activists published a series of investigations into spyware sold by an Israeli surveillance technology company (Marczak et al., 2018; Kirchgaessner et al., 2021). The reports revealed that at least ten countries were customers of the NSO Group, and their Pegasus software had been found on the devices of prominent lawyers, journalists, and human rights defenders in dozens of countries.

While the recent rise in off-the-shelf surveillance software is notable, mass surveillance of online information has been gaining popularity since the early 2000s, when governments started to invest heavily in their digital surveillance infrastructure in the context of the "war on terror" (e.g. Ball and Webster, 2003). In 2013, the global surveillance disclosures initiated by the former NSA employee Edward Snowden offered first insights into the full extent of the mass surveillance capabilities the United States and allied countries had established (Lowe, 2016). Since then, global investment into surveillance infrastructure has expanded (Human Rights Watch, 2014; Mackenzie, 2021), and the surveillance technology industry is booming (Wagner and Guarnieri, 2014). In 2014, the UN Office of the High Commissioner for Human Rights issued a report contending that digital surveillance is frequently used to specifically target political dissidents and members of the opposition (OHCHR, 2014: 3). In this book I focus on Internet surveillance, but modern surveillance technology goes far beyond Internet surveillance. CCTV, ID scans, facial recognition technology, biometric data (DNA, fingerprint, retina scans), heat sensors, and the collection of financial, social, and health-related personal information are all methods of surveillance that are gaining in popularity (see e.g. Xu, 2021).

Beyond disclosures and leaked documents surrounding surveillance infrastructure and technology, security researchers, digital rights organizations, journalists, and targeted activists have all contributed to public knowledge on the capabilities and advancements in digital monitoring. States may strategically communicate some of their surveillance capabilities in a effort to intimidate potential critics and deter people from engaging in unwanted behaviors. In general, surveillance capabilities remain at least partially hidden in order to be effective. In the next section, I discuss the kind of data state actors are interested in monitoring, and how some of the

From content to metadata

We can broadly distinguish between the monitoring of content produced and exchanged online, and the monitoring of metadata surrounding the content, its producers, and consumers. The content includes all forms of text, such as blog and social media posts, news articles, emails, short messages, as well as voice messages. It also includes media such as photos or videos of protests, instances of state abuse or corruption, documentation of certain groups of people, marches, signs, symbols, as well as the direct or indirect mentioning of sensitive topics. A lot of the content states will be interested in monitoring will also be the kind of content considered worthy of censorship. Both censorship and surveillance are concerned with controlling these types of data, but digital surveillance is oftentimes at least as if not more interested in metadata. Metadata is data that describes and can help classify other data sources. Metadata on the Internet has been defined as "a structured description of the essential attributes of an information object" (Gill, 2008: 23). Governments tend to be interested in metadata that represents individuals' online activities, as well as information that describes their real life and online network. Popular forms of digital meta data collected by governments include the location of individuals, number of devices and device usage, application statistics, browsing histories, contact lists, as well as the volume, timing, and frequency of interactions between different users.

Geolocation methods are manifold. With the support of telecommunications providers, governments can track mobile phone locations using information from the most recent cell towers a phone communicated with. Providers may also have insight into recent WiFi systems an individual's device has accessed. Targeted surveillance methods, which will be discussed below, may rely on intrusive technology that reports back a device's location consistently. Individuals also frequently self-disclose their location by sharing photos or even their location online.

The timing, frequency, and volume of communication between individuals or groups can be of core interest to governments, helping them reconstruct events, infer content, and establish hierarchies in opposition networks. Metadata about communication patterns tends to be more readily available for analysis than the actual content of communication, in particular as popular text-based chat providers have ramped up end-to-end encryption of written content (Friberg, 2016). Communication on open or semi-public social media websites can also be a source for metadata monitoring and analysis.

Even when content and metadata are available, social media network analyses frequently rely on posting and commenting patterns that can, similarly to chat monitoring, help establish central nodes and dynamics within opposition activity (Qin, Strömberg, and Wu, 2017). It can also help identify those who may not be publicly involved in activities aimed at challenging the government, but show sympathies or at least a certain degree of interest for anti-government thoughts and ideas. For example, many more individuals may follow anti-government social media accounts or read activist blogs and news outlets than are actively involved in promoting opposition content. Depending on the government's perception, sympathizers or interested citizens may be monitored closely for possible changes in behavior. Other forms of metadata exist that can also be interesting to governments, including individuals' browsing histories, contact lists, or number of devices used. Objects of interest may be when and how often users access certain websites and whether those websites are known to be critical of the government. Individuals who own more than one mobile device where the patterns of usage differ strongly may also be deemed suspicious. And having known opposition members saved in one's contact list, or being included in the contact list of a known opposition member, is likely to draw interest as well.

Mass and targeted surveillance techniques

Mass surveillance is aimed at indiscriminately monitoring data and metadata produced and consumed by the broader population in any given area. A popular tool used for this is based on the deep packet inspection technology (DPI) just discussed in the context of Internet filtering. DPI is frequently implemented by Internet Service Providers for non-political reasons, such as filtering out spam and potentially harmful code. Software that implements DPI is therefore usually designed to inspect, store, and filter content at the same time. Since the method allows providers to not only monitor the metadata associated with information exchanged online but can also store content it is a useful technique for actors interested in observing, searching, and triangulating data of interest. Where ISPs are state-owned, mass surveillance technology is often directly installed with the provider, and the data gleaned from monitoring users is made readily available to the authorities. If telecommunications companies are hesitant to implement controls governments may apply pressure, as suggested by the Office of the High Commissioner of Human Rights:

> Governments reportedly have threatened to ban the services of telecommunication and wireless equipment companies unless given direct access to communication traffic, tapped fibre-optic cables for surveillance purposes, and required companies systematically to disclose bulk information on customers and employees. (OHCHR, 2014: 3)

Mass surveillance can be facilitated by constraining the populations' ability to access the Internet anonymously or securely. Governments can mandate that individuals present identification prior to obtaining access to the Internet. This includes collecting biometric data for personal identification, such as fingerprints or retina scanning, and requiring government-issued identification for the purchase and registration of SIM cards or when using Internet cafés. They also reduce access to anonymizing software, such as virtual private networks, encrypted messaging apps, alternative DNS servers, or the Tor network. This can help reduce the amount of information that is hidden or hard to obtain for the government. Governments may also monitor who is using anonymizing software, operating under the assumption that they are doing so to hide their activities from the authorities.

Many forms of digital surveillance are meant to monitor the behavior and data of individuals, specific groups, or those at the periphery of said groups. Methods of mass surveillance can be used to identify and filter out individuals or groups of interest, for example by flagging users attempting to access content based on specific keywords, or from pre-defined sources. Targets are frequently selected through metadata by identifying individuals located at the site of a protest, or found in the address book of a known dissident. A variety of techniques exist that can easily be employed to monitor a more targeted group of individuals. Unencrypted text and multimedia content can be accessed without hacking the target's devices to gain illegal access. National security laws can mandate that companies build backdoors into devices or software that allow security and law enforcement agencies to access users' data under the guise of internal security. But not all companies comply with such orders, and individuals of interest to the state, such as human rights defenders, opposition members, or journalists, are increasingly become conscious of their own digital security risks (Marczak, 2016). Companies selling spyware that provides remote access to a target's device have therefore been welcoming more and more nation-states as customers. Governments also employ their own software specialists to build spyware, and usually make use of a variety of different tools to optimize monitoring strategies (e.g. Mackenzie, 2021).

Remote control access to a device through the injection of malicious software, or access via software backdoors are intrusive techniques, but are generally intended to covertly surveil the selected target. Covert surveillance is advantageous because it keeps the target from possibly adjusting their online behavior or device location. Beyond that, it has the added benefit of providing governments with access to the devices of individuals based abroad (Marczak et al., 2018). But repressive governments have also engaged in overt attacks on targets, for example by detaining them and demanding access to their social media accounts (SalamaTech, 2015).

Social engineering is a popular tactic used to gain access to a target's device without their knowledge. Attackers attempt to deceive the target so as to engage them in risky security behavior. Social engineering methods require attackers to understand the target's motivations, habits, or social networks. For example, when attempting to motivate a human rights activist to click on a malicious piece of software, attackers may lead the target to believe they are a victim of state abuse. To do so they might send a text message asking the activist for help in bringing their case to trial, while attaching the spyware disguised as a video showing alleged beatings by security forces. Such attacks are also called phishing attacks, which are often sent to targets as emails or text messages and are intended to coax users into either clicking on a link, opening an attached document, installing some software on their device, or asking them to provide their user credentials and password on a website.[12]

In 2019, the Moroccon activist Maati Monjib and human rights lawyer Abdessadak El Bouchattaoui both reported receiving a suspicious text message that encouraged them to click on an external link. Clicking the link would have led to the installation of software allowing the attackers to surveil their calls, chat messages (including encrypted ones), and the device's geolocation (Brewster, 2019). The software was attributed to the Israel-based NSO company and has appeared on human rights defenders, journalists, and opposition members' phones suspected to have been targeted by countries such as Togo, Saudi Arabia, and the United Arab Emirates (Marczak et al., 2018; Srivastava, 2020). The NSO software found on activists' phones in recent years is but one of many such forms of spyware that has been employed by governments. Software that provides authorities with remote access and interception tools is sold by a variety of companies, many of which are based in Europe and North America. For example, the Gamma International Group is based in the United Kingdom and Germany, and is best known for having sold a product called FinFisher that for many years provided governments around the world with a full surveillance toolkit (Wagner and Guarnieri, 2014).

Summary

There are a wide variety of technical tools that governments make use of in order to control cyberspace. Most of these tools are directed at managing the flow of information online within their own area of jurisdiction, but some methods, such as distributed denial of service attacks or the use of spyware, can target and affect users in other countries as well. This chapter has offered an overview of commonly used forms of online controls, showing how they act as information blocking or monitoring tools. The next chapter theorizes about the implications these tools have for violent forms of state repression.

3

Theory

This chapter outlines how online controls are changing the landscape of information control, and how they are linked to states' use of violent repression. I argue that online controls support violent repression because the choice of cyber control—censorship vs. surveillance—*enables* the use of some forms of violent repression and *limits* the use of other forms. While online controls and state repression are embedded in both the broader political context and repertoire of policy options available to the government, they are the two factors under consideration in this chapter.

In the realm of online controls, states may opt for controls geared towards censorship or choose to focus on maintaining Internet access and engage in surveillance. As the previous chapter established, censorship and surveillance are not mutually exclusive policy choices. States tend to employ a mixture of cyber controls, and the extent to which the effects of these controls are felt by the various segments of the population is subject to change both across and within countries. For the purpose of theoretically understanding the implications of various forms of controls, shutdowns of Internet access and the monitoring of a fully accessible Internet represent stylized ends of a spectrum.

Building on foundational work by Davenport (2007*a*: 2) and Goldstein (1978: xxviii), I define state repression as the actual or threatened use of physical violence against individuals or groups who are perceived to challenge the political status quo and power relationships because of their actions or beliefs. Repression is principally aimed at deterring individual or collective mobilization against the prevailing political and social order by raising both the physical and material costs of challenging beliefs and actions. States may opt for an escalation of violence by attacking and killing members of their countries' population indiscriminately, or they can choose to single out specific individuals or groups that are deemed threatening and eliminate them in a targeted manner.

To distinguish between different forms of repression I draw on research that has conceptualized violence with respect to the precision of the target.

Repression in the Digital Age: Surveillance, Censorship, and the Dynamics of State Violence. Anita R. Gohdes, Oxford University Press. © Oxford University Press 2024. DOI: 10.1093/oso/9780197743577.003.0003

THEORY 41

On the one end of the spectrum is targeted repression, where the receivers of violent coercion are selected based on specific individual or collective characteristics (Kalyvas, 2006; Steele, 2009; Wood, 2010). Such characteristics may be activity-based, such as when individuals are targeted for anti-regime activities like organizing protests, criticizing policies, or merely having voted against the government. Characteristics may also be identity-based, such as when individuals belong to ethnic or religious groups that are perceived to be a threat to the government's security and stability. While not always the case, targeted repression is frequently associated with a lower scale of violence. In contrast, indiscriminate, or untargeted, repression is defined as violence that does not discriminate between those individuals or groups that are considered a threat, and those who might be classified as "normal" citizens (Mason and Krane, 1989).

The nature, scale, and precision of state repression is fundamentally dependent on information. In the following section I discuss the relationship between information and repression and highlight ways in which the Internet is changing the architecture, speed, and distribution of information control.

3.1 The role of information in repression

Effective repression ideally targets those individuals or groups who pose a threat to the state, while sparing those who do not constitute a threat. The ability to discriminate between these subgroups requires high-quality information on current, growing, and future threats. There are a number of ways in which governments have traditionally obtained information to help guide both their repressive and distributive policies. One way in which governments obtain information about their popularity, and lack thereof, is through elections (see e.g. Gandhi and Lust-Okar, 2009). Electoral processes, whether they are conducted in fully free and fair ways or not, can provide leaders with updates on general levels of public support. They also provide a fine-grained look at geographic areas and sectors of the population that would like to see a change in leadership (Magaloni, 2006). Areas identified as having lower support for the incumbent may suffer distributive and repressive consequences in years following elections (Blaydes, 2010; Steele, 2011).

A traditional approach towards obtaining precise information on potential threats has been through the intelligence work of state security apparatuses. Informants trained to infiltrate, monitor, and report on the activities of potentially threatening individuals or groups often make up a large proportion of internal security personnel, in particular in non-democratic countries (Greitens, 2016).

Obtaining detailed information through the use of informants is very costly. Prior to the expansion of mobile communication technology and the Internet, the surveillance capacities of governments, while frequently pervasive, required intense human labor. Analog surveillance demands enormous recruitment and training efforts, as well as a delicate network for information transmission built on a combination of trust, deception, payoffs, and coercion. Maintaining a functioning network of informants that manages to infiltrate the sectors of a society where threats are most likely to be hidden is a massive endeavor. This example from Communist Bulgaria illustrates the challenge:

> The management of dissent required systematic surveillance of a wide spectrum of groups: the clergy and churchgoers, intellectuals and students, ethnic minorities, sympathizers of the old regime and of the formerly existing opposition parties, peasants who opposed land collectivization, and fringe political groups like the anarchists. To accomplish this, the DS [Bulgarian State Security] needed an informant network that was both large in size and high in quality. The size of the DS informant network grew from less than 1,000 in 1945 to as many as 55,000 by 1953.
>
> (Dimitrov and Sassoon, 2014: 14–15)

Many security services were quick to adapt to expansions of communication technology, such as landline telephones. The Ministerium für Staatssicherheit in the former German Democratic Republic was famously known for tapping phones all across the country and maintaining a dedicated staff charged with sifting through information gleaned from phone calls. Yet, the technical limits on the number of wiretaps meant that secret service agents were frequently relegated to physically eavesdropping on those identified as potentially threatening.

The ways in which access to information affects the choice of violent responses by states has been the subject of research by scholars studying conflict violence and those studying authoritarian survival more generally. Regarding the composition and focus of the security services in Communist Bulgaria and Ba'thist Iraq, Dimitrov and Sassoon (2014) argue that longer-term changes in repressive strategy in both countries were ultimately dependent on their ability to obtain high-quality information. The ability to access actionable intelligence was dependent on the strategic priorities by the respective party as well as their ability to penetrate networks of contention in certain sectors of the population. Their findings indicate that high-quality work by informants was directly tied to targeted repression, while lack of information ensued in mass repression. Blaydes (2019: 46), also studying the Ba'thist regime in Iraq, suggests that access to high-quality information is tied to the state's ability to infiltrate different societal groups effectively. In Iraq, the regime's hunger for high-quality insight into the activities of the country's Kurdish minority was met with linguistic, socio-cultural, and bureaucratic challenges (Blaydes, 2019: 46).

State capacity to monitor and identify challengers is also highly varied geographically (see Müller-Crepon, Hunziker, and Cederman, 2021). In his work on the logic of violence in civil war, Kalyvas (2006) argues that a core means of obtaining intelligence in the midst of warfare is through exercising geographic control over a certain territory. Sufficiently controlled areas allow state forces to identify hidden enemies by drawing on information shared by informants and collaborators who, because of the group's control, are less likely to fear retribution by those they are informing on.[1] Through the availability of information on the local whereabouts of insurgents, state forces are able to selectively target insurgents and their supporters, thereby employing violence more effectively. According to this logic, selective violence is preferable to indiscriminate violence, as it allows armed actors to clearly signal to civilians the benefits of collaboration; only those who choose to side with the enemy will be punished.

In sum, the varying willingness and ability to monitor and police certain localities and societal groups helps explain why and when security forces are more likely to engage in targeted violence, and when they are likely to resort to mass repression. Building and training an extensive network of informants to successfully infiltrate various parts of society requires extensive resources and at least some knowledge of the core threats the political leadership is facing. For this reason, even highly resourced states that heavily invest in surveillance may be caught off-guard by dynamic changes to the domestic threat landscape. Security services, like any bureaucracy, are slow to change, and their core competencies tend to be designed with one main objective in mind. In the case of security services that objective is dependent on the core threat a country faces (Greitens, 2016). When that core threat is replaced

44 REPRESSION IN THE DIGITAL AGE

with a new source of contention, it may leave security forces unprepared and unable to respond efficiently. Reorienting the focus of security services may take many years (Dimitrov and Sassoon, 2014: 21).

The double-edged sword of online information control

Traditional intelligence networks based primarily on in-person informing are usually built and put in place for the sole purpose of benefiting the authorities. While the infrastructure they rely on is resource-intensive, networks of in-person informants provide an asymmetric increase in access to information for the state. A fundamental difference between in-person and online surveillance is that the infrastructure online surveillance relies upon is multi-purpose. Its core component, Internet penetration, has been eagerly adopted by the public on a global scale and serves many financial, social, and political functions that are not directly linked to the state's surveillance objectives. Because this infrastructure is multi-purpose, it has expanded the precision, resolution, and nature of information, affording states access to highly disaggregated and networked information. From the perspective of intrusive state authorities, this type of information would at best have been available through laborious and delicate in-person informing in the pre-Internet era, and at worst would never have been available at all.

Precisely because online surveillance relies on a multi-purpose infrastructure, it brings with it new risks of stimulating anti-government thought and action. Online surveillance only works if the digital infrastructure is adopted and used by people, and if it is done so relatively freely. The more individuals have the ability to exchange and access information freely, the easier the monitoring and interception of critical information becomes. At the same time, the Internet was initially designed to facilitate the access and exchange of information, not act as a giant self-service spy-tool for inquisitive security services. As a consequence, states have been confronted with digitally enabled activists and movements (Earl and Kimport, 2011) that have adopted new online tools to bolster their coordinated strength in taking on the state (see e.g. Danitz and Strobel, 1999; Goldstein, 2007; Chowdhury, 2008). And as I discuss below, expanding digital infrastructures have also allowed non-state groups to improve their military capabilities by facilitating the calibration of weapons and targeting military locations.

Many countries have therefore accompanied the expansion of Internet penetration with the kinds of restrictions and censorship methods described in the previous chapter, even while knowing that such restrictions will also affect their own ability to monitor dissidents (Kalathil and Boas, 2003; Boas, 2006; Deibert et al., 2010).

Modern-day governments intent on controlling digitally mobilized citizens therefore face a fundamental trade-off: they can provide, or at least not actively hinder, access to digital communication and content and use the information gleaned from *surveilling* these channels to their own advantage. This strategy produces new and precise forms of information, but simultaneously provides the infrastructure for potential opposition groups to collectively coordinate and mobilize. Alternatively, they can *censor* their citizens' access to digital channels of mobilization by shutting down or restricting Internet access. While limiting the benefits for protest groups, this strategy also results in information loss. Both strategies thus provide attractive benefits, but also come at considerable cost.

To give an example, assume that a group of activists are planning an anti-government demonstration. A censorship strategy would assume that the protest can only be successful if the activists are able to reach out to fellow citizens via online social media platforms and motivate them to join the demonstrations. Shutting down accessibility to these platforms should—according to this logic—reduce the successfulness and size of such a demonstration. Alternatively, states might decide to make use of digital surveillance. For surveillance to work, the activists would *have* to reach out to their fellow citizens via social media in order for the state to monitor the potential number of protesters, and register each individual's name, location, level of motivation to participate, and—if possible—history of anti-government activities.

The implications for a state's coercive strategy will be dependent on this tradeoff. Where governments restrict network access, they will also be more likely to employ broader, more indiscriminate campaigns of violence against their own population. In contrast, maintaining network connections in order to digitally surveil citizens will more likely be used where states are interested in identifying specific, individual threats; therefore, incidences of highly targeted state terror will be more prevalent. In the following section, I discuss the logic of these two different strategies of online information control in more detail, and provide arguments about their constraining and enabling effect on the choice of violent, coercive strategy.

3.2 The logic of online surveillance

Online surveillance of entire populations, in particular of those identified as potential threats, is a highly rational policy option for governments who fear for their political survival. Knowing where the perceived threat is coming from, and who the most "dangerous" actors are, is a crucial component for governments who are resolved to stay in power. There are a number of ways contemporary online surveillance can support governments in maintaining political control. Mass surveillance is used to flag and *identify* dissidents, while monitoring known threats helps identify their networks and stay abreast of planned activities. Analyzing social media patterns can provide important information on the growth and spread of political unrest. Where protest does erupt, surveilling the entire population's response to it can help anticipate the potential for future dissent and assess how the protests are perceived at large. In general, surveillance will be covert, but in some instances states will partially reveal their monitoring activities as a way to deter the population from challenging state authority.

Identification

Online surveillance offers important and tempting opportunities for governments to gather timely and precise information on the identity of potentially threatening activists and dissidents. Individuals who are active in writing critical articles about the government and posting them online can be identified almost immediately, and their interaction and connection with other activists recorded and analyzed. Tracing individuals' locations through their IP addresses or the signals from their mobile phones has become a routine operation, and frequently leads to the arrest of online activists. State authorities across the world, including in Vietnam, Russia, Bangladesh, and Ethiopia, routinely harass and arrest bloggers for voicing critical opinions on government policies or conduct (Poetranto, 2012; CIPESA, 2014). In many cases, these arrests occur before any of these activists have even launched activities outside of the digital world (see Committee to Protect Journalists, 2014).

Online surveillance has also raised the bar of what good quality intelligence can look like, and expanded state authorities' imagination of what counts as dissent.[2] Someone interested in the status of a discriminated minority may have not uttered a word about this to anyone yet, let alone drawn public attention to their interest. But they may have decided to search for information online about this group, thereby automatically being digitally flagged as a potential troublemaker because of the search terms they used. Once flagged, authorities can also track their communications patterns and identify their private and professional networks.

Anticipation

The production of social media content has, to a certain extent, become a mirror of real-life, in that the number and nature of online commentaries tends to vary with actual events happening on the ground (Zeitzoff, 2011). Challenges to a state's political authority, for example through riots or protests, will quickly be discussed online, or might even be sparked by online conversations (González-Bailón et al., 2011; Barberá et al., 2015). Using digital surveillance to closely monitor the attitudes of the broader population towards both the challenger's actions and the government's initial reaction offers an important barometer of a society's general disposition towards the contemporary political climate. Bursts of activity, topic changes, and the geographic diffusion of online discussions can provide early warnings of growing and shifting social and political unrest (Chen and Xu, 2017; Qin, Strömberg, and Wu, 2017). Use of the information exchanged on social media to build network models of interaction between current and potential dissidents has been a strategy used by governments in countries such as China, Bahrain, Syria, and Egypt. Social media can also help governments identify "hidden influencers," individuals who are less visible within regular opposition networks but end up being crucial in building, framing, and maintaining protest mobilization (González-Bailón, Borge-Holthoefer, and Moreno, 2013).

A principal problem for authoritarian regimes is that they tend to suppress mass opinion for so long that they end up without a clear understanding of the political attitudes held by the majority of their population (Kuran, 1997). Lorentzen (2013) argues that consolidated authoritarian regimes actually have an incentive to permit local protest at fairly regular intervals in order to gather information about political dissatisfaction. In a similar way, monitoring the broader public's reaction towards minor protests can significantly enhance the government's understanding of potential grievances simmering at the surface of society (Gunitsky, 2015); discontent might turn into a critical threat if not countered in a targeted way.

48 REPRESSION IN THE DIGITAL AGE

Spyware that provides full remote access to the target's device can help security services monitor the whereabouts, behavior, and communications of dissidents and independent journalists (Telecomix, 2012; Srivastava, 2020). The combination of targeted intrusive surveillance of smaller groups and mass monitoring of public media sources affords states access to both the plans of core activists and the resonance their proposed actions might find in the broader population.

Intimidation

Improved identification and anticipation of dissent are direct instrumental gains that governments expect from the employment of online surveillance tools. A core function of large-scale societal monitoring that has been discussed by surveillance studies scholars for decades is the state's idea of achieving population control and discipline through deterrence (Lyon, 2001; Ball, Haggerty, and Lyon, 2012). Discipline through the threat of surveillance lies at the core of Bentham's famous plans for a panopticon, a correctional institution designed to allow for constant surveillance of prisoners while concealing the guards from the inmates' view. The assumption was that prisoners could be controlled without physical coercion if they were placed amidst an omnipresent surveillance infrastructure while never knowing whether they were actually being monitored or not (Bentham, 1995; Elmer, 2012). While the original idea of the omnipresent surveillance infrastructure was designed to control prison populations, surveillance researchers have highlighted the ways in which modern societies are incorporating elements of the panopticon into broader forms of societal control (Lyon, 2006).

The empirical focus of this book is on the informational value governments expect to glean from employing online surveillance methods. But the potential of using surveillance for social control is theoretically important in understanding when and why governments will expand and provide digital infrastructure (Greitens, Lee, and Yazici, 2020). To bolster the omnipresence of surveillance infrastructure, visible technology such as CCTV cameras and frequent ID checkpoints can support the message that at any given time, your behavior or communication may be watched and recorded (Xiao, 2019).

States can also strategically reveal their surveillance capabilities to selected parts of the population in order to communicate their ability and power. In January 2014 protesters on Kiev's central independence square Maidan Nezalezhnosti received a text message that they had been recorded as participants in a mass disturbance (Murphy, 2014). By revealing that they were monitoring the presence of protesters and were keeping tabs on who was participating, the government signaled its capabilities and readiness to use them. In other contexts, surveillance capabilities are revealed during interrogations. For example, ethnic minorities in Ethiopia have reported of being confronted with the history and content of their phone calls (Human Rights Watch, 2014). The partial revelation of surveillance techniques in and of itself becomes a repressive measure meant to intimidate and deter further anti-government activity. The message sent implies that the government not only knows *who* is challenging it—regardless of whether this information is correct or not—but that it has identified these challengers as a threat, and is willing and able to take action against them. The knowledge of surveillance and its consequences is intended to actively encourage self-censorship and compliance among the population.

Implications for coercive strategy

Online surveillance is a powerful tool that has the potential to support the repression of anti-government activity before it extensively diffuses and at the same deter action by those who know they are being watched. Monitoring and identifying dissents is more likely to be useful when and where governments have less knowledge about the potential threats. The less governments know about the concrete challenge(r)s they are facing the more online surveillance data can support the identification and location of those initiating dissenting action. Once opposition groups have become institutionalized with accepted leaders who speak openly for the entire group, covert information becomes openly available; the added value of surveillance decreases in comparison to the benefits gained from censoring anti-government speech. In concerted efforts to counter growing domestic threats, digital surveillance is likely to support the use of targeted acts of localized violence against those identified as critical to the protesters' future success.

Precise and high-resolution information is not always high quality. The collection of intelligence based on online surveillance does *not* automatically result in perfectly accurate information. Information collected on potential targets may be precise, for example by providing the exact location and full message and contact history of a suspected rebel leader. By extension, this information can allow security forces to target this individual with a high

50 REPRESSION IN THE DIGITAL AGE

level of precision. But the information may still be wrong for a number of reasons, including that the targeted individual is not in fact the suspected leader of a rebellion. What this demonstrates is that the correlation between online surveillance and targeted repression is enabled by an increase in access to precise information. Precise information can also be high quality, but it is not a precondition for security forces to act on it.

Because online surveillance only works when the Internet can be used, targeted repression is more likely to occur in contexts where governments provide access to the Internet. It, therefore, comes at a high price: for online surveillance tools to work, the target population needs to have access to the Internet. Unrestricted access to the Internet, in turn, provides opposition groups with all the advantages and potential of collectively organizing on the Internet (Steinert-Threlkeld et al., 2015; Larson et al., 2019).

It is important to note that not all modern surveillance infrastructure is multi-purpose, and therefore not all modern surveillance infrastructure requires governments to consider this trade-off with the same urgency. A prominent example is the Golden Shield Project (GSP), a surveillance system that was introduced by the Chinese Government at the turn of the millennium. The resources, capabilities, and sophistication of the Chinese surveillance and censorship apparatus make the country somewhat of an outlier (MacKinnon, 2011; Cairns and Plantan, 2016; Roberts, 2018; Chen and Greitens, 2021). At its inception, the GSP surveillance system encompassed wide-ranging linking of personal information in a networked database and helped the government identify potential threats emanating from the population (Xu, 2021: 316). In his study of the repressive effects of the GSP, Xu shows how the rollout of the project increased the authorities' use of targeted, preventive repression (Xu, 2021). His results support the theoretical expectation that high-quality information will be associated with a more targeted repressive strategy. In the case of the Golden Shield Project, user-generated exchanges online only make up a part of the entire surveillance apparatus. Xu shows that the project included:

> Internet surveillance modules that monitor important websites, online forums, and social media. Based on keywords searching software, these modules automatically discover and record public sentiments, and then report signs of social instability to local police.   (Xu, 2021: 316)

Disruptions of the networks available to the general public would thus likely be less impactful on the authorities' abilities to gather high-quality

THEORY   51

information since they would still be left with access to networked data on individuals' movement patterns, personal and professional details, and biometrics. But much recent research has demonstrated that the Chinese authorities tend to approach censorship with a certain level of restraint in anticipation of improved long-term support and stability (Lorentzen, 2014; Chen and Xu, 2017; Qin, Strömberg, and Wu, 2017; Roberts, 2018).

3.3 The logic of online censorship

Censorship is pursued under the assumption that certain forms of information have the potential to incite dangerous thoughts and actions among the population. It includes the restriction of individuals' freedom of speech as well as restrictions of various types of media. Authorities use various forms of repression and intimidation to encourage self-censorship by individuals in public- and semi-public spaces. In addition, the publication and broadcasting of critical viewpoints on TV, radio, or in newspapers is often tightly regulated by laws, economic sanctions, and political marginalization of such outlets (Whitten-Woodring and Van Belle, 2017).

Many traditional forms of censorship are time and labor intensive in their implementation. Shutting down newspapers, radio, and TV stations, or re-staffing them entirely with loyalists takes a considerable amount time, effort, and coordination. Reversing such actions to loosen censorship may take even longer. In contrast, online censorship allows states to more dynamically respond to changes in the political climate. Full or partial shutdowns of the Internet require technical and administrative coordination that, depending on the number of ISPs, can be implemented and reversed with relative ease. Adding or removing domains from a blacklist or launching DDoS attacks is a matter of writing a few lines of code and instructing some moderately skilled IT personel. This "just-in-time" approach towards online censorship allows governments and their security forces to apply temporary restrictions (Deibert et al., 2008) that can swiftly be reversed to allow regular access.

Restricting information exchange

Cutting digital communication channels can complicate the exchange of information that is critical of the government, making it increasingly difficult for individuals to assess the extent to which fellow citizens are also frustrated

52 REPRESSION IN THE DIGITAL AGE

with the political status quo. The role of information in lowering people's inhibition in joining anti-government activities is succinctly formalized in Lohmann's information cascade model, which assumes that protest and regime overthrow unfold across different stages:

> (1) People take costly political action to express their dissatisfaction with the incumbent regime. (2) The public then takes informational cues from changes in the size of the protest movement over time. (3) The regime loses public support and collapses if the protest activities reveal it to be malign.
>
> Lohmann (1994: 49)

Clearly, loss of public support does not always unavoidably lead to regime collapse, yet in their pursuit of political stability and longevity governments will be wary to take unnecessary risks. Restricting access to online communication can help hamper the spread and awareness of general public discontent. Reducing the volume of local "negative press" can make it increasingly hard for individuals to assess the extent to which fellow citizens are frustrated with the political status quo and perhaps willing to resist or fight to change it. As a consequence, citizens may revert to keeping their true opinions of government's performance to themselves (Kuran, 1997).

States therefore have a vested interest in making the public display of discontent as difficult as possible, to prevent the occurrence of such cascades, but the rise in information exchange across social media platforms has dramatically lowered these costs for anyone connected to the Internet (Edmond, 2013; González-Bailón et al., 2011). Restricting the exchange of information to avoid widespread diffusion during the critical second stage identified by Lohmann can be a rational and easy-to-implement strategy for governments.

Hindering collective organization

Beyond the exchange of information about individuals' political preferences, online communication has played a fundamental role in helping groups with common grievances collectively organize (Theocharis et al., 2015). The distinction between communication about dissatisfaction and communication about the logistics of organizing in light of dissatisfaction helps clarify the role online communication can play in opposition activity (Little, 2016). Messenger apps and social media are important for collective mobilization because they connect core activists with each other and with the periphery. Peripheral protesters are larger in numbers and include a broader cross-section of the population, making them crucial for sustaining the momentum and for providing situational knowledge during protest activities (Barberá et al., 2015; Steinert-Threlkeld, 2017).

The importance of online communication for the efficient coordination of anti-government activities explains why states may restrict access to the Internet, even when public dissatisfaction is already a well-known fact. Unanticipated restriction of online access can hinder collective mobilization. The sudden absence of vital news sources, location services, social media, and messenger apps means the collective organization of dissent must revert to slower forms of communication. Losing these channels can deal a significant blow to groups intent on maintaining a cohesive and efficiently organized opposition that also appeals to more moderate members of society. Evidence from China suggests that during heightened political tensions, the government focuses on censoring content calling for collective action (King, Pan, and Roberts, 2013).

But even where opposition groups have developed the capacity to maintain cohesion and control in the absence of network access, the shutdown of connectivity allows governments to further isolate groups from their core support network. In contentious contexts where opposition groups resist or even actively fight the government, garnering and maintaining support for the opposition can be a key strength of otherwise weak actors (Arreguin-Toft, 2001; Valentino, Huth, and Balch-Lindsay, 2004). In modern conflicts opposition groups increasingly rely on digital channels to reach both new potential supporters and fresh recuits. Material support no longer requires local interactions, since financial transactions can be made through mobile phones. Individuals in distant locations can demonstrate their solidarity by spreading messages as well as collecting financial support. When governments limit Internet accessibility in areas where opposition and resistance groups are located, they thus not only hinder said groups' abilities to organize and fight but also limit their access to moral and material support.

Restricting access to parts or all of the Internet for short periods of time not only stifles the spread of anti-government information, it also prevents individuals from collectively organizing themselves and maintaining order and discipline during concerted protest actions. In addition, this disorder can give governments a reason to violently intervene to "restore" order. If the disruption of digital communication channels is unexpected, governments

54 REPRESSION IN THE DIGITAL AGE

have the advantage of surprising their opponents, who have to regroup and coordinate activities via channels not dependent on the Internet.

Depleting opposition capabilities

Governments faced with armed internal rebellion have a particular incentive to cut Internet connections: stifling the opposition's military capability. Recent conflicts in Libya and Syria provide extensive footage of opposition fighters using online mapping services, such as Google Earth and Google Maps, to accurately locate military targets and to calibrate weapons to effectively reach said targets (Brownstone, 2011; Miller, 2012; Keating, 2013). New developments in geographical location systems made for personal use on devices such as smartphones and tablets have revolutionized the capacity to locate and target regime forces with a level of precision that was not available a decade ago. Cutting these connections will provide an operational advantage for state military and pro-government militas over oftentimes under-equipped and ill-trained insurgent groups.

Withholding infrastructure

When political challengers gain momentum in voicing their concerns about the legitimacy and credibility of incumbent regimes, displays of power and control can be an effective way to remind the domestic population of who has the capability to deny them basic infrastructural needs. Restricting online access in light of oppositional threats can also serve as a form of punishment of the population for allowing and possibly even supporting the formation of an opposition group that threatens the government. As with declarations of states of emergency, the denial of basic infrastructure can be blamed on threats to national security and the necessity for preventing any further harm.

Blaydes, in her study of Egypt's infrastructure development under Mubarak, shows how regions that supported the opposition in the 1984 elections were systematically disadvantaged in their infrastructure developments during the following decade (Blaydes, 2010: 65–76). Internet access is by now part of modern societies' core infrastructure; next to power supply, roads, housing, and water facilities, modern life is unthinkable without access to information and communications technology (Sandvig, 2013; Musiani et al., 2016). Large-scale counterinsurgency tactics such as sieges have traditionally been characterized by the denial of basic services, such as electricity, water, waste removal, and policing (Todman, 2017). It is thus not surprising that Internet access has joined the list of basic services now open to state manipulation.

State-imposed Internet shutdowns are thus timely reminders of the de facto power of ruling governments, and can send a clear signal to the domestic population that further opposition activities are seen as a threat and will, in turn, be punished. Outside of conflict situations, states have been known to selectively drag their feet on expanding digital access in areas deemed problematic (Weidmann et al., 2016). During protests the denial of online infrastructure is usually temporary and reversible, as demonstrated by short-term censorship and shutdown methods.

When censorship backfires
A population that relies on the Internet for both personal and professional reasons is likely to become skeptical of a government that cuts them off from these channels for extended periods of time. Worse, the denial of these basic services might even make a government appear to be somewhat desperate. Obstructing or even just partly restricting accessibility can actually provide incentives for a neutral population to search for ways to circumvent the bans, and possibly even search for more sensitive content (Hobbs and Roberts, 2018; Gläßel and Paula, 2019). Thus, when a large segment of the population cannot access online services for non-political activities because the government is trying to censor a small activist group, this can spectacularly backfire (Zuckerman, 2015).

Evidence suggests that following the outages in Egypt in 2011, an increasing number of protesters took to the streets to demonstrate against Mubarak's regime (Hassanpour, 2014). When Turkey's government decided to merely block access to Twitter in April 2014, the response was a national and international rallying of protests against Prime Minister Erdoğan (Tufekci, 2014). For this reason, overly ambitious network disruptions to prohibit the organization and coordination of a few select dissidents may quickly dispel the illusion of freedom for the majority of Internet users. This reinforces the attention given to activists and broadens their platform. The restriction of network access will then provide the final impetus for ordinary citizens to take to the streets and protest against repressive government policies.

Extreme censorship, such as nationwide shutdowns, can also attract huge international interest. The outcry across the world, in particular on social media, tends to be large when the Internet gets shut down, as recently happened in Iran, Myanmar, Uganda, and parts of Ethiopia. Since activists are connected around the globe, not least because of social media, the sudden blackout of information may even produce a boomerang effect, whereby activists in other countries pressure their own government to condemn the actions in the repressive state (see Keck and Sikkink, 1998).

Lastly, because users increasingly rely on online services for their livelihoods, censorship can lead to considerable economic losses. Companies all across the globe rely on messenger apps such as Telegram or WhatsApp to conduct their business. When the Mubarak regime shut down Internet services for five days in 2011, the Egyptian economy lost an estimated $90 million worth of revenues (Howard, Agarwal, and Hussain, 2011: 231). This figure only includes direct losses in revenues due to the absence of Internet and phone services; it does not include the shutdown of general communication services, such as those generated by tourism, call centers, and e-commerce, as well as potential losses on investment in the aftermath of the blackout (see OECD, 2011). One study examining the economic impact in India estimated that between 2012 and 2017, more than 16,000 hours of Internet shutdown cost the Indian economy around $3.04 billion (Kathuria et al., 2018: 10).

Implications for coercive strategy

While the technical implementation of disruptions provides a relatively cheap policy option, the repercussions of cutting off Internet access can clearly be extremely costly for the government. Restricting information access also affects the state's own ability to gather intelligence about the nature and characteristics of the protesters. To effectively target internal threats, governments are largely dependent on intelligence that they collect through tip-offs from their civilian supporters, and through monitoring the actions and declared intentions of dissidents. As soon as these dissidents are no longer able to communicate online, states automatically have a harder time monitoring the opposition's plans and location. Furthermore, the lack of network access prevents supporters from providing critical information to the government.

There are two main arguments that suggest why governments using Internet disruptions in light of domestic threats will implement them in conjunction with violent coercive strategies that are *larger in scale and indiscriminate* in terms of whom they target.

First, from a government's perspective, the benefits of disruptions—namely gaining organizational and operational advantages over the opposition—will only be worth the costs in situations where it perceives the domestic political threat to be *large*. Where a critical mass of citizens has already taken to the street and collectively organized a substantial amount of internal resistance and support, disrupting the Internet can act as an immediate attempt to limit further diffusion of the protests, and prevent them from turning into population-wide uprisings. Where only a small portion of a domestic population is seen as challenging the status quo, the disruption of the Internet would likely only lead to increased attention for those waging the anti-government campaign, and the disruptive response by the state could even lead to further support and solidarity with the protest movement.

Clearly, restrictions to digital communication only make sense if the expected support and solidarity that might possibly be generated towards anti-government groups in light of disruptions is negligible, when compared to the damage it is expected to cause to the opposition's capabilities to organize. This will most likely occur where the opposition has already reached a critical size and requires reliable communication channels to maintain its strength and momentum. The decision to visibly respond to critical domestic threats via a demonstration of control in the form of Internet restrictions suggests that a government is resolved and willing to counterattack the opposition with a heavy hand. As research on the logic of violence in civil conflict has revealed, state violence is likely to be indiscriminate in terms of whom it targets when the state perceives the majority of its population to be a threat (Valentino, Huth, and Balch-Lindsay, 2004; Kalyvas, 2006).

The second reason that suggests Internet disruptions will be accompanied by larger, indiscriminate campaigns of coercion relates to the constraining effects of the outage itself. When a government opts for the use of Internet disruptions to avert further spread of unrest, it simultaneously limits its own access to crucial intelligence significantly. Not only are anti-government groups barred from organizing online, but state forces now also lack access to this information. In addition, loyal civilian supporters of the government are hindered from sharing knowledge about developments on the ground with them. In short, states sabotage their own access to information about the identity and location of the most "dangerous" dissidents. The use of violence will inadvertently become increasingly indiscriminate.

Where states perceive the threat from opposition movements to be *large*, disrupting Internet accessibility presents a somewhat desperate measure to avert further damage. Once the choice for active network disruptions has been made, and the technical implementation is completed, the options for using violence will be severely limited: without up-to-date intelligence on the developments of anti-government activists, the government has less opportunity and capability to locate and target those individuals deemed most threatening. Strategies of violence employed by the state are then more likely to affect the domestic population indiscriminately than to target dissidents individually.

Summary of theoretical expectations

I argue that cyber and coercive control are coordinated and employed by state actors in response to perceived domestic political challenges. State actors opt for a specific form of cyber control to support and facilitate the use of a specific form of violent repression.

Online surveillance, through the collection of precise and highly specified intelligence on the intentions and location of critical players in anti-government movements supports security forces in employing targeted, individualized violence. Online surveillance is thus likely to increase states' use of targeted, individualized strategies of violent coercion against domestic threats.

When and where state actors prioritize censoring information, for example through the partial or full shutdown of access to the Internet, they are also more likely to engage in indiscriminate repression.

This chapter has illustrated the ways in which Internet access provides venues for organizing, exchanging ideas, and coordinating actions that challenge the state in fundamental ways. The Internet gives non-state actors access to the digital tools for protest and dissent, while at the same time creating opportunities for the state to penetrate sectors of society that were previously hard and costly to reach. The choice between Internet restrictions, leading to active censorship, and Internet provision, which can be used for digital surveillance purposes, presents states with a fundamental trade-off that ultimately constrains them in their choice of coercive strategy. This chapter has provided a first theoretical entry point to investigating the logic of these strategies of Internet control from the perspective of governments fearful about their survival, and has suggested mechanisms that link them to violent coercive strategies.

The next chapter turns to the use of digital controls and violent repression by regime forces in the context of the Syrian conflict.

4

Online controls and repression in Syria

A few weeks before the first mass protests ensued across Syria in March 2011, the regime led by President Bashar Al-Assad lifted a large number of bans on social networking platforms, including Facebook and YouTube. Up to that point, the Assad regime had controlled the most regulated media and telecommunications landscape in the Middle East (OpenNet Initiative, 2009*b*). Suddenly, Syrian citizens were able to digitally voice their anger and resentment towards a despotic regime with an appalling human rights record. At a time where citizens in neighboring countries were taking to social media to organize and broadcast their dissent, the decision to allow largely unfiltered access would appear to be a recipe for disaster, from the perspective of the Assad regime. Why, after years of extreme censorship, would a deeply autocratic government suddenly permit unrestricted access to, and exchange of, information? The following three chapters will explore this question by taking a look at how the regime's domestic control of the Internet has intersected with and influenced its use of violent repression to maintain political control. The present chapter provides an overview of the regime's digital politics prior to and following the uprising in 2011 and subsequent conflict. I conclude with a discussion of the data and measurement approach the next two chapters take in order to empirically investigate the relationship between cyber controls and violent repression.

4.1 Information control for regime stability

Intelligence gathering through monitoring of both the general population and across government agencies has been at the heart of the Syrian security strategy since its inception. Following the Ba'th coup in 1963 and the establishment of the State of Emergency Law, the intelligence services firmly established themselves as a core actor who would help guarantee the regime's rule by weeding out opponents early and rigorously. At the same time, the country's Armed Forces were ruthless in their use of indiscriminate violence

Repression in the Digital Age: Surveillance, Censorship, and the Dynamics of State Violence. Anita R. Gohdes, Oxford University Press. © Oxford University Press 2024. DOI: 10.1093/oso/9780197743577.003.0004

ONLINE CONTROLS AND REPRESSION IN SYRIA 61

against organized opposition, as first demonstrated in the shelling of Hama after an uprising of the Muslim Brotherhood in 1964 (Rathmell, 1996). When Hafiz al-Assad came to power through what he termed a "corrective coup" in 1970, he proceeded to build an intelligence service that was largely staffed by members of his own inner circle, including family members and other close ties from within the Alawite community (Hinnebusch, 2001).[1]

While the regime's intelligence services were primarily concerned with foreign policy issues, in particular related to Israel, Lebanon, and Egypt, domestic challenges offered opportunities for the services to further expand their discretionary power and resources. As Hinnebusch (2001: 81) writes "[t]he security forces and intelligence services *(mukhabarat)* are multiple, pervasive in surveillance of society, and feared for the arbitrary arrest, imprisonment and torture of dissidents which they have practised." Episodes of indiscriminate domestic force by the security services during the rule of Hafiz Al-Assad were apparent in the brutal crackdowns against militant Islamist groups in the early 1980s, following an assassination attempt against the president. The crackdown culminated in an offensive against the city of Hama, where in 1982 state forces used heavy weaponry including helicopters, fighter jets, and tanks, flattening entire neighborhoos and killing thousands of civilians (Atassi, 2012). The attack on Hama in 1982 became a key symbol for the regime's ruthless readiness to violently punish any and all challenges to its existence.

In addition to the demonstrated preparedness to use indiscriminate violence, the regime's internal intelligence services were also known to swiftly and defiantly deal with individuals sharing content that was deemed critical of the government. In the late 1980s, a number of journalists who had reported on issues related to corruption and mismanagement were subsequently targeted and killed by perpetrators linked to the regime (Wege, 1990: 93).

Hafiz al-Assad's success in maintaining political power for decades has therefore been, among other things,[2] attributed to his ruthlessness in using repression and surveillance against the general population as well as among the various intelligence services (Wege, 1990: 97). Grassroots opposition were silenced and dismantled through local-level surveillance and violent coercion. Elite-level challenges were apprehended and prevented by pitting the various intelligence services of the country against each other, and building an elaborate network of agencies spying on one another to prevent yet another coup (Hinnebusch, 2001; Baczko, Dorronsoro,

62 REPRESSION IN THE DIGITAL AGE

and Quesnay, 2018: 61). The extensive networks built to spy on both the population and across the various intelligence communities highlight the important role offline, or "in-person" surveillance played in maintaining and fortifying the regime's political power long before the advent of digital telecommunications.

Hafiz's son, Bashar, assumed power in the wake of his father's passing in 2000 at the age of 34. Bashar had been groomed as the heir to his father's iron rule of Syria ever since the death of his older brother in 1994. Initially, hope of political and economic reforms was projected onto the 34-year-old, not least because of his international work experience and carefully crafted image of being a technologically minded reformer (e.g. Harms, 2004). Bashar al-Assad was quick to replace key political and military positions with his personal network of loyal supporters that would help secure his own political survival (Perthes, 2006). Notable in the context of this study is the Makhluf family, related to Bashar al-Assad through his mother, which has become one of the most affluent and influential business powers in Syria. Rami Makhluf, al-Assad's cousin, remains in control of Syriatel, the country's key mobile network provider (Leverett, 2005: 83–84). The inherited structures of authoritarian government, paired with the installation of his own inner circle in key positions of influence, helped consolidate Bashar al-Assad's power as Syrian president in the following decade. While violent repression against popular voices challenging the government was still a key pillar of dealing with opposition, less overt methods relying on pervasive and multi-level surveillance of public and semi-private spaces were generally favored (Perthes, 2006). The following section explores the use of digital politics to consolidate political authority prior to the uprisings in 2011.

4.2 Digital politics pre-conflict

Press freedom and freedom of speech are theoretically enshrined in the country's constitution, but a host of policies and laws, including the Emergency Law put in place in 1962, grant the government the legal power to censor and control media and communications (OpenNet Initiative, 2009b: 2). First access to the Internet was established for government bodies in 1998. One year later the Syrian government, through the Syrian Telecommunications Establishment (STE), set in motion plans for its first nationwide monitoring system (Privacy International, 2016: 8). Only then was access to the Internet introduced to the general public (OpenNet

Initiative, 2009*b*: 2). According to the International Telecommunication Union (ITU), the percentage of the population with access to the Internet increased from 0 to 17% between 1999 and 2009. In the following decade, the official estimate of the ITU would double again.[3]

With continuous changes to Syria's telecommunications networks, the government steadily invested in new software solutions to improve their surveillance capabilities and paid increasing attention to technical solutions that would allow them to intercept in ways that would go undetected by their targets, including solutions for monitoring Internet communications via satellite connections. In 2004, the government started working with German software designed to intercept communication in real-time (Privacy International, 2016: 9). The software, called lawful interception management system (LIMS), allowed authorities to access a large variety of communication, such as digital calls, text messages, and emails. In 2008, the government explicitly requested bids for software solutions that would allow them to not only monitor but also filter unwanted content. According to documents obtained by Privacy International, STE was clear in communicating their need for solutions that would allow them to filter content containing politically sensitive messages, not just regular spam (Privacy International, 2016: 8).

Surveillance of online content being linked to offline repression predates the outbreak of the conflict in 2011. In 2007, Reporters Without Borders wrote that Syria was "the biggest prison for cyber-dissidents in the Middle East," after the government had repeatedly arrested individuals who had voiced criticism against the regime online (Reporters Without Borders, 2007). In addition to less visible monitoring and interception, the government actively filtered content and censored access to websites. In the years leading up to the 2011 uprising, Syrian authorities oversaw the pervasive filtering of political content and online tools such as social media services, email providers, search engines, and VoIP services, as well as the selective filtering of content related to social and security issues (OpenNet Initiative, 2009*b*).

In a concerted effort to control online content, the government also incentivized self-censorship by forcing Syrian-based websites and users into revealing their identity when posting or accessing content. For example, Syrian-based websites were forced to provide the full name and identity of the producers whose content they hosted. And a law introduced in 2008 required Internet cafes—at the time one of the most popular access points for Syrians to use the Internet—to record the identity of all customers (Oweis, 2008).

Citizens intent on accessing tools such as social media websites or VoIP services were overwhelmingly reliant on circumvention applications, such as VPNs and other types of proxy connections. In the early 2000s, access to circumvention tools was relatively easy, but the government continued to work towards closing loopholes through improved software, making it increasingly difficult for citizens to access forbidden content (Sands, 2008). While the lack of direct access discouraged some users, many opted for circumvention tools, which in turn not only provided access to forbidden sites, but also shielded them from regime monitoring (Baiazy, 2012). A byproduct of censoring access to unwanted services therefore resulted in the government not being able to intercept content of those who managed to get around the prescribed restrictions, thereby diminishing its own access to potentially crucial intelligence.

4.3 2011 uprising and repression

In March 2011, a group of young teenagers in Daraa were imprisoned and subsequently tortured for writing graffiti that criticized the regime. The protests that ensued following their imprisonment quickly spread across the country, not least because the incident was shared widely on social media (Leenders, 2013; Baczko, Dorronsoro, and Quesnay, 2018: 67). Within a short period of time, the initial protests calling for the release of the teenagers had turned into a mass movement calling for political change and giving voice to a multitude of grievances all over the country (Mazur, 2021). From the start, civil society actors and regular citizens made use of digital spaces to debate ideas, plan actions, and further mobilize. The mass mobilization that spread across Syria occurred in the context of civilian uprisings across numerous Arab countries, most importantly Egypt and Tunisia, which in the months before had demonstrated the potential for change that large and sustained political opposition could entail.

The regime almost immediately responded to the protesters with extreme brutality. In late April 2011, the regime laid siege to the city of Daraa, a tactic it would come to use repeatedly against cities over the course of the conflict. For ten days, state forces cut the city's access to water, power, and communication networks and used heavy weaponry to kill hundreds and injure thousands, all the while refusing access to humanitarian support (Todman, 2017: 13). This tactic was repeated in a number of other towns and cities in the following months. The concerted violent crackdown on protesters who called for the release of prisoners in Daraa was unequivocally aimed at preventing the diffusion of the protests to other parts of the country.

The use of widespread and brutal violence was intended to crush the uprising where possible, and at the same time hinder the opposition in establishing a unified, institutionalized, and broad movement that would have offered one clear alternative to the regime (Leenders, 2015). As will be discussed in the next section, the regime made use of a range of digital surveillance technologies to obtain information on the key opposition actors. To fracture the opposition, the regime strategically cooperated with selected groups, such as the early concessions made towards Kurdish groups who had traditionally been marginalized and discriminated by the regime. Sectarian divides were purposefully engineered: "The regime readily invented, built, encouraged and manipulated sectarian divisions that dramatically altered— and undermined—the uprising's dynamics" (Leenders, 2015: 252). In addition, radical Islamists who were previously incarcerated were released from prison; many would join and lead radical armed opposition groups that would come to the fore in the coming years (Baczko, Dorronsoro, and Quesnay, 2018).

In the early stages of the conflict, the regime's brutal crackdown mimicked the extreme brutality of repression used against protesters under Hafez al-Assad in the 1980s (Atassi, 2012). The assumption was that a disproportionate repressive response would be as effective at deterring the population from supporting challengers as the 1982 offensive in Hama had been in helping secure Hafez's tenure as president. This time around, the strategy proved ineffective at quelling the protests. Instead of retreating, protestors and other anti-government activists continued to organize and take to the streets, calling for political change. Brownlee (2018: 190) points to the importance of social media: "The act of uploading photos or videos onto YouTube documenting the regime's brutality paradoxically encouraged more people to join civil resistance despite the high degree of risk and uncertainty."

As the protests progressed and state repression intensified, armed opposition groups increasingly confronted the regime. Defectors left the military to join these groups, often after witnessing the brutal repression of their own friends and family (Neistat and Solvang, 2011). In the fall of 2011, armed anti-regime groups, notably the Free Syrian Army, ramped up their use of force in an attempt to resist the government's heavy handed response (Neistat and Solvang, 2011). In reflecting on the differences between 1982

66 REPRESSION IN THE DIGITAL AGE

and 2011, one Free Syrian Army (FSA) member remarked: "His father destroyed Hama in a few days, but there was no TV there and no Internet to show the world [. . . .] But today we have the Internet, we photograph and film and have Al Jazeera, so people know. They can see what is happening" (Peterson, 2012).

Determined to squash the opposition, the regime made more concerted efforts to not only target civilians but also damage civilian infrastructure (Todman, 2017). As the protests failed to be quelled and the opposition increasingly evolved into an armed insurgency, the regime's strategy shifted. Heavy artillery against rebel strongholds was first employed in the early months of 2012 (Holliday, 2013: 15). Since then, artillery fire and airpower have become a core strategy used against the Syrian population. Whereas regime forces had previously attempted to fight the opposition through repressive offensives, they now moved towards subsequently establishing military control over towns and cities (Holliday, 2013).

Throughout the conflict, state repression has been perpetrated by a number of different groups that are either directly or indirectly controlled by the regime. The regular state forces, also known as the Syrian Arab Armed Forces, include the Navy, Air Force, and Army. In 2011, the Armed Forces were reported to have comprised roughly 300,000 personnel (OHCHR, 2011). The Army includes a number of specialized divisions, such as the Republican Guard, whose primary task is countering international security threats, as well as the so-called 4th Divison, presumed at the outset of the conflict to be under the control of the president's brother (OHCHR, 2011; Holliday, 2013).

In addition to the Armed Forces, the state's security sector is comprised of a multitude of rather opaque intelligence and security units. These include the military and Air Force intelligence, and a variety of police forces. The regime has also made extensive use of pro-government militias. The *Shabiha*, a predominantly Alawite group, played an early and important role in repressing opposition actors, often with egregious violence, in particular against Sunni rebels (Hinnebusch, 2012: 107). Along with the *Shabiha*, local self-defense committees, often comprised of other minority groups, took up arms to help protect their neighborhoods and regime facilities (Holliday, 2013: 18).

In a report published in November 2011, only a few months after the outbreak of the protests, the UN Human Rights Council wrote that it had documented "patterns of summary execution, arbitrary arrest, enforced disappearance, torture, including sexual violence, as well as violations of children's rights" (OHCHR, 2011: 1) perpetrated by the Syrian military and security forces. Victims included regular civilians, members of the armed opposition, activists, journalists, medical personnel, as well as defectors from the security services (Neistat and Solvang, 2011). Human Rights Watch reported that commanders in the security forces had given orders to kill protesters and bystanders, asserting that the protests needed to be stopped "by all means necessary" (Neistat and Solvang, 2011). In addition, civilians had been arbitrarily detained, tortured, and in many cases either executed or arrested. Further details on the patterns of violence committed by the regime in the first years of the conflict will be discussed in Section 4.5.

4.4 Digital politics following the uprising

A few weeks prior to the Daraa incident, and as large protests in the region were already underway, the Syrian authorities reversed a multi-year ban of popular social media sites, including Facebook, YouTube, and Blogspot. While the move was seen by some as a concession by the regime towards improving the opportunities for freedom of expression, human rights advocates quickly voiced their concern about the government's motives behind the lift, given its long-standing investment in in-person and online monitoring (Preston, 2011). The regime's heavy reliance on digital monitoring software and various forms of hacking and spying following the unblocking of these sites suggests that its intentions behind lifting the ban were to obtain information on the location, identity, and extent of opposition activities within its own borders.

After decades of controlling a highly censored media landscape, lifting the ban offered the regime a low-cost way to expand surveillance and gain a clearer picture of state enemies (see e.g. MacKinnon, 2012). But at the outset of the uprisings, both digital mobilization and the use of social media to share the unfolding events with the outside world initially proved to be challenging for the regime. While many Syrian Internet users had already been active on Facebook prior to lifting of the ban, the change in accessibility of social media websites helped stimulate further online activity on both semi-anonymous and non-anonymous platforms (Brownlee, 2018). Monitoring these platforms effectively required a steep learning curve for the authorities.

The regime's intricate surveillance infrastructure presented a considerable obstacle to the mobilization and institutionalization of the protest movement, in particular in the early phase of the protests. Protesters were often keenly aware of the fact that their communication was being heavily monitored, and some proceeded to cover their faces during public protests to avoid being identified and targeted (Baczko, Dorronsoro, and Quesnay, 2018: 77–79).

Yet evidence collected from military facilities that were abandoned when anti-government groups took over Raqqa in March 2013 suggest that the regime's security apparatus initially had very little intelligence on who the core opposition actors were (Leenders, 2015: 251). This indicates that initially the opposition managed to evade the traditional monitoring and surveillance tactics of the regime to a certain degree.

The government's decision to provide access to social networking sites thus simultaneously supported its own intelligence gathering on the evolving networks and locations of key actors of the nascent civilian uprising, while also providing this opposition with new spaces to collectively plan and organize.

Like many fellow autocrats in the region, the regime was not prepared to effectively deal with the sophisticated use of social media to share pictures, videos, and live reports from mass demonstrations in the early days of the conflict (Miller and Sienkiewicz, 2012). Prominent international media platforms, such as Al-Jazeera, were crucial in channeling and spreading content produced by citizen journalists streaming visuals from the contentious events taking place all over the country (Sultan, 2013). State run media responded with extreme and elaborate conspiracies aimed at diverting attention and focusing on the role of alleged foreign instigations through Israeli Zionists, Qatar (where Al-Jazeera is based), and the US (Alrababa'h and Blaydes, 2021).

Digital surveillance in Syria from late 2011 onwards took on many forms, including the use of imported surveillance and filtering software (Chaabane et al., 2014), targeted malware attacks against opposition actors (Telecomix, 2012; Regalado, Villeneuve, and Scott-Railton, 2015), as well as the employment of a so-called Syrian Electronic Army (Al-Rawi, 2014). In his speech at Damascus University in June 2011, Bashar al-Assad explicitly mentioned the young people's role in responding to the protesters, asserting that "[t]here is the electronic army which has been a real army in virtual reality (Al-Assad, 2011)." A number of security branches within the regime forces are concerned with controlling the telecommunications sector. The branch known as "Branch 225," is reportedly the key communication branch linked to the STE, the ISP active within Syria, as well as other companies involved in providing telecommunications access (Baiazy, 2012; Syrian Network for Human Rights, 2013).

Experts began reporting on the targeting of Syrian activists through pro-government malware within the first year of the conflict (Poulsen, 2013). The types of attacks and tools used changed over time and included, among others, so-called Remote Access Tools (RATs) often distributed through various types of social engineering. Efforts to obtain remote access of users' accounts and devices were described by security researchers as a combination of "fake security tools, fake Skype encryption, and a steady stream of intriguing bait documents and malicious links, tailored to the interests, needs, and fears of the opposition" (Galperin, Marquis-Boire, and Scott-Railton, 2013: 2).

Throughout the conflict, pro- and anti-government groups have employed low-level cyber attacks (Kostyuk and Zhukov, 2019: 24). Regime forces frequently obtained access through the employment of general phishing and targeted ("spear-phishing") attacks. Malware has also been distributed through download links posted on regime critical Facebook pages (Galperin, Marquis-Boire, and Scott-Railton, 2013). Once the attackers obtained a user's credentials or access to their devices more generally, they were able to infiltrate the user's accounts and files, and glean plans on opposition activities as well as identity and location details of other activists (Regalado, Villeneuve, and Scott-Railton, 2015).

The types of malware and phishing attacks used throughout the con-flict have ranged from very crude man-in-the-middle attacks, such as fake websites masquerading as the official Facebook page, to more specialized technology providing full remote access to individuals' digital presence. Continuing their long-standing tradition of working with foreign moni-toring technology, the regime has repeatedly purchased access to surveil-lance products by companies such as Blue Coat Systems (Telecomix, 2012; Reporters Without Borders, 2013).

Anecdotal evidence suggests that opposition members and activists exposed to malware have been arrested, and have had interrogators mention interception of digital information to them (Marczak et al., 2014: 7–8). These types of attacks would allow the attackers to help intelligence services map out anti-government activist networks more accurately. While the specific

70 REPRESSION IN THE DIGITAL AGE

identity of the attackers is not always clear, reports contend that the major security branches of the regime operate their own so-called information rooms, which are staffed with young IT students who have been tasked with obtaining as much information from the activists' social media accounts and devices as possible. Once arrested, individuals have frequently been forced to share the passwords of their digital devices, as well as social media accounts, allowing the information rooms to gather further information (Baiazy, 2012; Hashem, 2015).

Throughout the conflict, the regime has maintained a diverse set of control measures designed to block access to content deemed politically sensitive. As telecommunications remain highly centralized, the government has continued to maintain a high level of control over the country's networks, allowing it to implement various froms of censorship with relative ease. Access to websites has been restricted through filtering software, but websites maintained by members of the opposition have also faced frequent distributed denial of service attacks (DDoS) aimed at prohibiting access to its content beyond Syrian borders.

Next to content and platform-specific filtering, the regime has implemented frequent and irregular shutdowns of the country's communication networks. These shutdowns have occurred at the national level and at the regional level (Freedom House, 2015). While the country-wide network outages have simultaneously been accompanied by the disruption of cell phone services, there has been more variation in accessibility of cell phone services at the regional level, as the data presented in the next two chapters confirms (BBC News, 2012b).

Nationwide shutdowns were repeatedly recorded between 2011 and 2014, and almost every shutdown was accompanied by broad international news coverage and outrage from government and non-government actors from outside of the country. By contrast, only limited attention has been granted to regional and local limits to Internet accessibility. This stark discrepancy in international attention may help explain the more frequent and persistent use of local limits to accessibility.

4.5 Studying repression in Syria: data and measurement

To study the dynamics between online controls and the nature of state repression, this section presents data and summarizes the various steps involved in creating a measure of regime violence for the first four years of the Syrian conflict. Collecting detailed information on violent incidences, in particular when perpetrated against civilians, is highly challenging, not least because it provides proof of serious crimes having been committed. Conflict actors and parties involved therefore have a general interest in hiding their atrocious behavior and shifting responsibilities of wrongdoing to their enemies (Slim, 2007). Core challenges to studying political violence tend to be related to the availability of sources, though different data projects may arrive at very different results even when they attempt to cover similar ground (Eck, 2012). Morgues, hospitals, local media workers, religious groups, armed groups, and government and military reports all provide a certain snapshot of violent events. These snapshot views are aimed at fulfilling certain internal organizational goals. The majority of data on violent incidences remain dependent on journalistic sources, and ample research has demonstrated that in general, media agencies tend to pursue their own agendas (Davenport, 2010; Schrodt, 2012; Dawkins, 2020). Usually, this does not involve providing a census of all violence occurring in contentious situations (Earl et al., 2004). Journalists who work in highly unstable countries face extreme working conditions and must often deal with life-threatening danger to themselves (Arsenault, Himelfarb, and Abbott, 2011). Changing security situations affect the accuracy and completeness of real-time reporting, and can lead to ex post corrections of previously reported content.

Nevertheless, disaggregated research on contentious politics places high demands on the quality of information needed to test its empirical implications (Hoover Green, 2019). The measures introduced here set a high standard for achieving accurate measurements of state violence by addressing three core problems. First, they address the problem of over-reporting violence, by ensuring that all documented violent events are accounted for only once. Second, they provide a measure of violent strategies that move beyond documented body counts. Details on the circumstances of each individual killing are incorporated to establish when violence was targeted or untargeted. Third, to move beyond documentation, the following analyses account for reporting biases through the use of multiple-recapture estimation techniques.

Operationalizing state repression

State repression is operationalized through lethal government violence. The data I rely on includes both non-combatant and combatant victims killed by Syrian regime forces and pro-government groups. For the time period under

72 REPRESSION IN THE DIGITAL AGE

consideration, the data do not allow for an exact classification of victims into combatants and non-combatant categories. In the early years of the Syrian conflict, deaths at the hand of regime forces were classified as "martyr" deaths by the recording groups, indicating that state military, paramilitary, and other higher-ranking government officials are excluded. Since the object of inquiry here pertains to the study of violence perpetrated by the government against whomever it deems threatening to its political stability, this can include ordinary civilians and those who have mobilized an armed struggle against the government. From the position of the government, anyone who is not in active support of its regime is generally seen as a threat and treated as an anti-government combatant or collaborator, which is one of the main ways states justify the killing of non-armed citizens during episodes of civil conflict (Valentino, Huth, and Balch-Lindsay, 2004; Slim, 2007; Parkinson, 2013).

Sources and data access

Four data sources form the basis of the measure created to understand the Syrian regime's repressive strategy. The Syrian Center for Statistics and Research (CSR-SY) is a network of reporters, researchers, and academics that operate both within and outside of Syria. The Damascus Center for Human Rights Studies (DCHRS) maintains several documentation projects, in addition to lobbying and advocating for Syrian human rights and working to draw attention to the situation in Syria. The Syrian Network for Human Rights (SNHR) conducts monthly reviews of their records and subsequently updates their data with newly discovered or verified information on victims. The Violation Documentation Centre (VDC) has for the past ten years published information on victims who were killed in Syria. In order to assure the highest possible quality standards in combining documented evidence from different sources, records of fatalities are only included if they are identifiable by the victim's full name, date of death, and governorate in which the death occurred (Price, Gohdes, and Ball, 2016). The records are consistent in providing information at a daily level for each of Syria's 14 governorates. Many of the records include semi-structured geographic information that specifies locations at the district or city-level, but due to lack of consistent availability I only analyze the data at the governorate level. All four data sources further provide unstructured information on the circumstances of the victim's death, which is what will be used for the classification of targeted and untargeted repression.

Data from these four sources used in this book are based on joint work with the Human Rights Data Analysis Group, for whom I have worked as consultant for the past decade. The data used here are a snapshot of this work, which covers the aforementioned sources and the time period from the beginning of March 2011 until the end of April 2015. Since the beginning of the Syrian conflict, all four groups have periodically shared their data with HRDAG for the purpose of cleaning, processing, and establishing an integrated database of documented killings.[4]

Record-linkage

To create a complete and accurate list of documented killings potential duplicates within individual lists have to be identified and removed, and victim identities need to be linked across lists, in order to arrive at an overall number of documented victims. The identification of duplicates within a given source is termed de-duplication. The identification of duplicates across different sources is termed record-linkage, or matching. De-duplication and matching were completed in the same process by compiling one list that includes all records from all four sources, and searching for records that have the same information on the victim name, as well as place and date of death. Where available, information on the age, sex, and date and location of birth was additionally used in the identifying process. The record-linkage process is performed through semi-supervised machine learning (see Price, Gohdes, and Ball, 2016).

Figure 4.1 plots the de-duplicated number of records by each source and compares them to the number of unique, matched records integrated from all sources. The integrated number of reported victims of lethal violence (solid line) is higher than each individual source, which means that the different sources are contributing records that are not found in other sources— they are not mere replicates of each other.

The frequency of individual records reported across different data sources can also be interpreted as the reporting *density*. Figure 4.2 breaks down the density of reporting for each Syrian governorate. Rural Damascus has by far the highest number of reported government killings in the period under consideration. Aleppo and Homs have a similar number of incidences

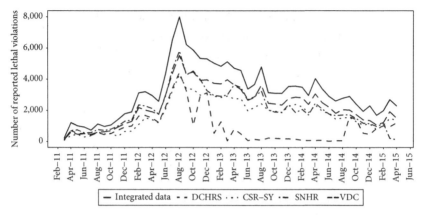

Fig. 4.1 Individual sources, and integrated data, over time, Syria, March 2011–April 2015.

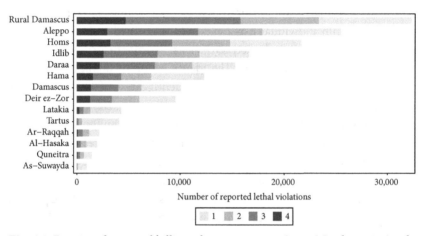

Fig. 4.2 Density of reported killings, by governorate, Syria, March 2011–April 2015.

that were reported by all four sources, but many more cases were only picked up by one, two, or three of the documentation groups in Aleppo than in Homs.

A simple assumption to make is that the reporting density of violent killings is related to the number of violent killings that occurred in the first place. If each documentation group is reporting many killings that were not picked up by others, it is likely that there are many more incidents that went completely unreported. To illustrate this point, let us assume that a group of four government agents are given the task of providing a census of the number of protesters on a certain day in a capital city. Each agent walks all around the city, and each does her best to take a photograph of every protester with her smartphone. At the end of the day, the agents get together to compare their pictures. If all four agents took pictures of the same protesters, they can assume that the group of protesters is probably not much bigger than those captured by all of them. But if they compare their pictures and realize that every agent has caught a significant number of protesters on camera that none of the others saw, they will realize that the crowd was much larger than any of them had anticipated. This will lead to the conclusion that had they employed a fifth or sixth agent, the number of new pictures would probably have grown accordingly. In a similar way, the light gray sections in Figure 4.2 indicate that a significant number of victims killed by the Syrian government have not been documented.

Sticking with this hypothetical scenario, let's assume that the agents' smartphones run low on battery during the course of the day, but only one of them has brought a battery pack. The other three have to find a place to charge their phones. Two of the agents have phones with minimum storage and therefore have to upload their videos and photos to a server to make room for more records. But at the height of the protest, mobile bandwidth slows to a crawl and they are forced to find a place with WiFi connection to continue their work. All of these technical hiccups mean that at the end of the day, important scenes were not caught on camera because of infrastructure challenges. But because the agents took so many photos and videos, they still have so much data that their superiors will probably not notice.

What this scenario shows us is that reporting patterns are dependent on a whole range of factors, and variation in infrastructure availability, including Internet accessibility, is one of them (Price, Gohdes, and Ball, 2015). Variation in reporting can seriously affect our empirical results, in particular when attempting to compare patterns of categories of violence that occurred under different circumstances.

Accounting for unreported violence

The record-linkage process across the four data sources allows us to create a single list with one row for each uniquely identifiable victim. Each row contains information about which source(s) recorded information about that victim. For example, this would allow us to know that victim A was documented by sources 1 and 3, and victim B was documented by sources 2, 3, and 4, and so on. We could then assess the overlaps—or intersections—between sources. These intersections can be used to estimate 4-system multiple recapture models that can predict the number of unreported regime killings (Lum, Price, and Banks, 2013; Hendrix and Salehyan, 2015). Multiple recapture estimation fits a model of the reporting process based, in this case, on four sources of reporting, in order to predict what went unreported. I make use of a set of multiple recapture models developed by Madigan and York (1997), which are designed to deal with dependency between different sources as it occurs when different data collection efforts occasionally work together or have the same primary source (Price, Gohdes, and Ball, 2016).[5]

For the purpose of this study, it is particularly important to discuss dependencies in reporting patterns that pertain to differing information access. Internet accessibility may increase information access, thereby allowing for a higher level of reporting where the Internet is accessible (Weidmann, 2016). In the next two chapters I address this possible source of underreporting by estimating separate multiple recapture models for various quantities of interest (see Sekar and Deming, 1949).

Summary of empirical approach

This chapter has shown the Syrian government's long history of mass surveillance and censorship of its population. Due to the monopolization of the telecommunications sector, the government remains in control of the national Internet infrastructure.[6] I therefore assume that where Internet accessibility is limited, it is limited intentionally, and where it is not limited this freedom of access is equally intentional. I also assume that surveillance technology is being employed where Internet accessibility is available. In the following two chapters, I study the interplay between government-implemented Internet controls and the use of violence repression during the Syrian conflict.

Table 4.1 provides an overview of the next two chapters analyzing repression in the Syrian conflict. I investigate how nationwide and regional cyber controls are implemented in conjunction with different forms of repressive strategies. The next chapter looks at nationwide shutdowns and the ways in which they coincide with larger government offensives. It delves into various mechanisms that could explain the co-occurence of shutdowns and changes

Table 4.1 Summary of empirical approach to study cyber controls and repression in the Syrian conflict.

	Nationwide shutdowns & government offensives	Internet accessibility & targeted violence
Time period	March 2011–March 2014	June 2013–April 2015
Type of control	Nationwide shutdowns	Regional accessibility
Repressive strategy	Number of killed	Proportion of targeted vs. untargeted killings
Geographic unit	National—and governate level	Governorate level
Accounting for reporting bias	Analysis of reporting patterns before, during, and after shutdowns	Estimating unreported targeted and untargeted killings

in state violence, and provides multiple empirical tests to isolate the most plausible mechanism. In studying nationwide shutdowns of the Internet that occurred in the first three years of the Syrian conflict, the results show a significant and substantive increase in daily regime-perpetrated killings at both the national and governorate level. A careful analysis of the reporting patterns of violence before, during, and after shutdowns suggests that the Internet blackouts were selectively and purposely implemented with the launch of larger repressive campaigns. Chapter 6 studies the relationship between regional levels of Internet accessibility and the Syrian regime's repressive strategy. Beyond the empirical implications formulated in the theory chapter, it asks under what conditions surveillance will be most useful to repressive rulers. Repressive strategies are operationalized as the proportion of targeted versus untargeted killings, measured at the governorate level. Violence is measured as combined numbers of documented and estimated unreported killings in order to account for reporting patterns that may be correlated with Internet accessibility. A range of empirical models suggest that the relationship between Internet accessibility and targeted repression is mediated by local conditions that determine whether the regime is able to rely on more traditional forms of intelligence or whether digital surveillance will enhance their ability to target those deemed threatening to their political survival.

5

Nationwide shutdowns and government offensives

On Friday, June 3, 2011, Syrians turned out in massive numbers onto the streets after prayers to once again protest the regime. In the early days of the uprising, protesters started giving the Friday demonstrations specific names to be spread on social media. Participants from all sectors of society were encouraged to join the crowds after Friday prayers (Friedman, 2011; Cherribi, 2017). The protests on the first Friday in June 2011 had been dedicated to the children who had been murdered during demonstrations in prior months. Reports suggested that in Hama alone, more than 50,000 people took to the streets to mourn the loss of children and demand change (BBC News, 2011*b*). While the government had already been engaged in heavy-handed responses against protesters in the weeks before, this Friday was different. For the first time since the protests had commenced in Daraa, Syrians were subjected to a nationwide Internet shutdown. Across the country, access to mobile networks, DSL, and dial-up connections were fully interrupted (Flock, 2011). Simultaneously, as thousands took to the streets in Hama, the regime's army continued its military offensive in Rastan, a city to the south, with heavy bombardment, shelling, and sniper attacks (BBC News, 2011*b*; Human Rights Watch, 2011). Throughout all of this, digital communication largely came to a halt.

The following day, when access to the Internet had been restored, the extent of violence slowly became visible. Witnesses uploaded videos and photos to social media showing members of the regime's security forces firing directly into Hama's protesting crowds, reportedly killing at least 53 people (BBC News, 2011*b*). The videos documented extensive use of force by security forces, but also showed the vast size of the crowds, underlining just how many people had decided to defiantly and publicly show their disapproval with the regime's actions (Sehegal, 2011). The full shutdown of access marked a new chapter in the regime's use of digital controls.

Repression in the Digital Age: Surveillance, Censorship, and the Dynamics of State Violence. Anita R. Gohdes, Oxford University Press. © Oxford University Press 2024. DOI: 10.1093/oso/9780197743577.003.0005

Over the course of the next three years, it would go on to shut down nationwide access to the Internet six more times.

In the spring of 2013, the security forces of the Syrian regime launched a military campaign on the southern town of Khirbet Ghazaleh, less than half an hour away from where the uprising against the government had first begun in 2011. Located in the Southern Daraa governorate and close to the Jordanian border, Khirbet Ghazale had long been of significant economic importance because the highway running through it was used to transport and trade goods between countries in the region and Europe (Al-Khalidi, 2013). As the conflict progressed and fighting intensified, Khirbet Ghazaleh had also become of strategic importance to opposition groups receiving weapons supplies via Jordan (Al-Khalidi, 2013; Borger and Hopkins, 2013). In April 2013, opposition groups established important gains in the south, including the capture of Khirbet Ghazaleh and besieging the center of Daraa (International Crisis Group, 2013: 14). On May 7, international media outlets reported the full shutdown of all Internet access across Syria (Fisher, 2013). Incidentally, this was the same day then US Secretary of State John Kerry and Russian Foreign Minister Sergei Lavrov issued a joint announcement that they had agreed to convene a meeting on Syria (BBC News, 2013). The following day, with the nationwide shutdown still in place, the government reported that it had regained control of Khirbet Ghazaleh (The Economist, 2013).

The two-day shutdown in early May attracted considerable attention from digital rights groups and Internet security companies, who published technical analyses suggesting an intentional withdrawal of access (Qtiesh and Reitman, 2013). In 2013, Syria had four cables that connected it to the rest of the world's Internet. Analysts suggested that the rapid blackout was due to withdrawals of all Border Gateway Protocol routes, essentially removing the Syrian IP space from the World Wide Web (Gallagher, 2012; Prince, 2013).

The killings of protesters in Hama in summer 2011 and the offensive aimed at recapturing Khirbet Ghazaleh in spring 2013 suggest that Internet shutdowns are employed by governments in conjunction with different forms of repressive activities. The violence perpetrated in the summer of 2011 was largely in the context of the repression of mass anti-government protests as well as campaigns coined as counterinsurgency. In contrast, by 2013 the situation had escalated into a civil war characterized by a multitude

80 REPRESSION IN THE DIGITAL AGE

of foreign interests and influences, and an increasingly fractionalized domestic opposition (International Crisis Group, 2013). Yet, during both phases of the conflict, nationwide shutdowns were used.

Up until now we have discussed the advantages governments hope to gain from censoring content and access to the Internet and have also seen how more subtle forms of shutdowns may prove useful that are not as extreme as what Syrians witnessed in June 2011. Each shutdown was accompanied by broad international coverage, drawing intense criticism from public and private leaders alike. This shows how, in contrast to censorship of content or individual domains, actual "blackouts" tend to provoke widespread condemnation and may damage a country's reputation profoundly. Why then, did the Syrian government purposefully and repeatedly engage in a full information blackout?

This chapter focuses on circumstances where Internet access has been purposefully cut for a short, specific time period. I discuss two core motives for governments to shut down the Internet temporarily. The first motive targets the opposition's efficacy. Short shutdowns are likely to impede the opposition's capability to successfully coordinate and challenge the government, thereby improving state security forces' chances of crushing the opposition. Where Internet shutdowns are primarily aimed at weakening the opposition, they are likely to be part of a concerted, coercive response tactic. The second motive relates to the domestic and international audience costs of visible opposition activity and government response. Where Internet shutdowns are primarily employed to avoid such audience costs, we should expect to see a change in violent state repression that is finely attuned to the period of the outage so as to avoid documentation.

Both motives can play a role when weighing the benefits of shutting down the net against the costs. Large coercive offensives against the opposition often produce gruesome images that are shared across social and traditional media, thereby provoking further domestic backlash and international outrage against the government. The fact that Internet shutdowns can also significantly impede documentation of atrocities may be a useful side-effect that helps improve the government's chances of crushing the opposition. Likewise, governments intent on hiding atrocities from the outside world may welcome the reduced capabilities of their proclaimed enemies while the Internet is inaccessible. Despite overlapping motivations, there are a number of reasons why it is useful to understand states' primary objectives when engaging in network disruptions. First, it helps us understand when and where we might observe an Internet shutdown. Second, states' repressive incentives to shut down the net may affect the type of violent response that accompanies the blackout. A better understanding of the timing and purpose of network shutdowns can help opposition groups, the domestic population, as well as the international community to better anticipate and respond to outages.

Between 2011 and 2014, the Syrian government implemented seven nationwide shutdowns. During these early years of the conflict, I show how regime forces repeatedly used nationwide Internet shutdowns when facing intense confrontation from opposition groups. I argue that the primary motive for shutting down the Internet in Syria can be attributed to the operational advantages a blackout would provide the Syrian security forces in their coercive repressive response to opposition challenges. The history of overt repression and disregard of potential international condemnation suggest that reputation-saving motives likely played a secondary role in the government's repressive considerations. By the time the first shutdown had occurred three months into the 2011 uprising, local citizen journalists and international news reporters had already extensively covered the widespread repressive state response. Nevertheless, the frequent targeting of members of the media demonstrates that the regime was not entirely indifferent to coverage of the conflict. According to the Committee to Protect Journalists (CPJ), Syria was the most dangerous country to work in as a journalist during 2012, 2013, and 2014, with killings and kidnappings of press staff occurring on a regular basis (Beiser, 2013). Between 2011 and 2014, CPJ reported that 80 journalists had been killed in Syria, 47 of whose killings were attributed to government, military officials, or paramilitary groups (and 20 by unknown perpetrators) (Committee to Protect Journalists, 2021).

5.1 Understanding full shutdowns

Concerted repression

A core goal of state repression is to raise the cost of collective action that may threaten the status quo. According to this argument, Internet shutdowns can function as part of a state's larger repressive strategy. Cutting access to the Internet completely means the collective organization of dissent and rebellion must revert to slower forms of communication, which can lead

82 REPRESSION IN THE DIGITAL AGE

to significant delays and inefficiencies for opposition movements. Online message systems have revolutionized the way in which resistance groups and insurgencies stay connected, and losing said access can deal a significant blow to groups intent on maintaining a cohesive and hierarchical opposition to the government.

Beyond protest and other forms of non-violent resistance, the ability to coordinate personnel, material, and last-minute strategies via mobile phones and the Internet is also a vital channel by which opposition groups are able to organize physical attacks against the government. Shutdowns are likely to temporarily disrupt the efficacy of opposition fighters' ability to coordinate, thereby impacting opposition groups' capabilities to carry out targeted attacks against the government's security forces. Location-based services, such as Google Earth and Google Maps, are used by ill-equipped rebel groups to locate military targets and to calibrate weapons accordingly (Miller, 2012; Keating, 2013). Faced with an army that is superiorly equipped with weapons, technology, and trained soldiers, opposition groups frequently conduct asymmetric warfare (Kalyvas and Balcells, 2010), where reliance on all available means of combat is pivotal.

Opposition groups are often keenly aware of the ways in which governments control the digital sphere. Early on in the conflict, Syrian opposition groups established alternative ways to communicate using two-way satellite devices (Perlroth, 2013b). Yet accessing the Internet through the same conventional means used by the rest of the country's population can still provide more security than relying on less broadly used channels such as satellite connections. Security researchers have demonstrated how satellite mobile devices produce traceable signals that allow governments to simply locate users and trace messages (see Driessen et al., 2012).

For years, researchers have warned how signals intelligence may be deployed to locate and target opposition members (Perlroth, 2013b). Locating and targeting rebels who communicate outside of conventional structures offers a clear coercive advantage for the state when compared to their use of ordinary network connections. The killings of two journalists in Homs in February 2012 support the notion that governments are making use of this technology. Security specialists contend that the Syrian government is likely to have directly targeted the houses from which they had traced the phones' signals (York and Timm, 2012). Consequently, although opposition groups might possess alternative ways of connecting via cell phones and the Internet, the increased usage of satellite devices is likely to improve the regime's capability of identifying armed fighters among the civilian population.

Finally, even when opposition groups have developed the capacity to maintain cohesion and control in the absence of digital tools, the shutdown of the Internet allows governments to further isolate groups from their support network of civilian sympathizers and foreign supporters.

Reputation saving

Ever since mobile phones and social media found themselves in the hands of protesters, they have been used to share information about government behavior. For governments faced with an opposition demanding change, the repressive effect of shutdowns may thus not always be a priority. Instead, governments may block the Internet in order to hide violent acts from international scrutiny while controlling the overall narrative of the contentious episode. Where state actors are afraid of receiving increased international attention and scrutiny for repressing their citizens, cutting the Internet can help limit the extent of information leaving the country. Network disruptions may provide governments with a chance to use widespread repression against the population without creating a national and international audience. Against the threat of naming and shaming, which could potentially provoke concrete consequences such as sanctions or a foreign intervention, an information blackout is a small price to pay. Although authoritarian governments frequently engage in violent repression, even when the international community is watching, the less real-time information is available, the more likely leaders will be able to plausibly deny responsibility for these atrocities (Mitchell, 2004).

The argument that Internet shutdowns may be used to cover-up atrocities has also been voiced in the context of the Syrian conflict. When the Internet was shut down in late 2012, Amnesty International lamented that:

[a]s fighting intensifies [...] we are extremely worried that the news that internet and mobile phone services appear to have been cut throughout Syria may herald the intention of the Syrian authorities to shield the truth of what is happening in the country from the outside world.[1]

84 REPRESSION IN THE DIGITAL AGE

Where reputation saving is the primary objective for Internet shutdowns, the main goal will therefore be the absence of detailed information regarding atrocities committed during the blackout. Put differently, from a government's perspective a successful shutdown would reduce the extent to which state-perpetrated violence is reported on. In light of a digital blackout, individuals and groups who document and disseminate the details on repressive events may have a harder time collecting information on individual victims. Fewer witnesses of repressive events will be able to directly share their visual content within their networks, thereby reducing the overall availability of real-time evidence.

Why nationwide shutdowns are likely to be infrequent

Short-term nationwide shutdowns that are implemented in anticipation of gaining temporary advantages over an actively resisting opposition are likely to be an infrequently and irregularly used repressive tool. The most obvious reason is that governments pursuing a counterinsurgency strategy in response to political threats will be particularly interested in maintaining access to opposition groups' digital communication for surveillance purposes. When state-run mobile phone and Internet services are generally accessible, opposition groups are more likely to make use of them. Longer periods without access to state-provided network services should increase the probability of rebel groups finding alternative means and services, such as satellite phones and modems, network access via neighboring countries, or dial-up connections. If opposition groups decide to reorganize entirely and banish mobile and virtual communication from their coordination repertoire, the government's benefits from shutting down network services are likely to be low because insurgent coordination will continue via offline channels.

Given the incentives and costs for governments to shut down their networks, cutting all Internet access is likely to be most effective in stifling opposition capability when used on an infrequent, temporary basis. Overuse of this most extreme form of censorship may even be counterproductive. If Internet shutdowns precede all forms of military actions and occur on a regular basis, civilians and opposition groups will be able to use them as an "early-warning system." Building on this, I argue that network outages are likely to be consistently associated with increased fighting. Conversely, not all periods of intense fighting are likely to be accompanied by a network shutdown. In short, disruptions will consistently be part of larger military campaigns, whereas not all military campaigns will entail disruptions.

Repressive implications of a shutdown

Given the principal motives of temporarily shutting down the Internet, a variety of repressive implications can be derived. I will test repressive implications with respect to the timing of both the shutdown and possible increases in violent repression, as well as possible increases in the extent to which violence remains underreported during a shutdown. Furthermore, the victims against whom violent repression is directed are likely to be dependent on the motives for the shutdown, as well.

If the primary motive of an Internet shutdown is concerted repression aimed at improving government-aligned fighters' chances of repressing the opposition, then regime forces are likely to be involved in increased fighting directly prior to and during the period of the outage. A main observable outcome will be an increase in the activity of government security and paramilitary forces during and in the immediate period surrounding outages. Pro-government fighter activity is approximated by the number of people killed by pro-regime forces. According to the theoretical expectations laid out above, I expect short, unexpected network outages to be accompanied by significantly higher levels of military activity, and thus significantly higher numbers of people killed. Empirically, I expect increases in violence immediately preceding disruptions to be consistent with the coercive response hypothesis. In addition, if we assume that the shutdown is ordered for tactical reasons that are not related to covering up atrocities, then concerted repressive offensives may continue beyond the shutdown as well. This would suggest that associated increases in violence may be visible in the days immediately following the shutdown. Increased military activity, measured as intensity of regime violence, immediately *prior*, *during*, and *after* shutdowns therefore likely indicates the strategic value of shutdowns in government repression policy: *All else equal, Internet shutdowns and the days immediately before and after the shutdown are likely to be accompanied by a significant increase in violent state repression.*

If the main intent behind shutting down the Internet is to cover up prosecutable war crimes against unarmed civilians, my expectation for the security forces' violent strategy would be a significant increase of violence that is limited to the Internet outage itself. Taking into account timing of when repressive violence increases versus the timing of network disruptions is therefore important. If governments care about the news of atrocities traveling beyond the battle grounds, they are likely to only *commence* with the violence once the network is disconnected. A substantive increase in violence prior to shutting down the Internet might even draw more attention to coercive activities, which would be counterproductive to the intention of reducing audience costs and saving the government's reputation. Furthermore, if the reputation-saving strategy were to be effective, we would expect to see the proportion of violence that is *not reported* increase during the shutdown. Documentation of violent events is seldom entirely accurate and complete, yet Internet shutdowns have the potential to disrupt information flows in a way that would lead to a disproportional reduction of reliable evidence on violence. Shutdowns aimed at hiding atrocities should therefore show no signs of an increase of violence *prior* to the outage, and if successful, should hide a large increase in undocumented fatalities *during* the disruption. In the case of a reputation-saving strategy, the expectation would therefore be that *all else equal, Internet shutdowns are likely to be accompanied by a significant increase in violent state repression, as well as an increase in the proportion of undocumented instances of violent state repression.*

Beyond these two arguments put forward, there might be other observed changes in the violence that are associated with Internet shutdowns. These could be dependent on changes in opposition and civilian behavior. Research on the effects of the Internet shutdown in Egypt in 2011 found that the digital blackout coincided with an increase in both the turnout and number of locations where protesters took to the streets (Hassanpour, 2014). Therefore, an alternative argument for changes in the level of violent repression used would be if governments decided to violently crack down in response to increased protest turnout. Empirically, a protest response strategy would predict a substantial increase in violence that is limited to the *immediate aftermath* of temporary Internet shutdowns.

Table 5.1 summarizes the expectation of these three possible strategies (concerted repression, reputation saving, protest response) that may explain

Table 5.1 Expected effects for network disruptions and violence.

Repressive Strategy	Documented violence	Undocumented violence (%)	Timing of change
Concerted repression	increase	no change	prior/during/after shutdown
Reputation saving	no change/increase	increase	during shutdown
Protest response	increase	no change	after shutdown
None	no change	no change	—

a change in violent state repression coinciding with Internet shutdowns. Empirically, I investigate these strategies by analyzing the dynamics of documented and undocumented repression immediately before, during, and after an Internet shutdown. The forth possibility is the absence of any relationship between violence and shutdowns, which would suggest that shutdowns are not directly related to a government's repressive strategy.

Data

Nationwide Internet shutdowns that occurred between March 2011 and the end of 2014 are determined through information collected by the Google Transparency reports on traffic disruptions in Syria.[2] Suspensions of traffic that lasted between a few hours and three days occurred in June 2011, July 2012, November/December 2012, January 2013, twice in May 2013, and February 2014. To investigate the different repressive strategies associated with shutdowns, I code a number of dichotomous variables. The first variable takes on the value of 1 on days where the Internet was shut down, and a 0 for days of normal connection. The second variable sets the treatment at $t - 1$, the day *prior* to the disruption. The third variable looks at the time window of the disruption and codes the day prior to, the days of the disruption, and the following day as 1, and the rest as 0. To control for decreasing or increasing effects over time, I include a measure that accounts for the number of previous outages, as well as a variable that measures the time since the last outage, as recent outages might positively or negatively affect the dynamics of violence.

5.2 Internet shutdowns and documented violence

Government offensives against opposition groups tend to be localized. Consequently, it is useful to look at regional variation in the use of violent repression in the context of nationwide shutdowns. The maps in Figure 5.1 show the difference in average levels of documented violence across Syrian governorates during three of the seven nationwide Internet shutdowns between March 2011 and March 2014. The numbers are derived by comparing the average daily levels of documented violence during the shutdown days to the average daily number in the week before and the week after each respective

88 REPRESSION IN THE DIGITAL AGE

shutdown. A positive change in the number of documented victims of lethal regime violence during the first nationwide shutdown is visible in Hama, which coincides with the mass protests in honor of killed children discussed earlier. The top row in Figure 5.1 shows the reported number of daily killings for the governorate of Hama between May and July 2011. Documentation patterns can mask the full extent of violence perpetrated, an issue that I will address through multiple-recapture estimation later in this chapter. Yet even the documented pattern of violence suggests a substantial increase in killings in Hama during the days the Internet was shut down all across the country.

On July 14, 2012, five days prior to what would be the second Internet shutdown, the Free Syrian Army launched an offensive in and around Damascus which they named "Damascus Volcano and Syrian Earthquake," intended to "liberate Damascus" from regime control (Osborn, 2012). According to Damascus residents, the FSA's offensive constituted the most intense fighting the country's capital had been subjected to since the start of the uprising (Osborn, 2012). Four days into the offensive, Deputy Defense Minister Assef Shawkat, one of Assad's closest advisors and brother-in-law, was killed through a bomb attack launched by FSA forces on the headquarters of the National Security Bureau (NSB) (BBC News, 2012a). In addition to Shawkat, the attack killed a number of senior members of the regime's military forces, and was celebrated by opposition forces as a serious attack on the regime's stability. The following day, on July 19, security forces commenced an intense retaliation against the opposition with heavy bombardment, aided by tanks and helicopter gunships. That day, the Internet was cut all across Syria. An anonymous security source told Al-Jazeera that following the attack against the NSB, the army had "decided to use all the weapons in its possession to finish the terrorists off (Al-Jazeera, 2012)." Although fighting had been ongoing prior to the shutdown, the second map in Figure 5.1 shows an increase of more than 50 cases of documented regime killings on the day of the shutdown, when compared to the days before and after the shutdown.

The third map and figure show the dynamics of documented daily killings during the fifth nationwide shutdown on May 7–8, 2013. The map shows a positive change in the number of documented killings during the shutdown, which corresponds with the fighting in Daraa described at the outset of this chapter. The graph shows that documented violence roughly doubles during the first day of the Internet shutdown. Another nationwide Internet

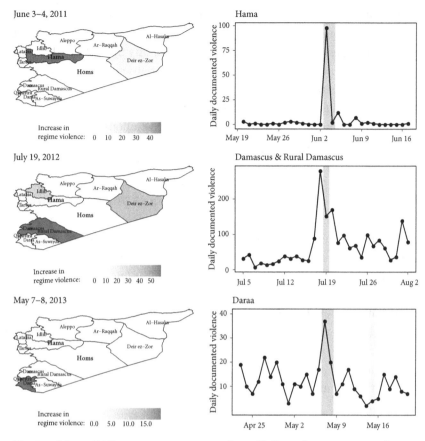

Fig. 5.1 **Maps:** Difference in average number of killings by governorate during three of the seven nationwide Internet shutdowns that occurred between 2011 and 2014. Difference is calculated by comparing average daily killings during the shutdown to average daily killings in the week preceding and the week following the shutdown. Only positive differences are reported to highlight core areas of fighting. **Graphs:** Daily numbers of documented regime killings for select governorates. Gray bars indicate days with nationwide Internet shutdowns.

shutdown occurred a week later, yet it is not reflected in immediate changes in documented conflict intensity in the southern part of Syria.

It is noteworthy that none of the nationwide shutdowns coincide with changes in documented violence in the north-eastern governorate Al-Hasaka. Early on in the conflict, opposition groups established quasi-administrative structures in the north-eastern governorate (MacFarquhar and Saad, 2012), and were subsequently cut off from central government services, including the Internet. We will investigate regional variations in Internet accessibility in the next chapter, which confirms that Al-Hasaka and Ar-Raqqah experienced very low levels of accessibility throughout the early years of the conflict. Evidently, the near constant absence of government-provided Internet means that nationwide shutdowns will bear no correlation with increases in government offensives.

Shutdowns implemented as part of a coercive response need not necessarily be implemented prior to the commencement of fighting. Shutting down the network amidst fighting is likely to constitute a military strategy. Aggregate levels of documented regime violence for all of Syria show a trend that is compatible with this conjecture. Figure 5.2 shows the aggregate average daily number of documented killings in the days leading up to any of the nationwide Internet shutdowns that occurred during the first four years of the conflict, as well as during the shutdown and in the week following a blackout, when the country comes back online. Although merely descriptive, the pattern suggests that overall, regime violence is substantially higher immediately before, during, and after a nationwide Internet shutdown. When comparing the average daily number of documented instances of lethal regime violence across all shutdowns, the number increases from approximately 150 to almost 180 per day prior to an outage. The average daily numbers remain high during the shutdown and then rapidly decrease two days after the shutdown.

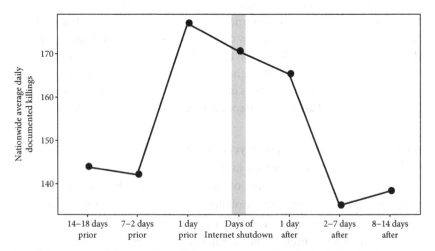

Fig. 5.2 Average daily number of documented killings in Syria in the days leading up to a nationwide Internet shutdown, as well as the days following a shutdown.

NATIONWIDE SHUTDOWNS AND GOVERNMENT OFFENSIVES   91

Table 5.2 Nationwide Internet shutdowns and documented regime violence.

	Model 1 Prior	Model 2 During	Model 3 Post
Pre shutdown $(t-1)$	0.171 (0.082) **18.7%**		
Days of shutdown (t)		0.103 (0.079) **10.9%**	
Post shutdown $(t+1)$			0.071 (0.073) **7.4%**
# days since	0.000	0.001	0.000
ω	0.106 (0.001)	0.106 (0.001)	0.105 (0.001)
N	994	994	994
LLF	−5472.85	−5473.844	−5474.448
AIC	10949.7	10951.687	10952.896

Poisson Exponentially Moving Average (PEWMA) Model.
Standard errors in parentheses. Predicted percentage changes in bold font.

Table 5.2 reports the multivariate analysis of daily regime killings between March 15, 2011, and March 31, 2014. In view of the fact that the conflict in Syria intensified over time in the first four years, the number of regime killings follows a generally increasing, non mean-reverting trend. To account for these dynamics, I estimate a Poisson exponentially weighted moving average model (PEWMA), as formalized by Brandt et al. (2000). PEWMA is a structural time series model that nests a Poisson model, where observed counts at time t are modeled as a weighted average of counts at previous time points (Brandt et al., 2000: 827).[3] Since the interpretation of the coefficients is not straightforward, I calculate the predicted percentage changes in killings for the same three treatments of interest (prior, during, post shutdown) used in the difference of mean tests. Table 5.2 reports the results of the three models. The model predicts that on average, the level of violence increases by 14.9% on the day prior to an Internet outage. During the actual blackout, violence is predicted to increase by 10.0%, and when looking at the day following a shutdown, the average increase is predicted to be 6.7%. Although not all governorates are affected by fighting in the same way, the aggregate national evidence offers support for the hypothesis that outages are preceded and accompanied by significant increases in violence.

I next analyze daily levels of documented violence at the governorate level, estimating a time-series cross section fixed-effects Poisson model, where the 14 governorates are the fixed units. I simulate the expected change in the number of regime fatalities in each Syrian governorate on the day before $(t-1)$, during (t) and day following $(t+1)$ a shutdown. Figure 5.3 shows all 14 governorates along the x-axis and plots the expected change in fatalities including the 95% confidence interval on the y-axis. The results show that the expected change in documented regime violence is significantly higher on the day prior to the shutdown (square dot), but the change remains significantly different from zero during and immediately after a shutdown, as well. None of the confidence intervals include zero, which means that during Internet shutdowns and in the time right before and after, we can observe statistically significant higher levels of documented violence across all Syrian governorates. The substantive effect varies clearly across governorates, which is not surprising given the significant regional differences in the levels of violence experienced. In Rural Damascus, Aleppo, and Homs, shutdowns are associated with an expected increase of three additional documented fatalities. The patterns remain similar on the day following a shutdown.

On days prior to shutdowns, the estimated expected changes in violence are substantially larger. The expected increase in conflict fatalities in Homs,

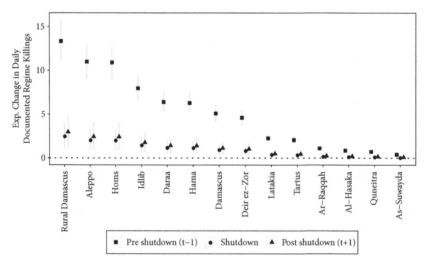

Fig. 5.3 Expected change in daily documented regime killings during a shutdown.

Rural Damascus, and Aleppo are above ten documented killings. In Idlib, Daraa, Hama, Damascus, and Deir ez-Zor, that number is still expected to be above five. All three models offer support for the argument that the Syrian government is pursuing a concerted repressive strategy: governorates in Syria experience a significant increase in documented regime killings on days where the regime shuts down the Internet. Furthermore, a first substantial increase in violence occurs one day prior, an increase we would not expect if the regime were interested in covering up atrocities during blackouts or cracking down on a higher number of protesters as a result of the shutdown.

Although the evidence is compatible with the argument put forward in this chapter, Syria witnessed only seven nationwide shutdowns in the first four years of the conflict, and the associations presented here may be due to chance. In order to check whether the timing of the shutdowns may have randomly fallen into conflict periods that were generally associated with a higher level of violence, I run a series of placebo tests using time-shifted placebos. I move the treatment, defined as the day of a shutdown at time t, within an interval from $t - 30$ and $t + 30$.[4] For each placebo date, the national-level time-series count model is estimated and the predicted percentage change of violence on days with the treatment is saved.

Figure 5.4 plots the predicted changes, as well as the actual treatments at t (the disruption) and $t - 1$ (the day prior the disruption). The placebos predict a change in violence that is below zero. Importantly, the predicted change in the weeks following the shutdown are also below zero, offering

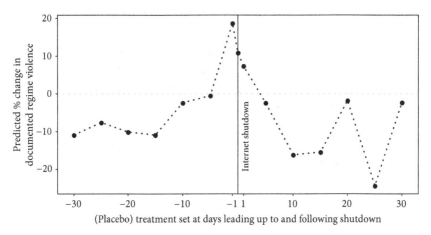

Fig. 5.4 Time-shifted placebo test, nationwide shutdown.

94 REPRESSION IN THE DIGITAL AGE

further support to the notion that the government was not responding to an increase in protest following the disruption.

5.3 Underreporting during shutdowns

The reported patterns of violence point towards a concerted repressive strategy, but this does not address the possibility that reporting patterns may be significantly different during information blackouts. The fact that we observe an increase in reported violence during shutdowns suggests that covering up repression was not fully successful during the nationwide shutdowns in the first four years of the Syrian conflict. Nevertheless, we may still observe significant differences in reporting patterns before, during, and after shutdowns that help us shine a light on some of the ways in which they affect the work of those groups leading the painstaking effort to expose the victims of conflict. Civil society groups have been doing their very best to document all deaths that were in some form or other visible. But when we attempt to examine the effects of information technology on conflict dynamics, the potential to draw biased conclusions might arise precisely because changes in said technology are correlated with groups' abilities to observe and record violence. For the present analysis, it is therefore of paramount importance to obtain an estimate of *all* fatalities, not just of those documented.

Here I now rely on the multiple recapture methods introduced in the previous chapter. I isolate the number of documented fatalities by governorate for the days without Internet, and estimate the number of undocumented killings before during, and after a shutdown. Since the degree of underreporting is likely to vary across time and space, I select the fixed period of three days before and three days after each network disruption and estimate the level of underreporting at the national level and for each respective governorate.

Figure 5.5 shows the degree of underreporting in violence for the three-day period prior to, during, and the three days following the shutdowns. Each point represents an estimate for the percentage of killings that went unreported during a given time period. The top left panel reports the combined proportions for all shutdowns, which suggest that, overall, underreporting was somewhat higher prior to and during a shutdown than in the days thereafter.

NATIONWIDE SHUTDOWNS AND GOVERNMENT OFFENSIVES 95

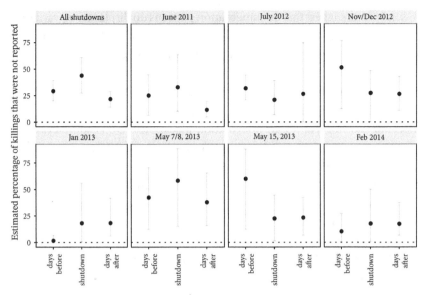

Fig. 5.5 Reporting patterns of violence in the three days before, during, and three days after each shutdown. Points refer to estimated percentage of killings that were not reported.

The remaining panels report numbers for each individual shutdown. The individual shutdown periods have a lower number of observed killings than the aggregate estimation for all shutdowns, which means that fewer observations are available to model the reporting process in the multiple recapture estimation. As a consequence, the estimates come with more uncertainty as captured by the 95% confidence intervals. The estimated rates of underreporting for the individual shutdowns vary. In some cases, such as July 2012, November/December 2012, and mid-May 2013, the estimated percentage of killings that were not reported is higher prior to the shutdown than during and afterwards. Other shutdowns illustrate the overall picture more closely, such as June 2011 and early May 2013, where the point estimate for the percentage of unreported killings is slightly higher prior to and during the shutdown itself. Next to the *relative* level of reporting, it is also apparent that the *absolute* level of reporting varied quite substantially between the different shutdowns. In early May 2013 they were around 50%, which would mean that only half of all killings that occurred were recorded. When access was cut less than a year later, in February 2014, estimated underreporting rates were less than 20%.

96 REPRESSION IN THE DIGITAL AGE

The results suggest that documentation patterns do display some variation surrounding the nationwide shutdown of the Internet. Underreporting is higher in the days prior to a shutdown than it is in the days following a shutdown, which suggest that in general, information blackouts had no lingering repercussions on the documentation of violence. The higher rate of underreporting during shutdowns suggests that even if the network blackout did not lead to an information blackout, there is some evidence of a dampening effect on documentation. The underreporting rates also add context to the findings presented in Table 5.2 and Figure 5.3, which both report lower levels of changes in violence during shutdowns than the day before. Because these analyses rely on reported numbers, the lower levels of reporting during shutdowns likely lead to a reduced effect size. Multiple recapture estimation requires a sufficiently large amount of data to estimate levels of underreporting, which makes a reanalysis with adjusted daily estimates is not possible.

Lastly, broader conflict dynamics may also help explain the higher levels of underreporting before and during shutdowns. If Internet shutdowns are implemented in tandem with broader military and repressive offensives, levels of underreporting before and during a shutdown are also likely to be a side-effect of an increase in absolute levels of violence. Rapid increases in the intensity of violence can make it even more challenging for documentation teams to keep track of the numbers and details of those who were killed.

Discussion

This chapter has investigated why state actors might have an incentive to include nationwide Internet shutdowns in their broader military strategy. I investigate the relationship between nationwide Internet outages and the use of violent repression by a government fighting to maintain political control. Scarce and sudden disconnection from essential communication networks is likely to weaken opposition groups' propensity to organize. That more violence is hidden from view during disruptions might turn out to be a welcome side-effect for governments seeking to maintain international legitimacy and internal control.

The evidence presented here suggests that the Syrian regime implemented large-scale disruptions selectively and purposely in conjunction with launching larger repressive campaigns. Not all such campaigns co-occur with Internet outages, but when they do, they tend to be preceded and accompanied by a substantial increase in violence. The findings speak to one part of the argument presented in Chapter 3, showing that mass censorship of digital infrastructure is likely to support mass and indiscriminate repression.

Even in conflicts that are under as much national and international scrutiny as the Syrian conflict has been, it is important to analytically distinguish between the empirical implications for *documented* violence, and the empirical implications for *actual* levels of violence: cases that are observed and those that are either intentionally or unintentionally hidden from documentation. The empirical expectations advanced in this chapter clearly distinguish between implications for the reporting of violence, and all perpetrated violence. Distinguishing between the events for which we have access to data and those that are hidden to varying degrees and can be approximated by estimating rates of underreporting helps sharpen our understanding of how disruptions in technological infrastructure affect broader conflict dynamics.

At the same time, the theoretical discussion advanced in this chapter suggests that these findings are likely to be context-dependent. Internet shutdowns that last longer than the ones imposed in Syria might have a more profound effect on documentation processes. Governments that are highly dependent on the support of international actors who value human rights are likely to have a greater interest in covering up their repressive actions. The same dynamic may be observed in countries that are not yet caught in conflict but where governments fear that publicly shared evidence of repression could spark a revolution. As we will see in Chapter 7, in such cases Internet shutdowns will likely be accompanied by a change in repressive strategy that is aimed at silencing, intimidating, and covering up excessive state violence.

The analysis in this chapter has focused on quantitative changes in the degree of lethal violence used by Syrian state forces, establishing an association between censorship and the scale of violence. What it has not shown is whether and how the *type* of violence changes with different degrees of network accessibility. The next chapter turns to this question by studying regional variations in cyber controls and the degree of targeted repression used by state authorities in Syria.

6

Internet accessibility and targeted violence

Thus far, we have established the pervasiveness of online controls used by the Syrian regime throughout the conflict, and the evidence presented in the previous chapter suggests a clear relationship between large-scale repression and nationwide shutdowns. Moving away from full shutdowns, this chapter asks when Internet accessibility will be particularly useful for governments who are looking to improve their ability to locate, monitor, and target their supposed enemies.

6.1 When is online surveillance useful?

The usefulness of online surveillance for informing states' repressive strategies is likely to vary in a number of important ways. From a global comparative perspective, the benefits of online surveillance will be dependent on a state's capacity to implement surveillance technology, train analysts (see Chen and Greitens, 2021), and feed the extracted information into the established workflow of its security services. The benefits may also be dependent on the level of Internet penetration within a given country and the degree to which opposition or dissident groups rely on online communication to organize and recruit new members (Macías-Medellín and Atuesta, 2021).

I focus here on within-country variation, and argue that online surveillance will be particularly useful where traditional forms of information gathering are proving to be less effective. Local variation in general support for the government will impact local state forces' capacity to collect high-quality information. In addition, established networks of informants may have been disrupted through changing local security situations (Shapiro and Weidmann, 2015). With lacking security and dysfunctional channels of communication, the population may be less willing to share tips on the whereabouts of dissidents. In contexts where the government is fighting

Repression in the Digital Age: Surveillance, Censorship, and the Dynamics of State Violence. Anita R. Gohdes, Oxford University Press. © Oxford University Press 2024. DOI: 10.1093/oso/9780197743577.003.0006

armed internal opposition groups, citizens are more likely to feel safe in sharing such information where the government exhibits a strong local presence, such as when it controls the majority of the territory (Kalyvas, 2006). Online surveillance is thus likely to be particularly useful for governments in areas that are not fully under their control.

Where traditional means of obtaining such information are available, states are likely to be less reliant on online surveillance to obtain high-quality intelligence. For example, in areas traditionally known to exhibit strong loyalties to the ruling regime, for example through ethnic, religious, or political linkages, online surveillance may play less of a role in acquiring information about "enemies of the state," as government supporters may be more willing to freely share such information with state authorities. Disruptions to the Internet that aim at limiting access to online content can even backfire in such areas, as those loyal to the government may feel they are being unnecessarily punished.

Observable implications

There are a number of empirically observable factors that are likely to correlate with digital surveillance providing additional information to governments. Importantly, a precondition for surveillance to be possible is Internet accessibility. Higher levels of Internet accessibility indicate a government's improved ability to make use of surveillance technology. My theoretical expectation is that online surveillance will be positively associated with a targeted repressive strategy. However, *this positive association will be more pronounced in areas where the government and its security forces have fewer opportunities to make use of traditional forms of information collection.*

The first observable factor through which I test this hypothesis is by comparing the impact of Internet accessibility on targeted state violence in areas controlled by the government versus areas where control is contested. I expect that in areas controlled by the government, the added value of Internet accessibility in providing intelligence will be less pronounced than in areas where control is contested. The second observable factor pertains to ethnic group presence. I expect that in areas where ethnic groups known to display higher levels of loyalty towards the government are present, the added value of Internet-based intelligence will be lower than in areas without such groups being present.

The remainder of this chapter proceeds as follows. I first discuss variations in regional Internet accessibility in Syria, before introducing a new measure

100 REPRESSION IN THE DIGITAL AGE

and operationalization of violent strategies and present descriptive patterns of civilian victimization in Syria between 2013 and 2015. I then present empirical evidence for the just-mentioned hypothesis, focusing first on the relationship between Internet accessibility and targeted violence, and then taking into account armed group control and regional ethnic group presence. I discuss these results in light of the broader theoretical argument pertaining to repressive dynamics and cyber controls.

6.2 Regional Internet accessibility in Syria

Throughout the course of the conflict, accessibility to the Internet varied profoundly across Syria. Figure 6.1 shows the level of network accessibility (Mobile Phones, 3G, and 2G) by governorate for the time period of this study, June 1, 2013–April 30, 2015. The data were collected by the Syria Digital Security Monitor (SDSM), a project funded by the SecDev Foundation.[1] Starting in June 2013, SDSM surveyed all Syrian districts every two weeks[2] in order to establish the degree of digital accessibility across the country.

Where the lines spike, regular or full Internet access is available. Some areas, such as Tartus, which is predominately government-controlled, and Damascus have had relatively uninterrupted Internet access for the majority of the time under investigation. The northern governorate of Ar-Raqqah, an IS stronghold throughout the period under investigation, is the only one to have been almost entirely cut off from both Internet and mobile phone access during the period under investigation (Al-Hussien, 2017). Many regions, however, have been subjected to high levels of fluctuation, including Hama, Homs, Idlib, Daraa, Aleppo, and the region surrounding the capital of Damascus (known as Rif Dimashq or Rural Damascus). These regions have been at the center of some of the worst fighting between regime and opposition forces, yet average levels of government control vary between them.

While there have been frequent reports of network infrastructure being destroyed as a byproduct of military offensives, the data presented here suggest that accessibility did not continuously decrease during this period under investigation. A continuous decrease in Internet and Mobile Phone accessibility is something we might expect to see if these changes were solely tied to technical failures stemming from irreparable damage by destruction of infrastructure. Instead, the data suggest that access is frequently lost

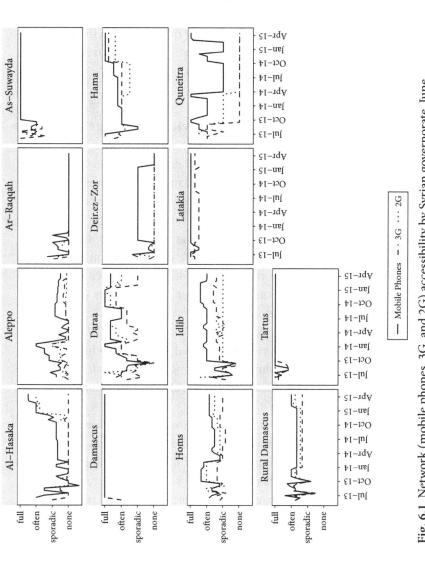

Fig. 6.1 Network (mobile phones, 3G, and 2G) accessibility by Syrian governorate, June 2013–April 2015.

102 REPRESSION IN THE DIGITAL AGE

for short periods of time and then increases again, only to decrease in the following month. These more systematic patterns have been widely identified as being implemented by regime forces, with anecdotal evidence identifying the timing of localized outages being related to military sieges and other forms of broad offensives. From a technical standpoint the systematic nature of the shutdowns suggests that they have been implemented through technical configurations, and not through physical failures or cut cables (e.g. Perlroth, 2013a).[3]

6.3 Measuring the regime's violent strategy

Quantifying variations in a government's repressive strategy is challenging, in particular when trying to study patterns that move beyond scale. I conceptualize the government's violent strategy as consisting of two components, namely the perpetration of targeted and untargeted killings. Comparing the number of targeted and untargeted killings to each other allows me to account for both types of violence within the same empirical model. For every time period t and governorate j, I model the number of targeted killings (y_{jt}) as compared to the total number of killings per observation (N_{jt}), which is the sum of targeted (y_{jt}) and untargeted killings (z_{jt}). Building on work by Kalyvas (2006), Steele (2009), and Wood (2010), I define targeted violence as instances where a victim was killed either due to individual or collective characteristics. In contrast, all incidences where the victim was not selected on the basis of individual or collective characteristics are defined as untargeted violence.

Since it is not possible to measure the government's intent directly, I rely on documented information regarding the circumstances of violence to infer the probable intent. I use supervised machine-learning to classify over 65,000 aggregated reports on individual killings that were committed by the Syrian regime (and pro-government forces) between June 2013 and April 2015 (see Price, Gohdes, and Ball, 2016). In the hand-coded training set, records are classified as *targeted* killings if the circumstances described in the aggregated report (1) indicate that the victim was selected based on his/her specific characteristics (e.g. "killed because he refused to[...]," "dissent"), and/or (2) indicate that the method of killing was of a selective nature (e.g. executed by sniper, hanging, beheading, set afire), and/or (3) the method of killing was accompanied by other violations of a selective nature (e.g. arrest, detention, prison, "found with hands/legs tied"). The majority of targeted killings are classified based on method of killing, or accompanying violations (e.g. torture) that indicate targeting.

Records are classified as *untargeted* killings if the circumstances described in the aggregated report (1) indicate that the victim was not selected based on his/her specific characteristics (e.g. "stepped on a landmine"), and/or (2) indicate that the method of killing was not selective (e.g. airplanes, explosion, bombing, shelling, mortar, chemical, toxic cases), and/or (3) the method of killing was not accompanied by other targeted violations.[4]

To classify the remaining records I use the gradient booster *xgboost* (Chen et al., 2017).[5] The classified records are then used as the basis to estimate unreported levels of both targeted and untargeted violence using multiple recapture estimation as introduced in Chapter 4, Section 4.5.

Figure 6.2 shows the dynamics of targeted and untargeted violence over time, using the same two-week intervals used in the analysis. The graph shows the variation in the different types of violence over time, as well as the variation in estimated underreporting based on the multi-recapture

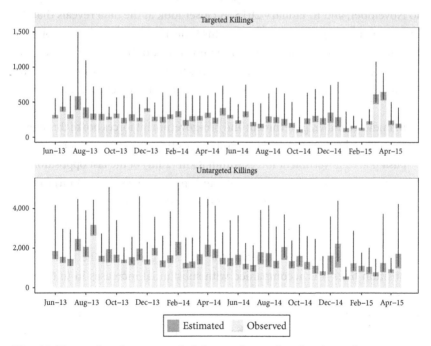

Fig. 6.2 Targeted and untargeted violence, observed and estimated counts, over time.

104 REPRESSION IN THE DIGITAL AGE

modeling. While the numbers are presented at the country-level, defining events of the conflict coincide with changes in the pattern of violence. It also suggests that patterns of targeted and untargeted violence do not merely coincide with each other, instead there are distinct dynamics to be found in both types of repressive strategy. In the second half of August 2013, a chemical attack attributed to the Syrian government was perpetrated in eastern Ghouta, on the outskirts of Damascus. The attack led to a sharp increase in casualties resulting from this indiscriminate attack on civilians' lives. Figure 6.2 displays a sharp rise in the number of untargeted killings in the second half of August 2013. No comparable increase is discernible in the dynamics of targeted killings, which matches the key events of this time period.

A further notable dynamic is visible in December 2014. While there is a small increase in targeted violence, the estimates suggest that there was a noteworthy increase in untargeted violence in the last month of 2014. This increase was, however, less documented than previous levels of violence, as indicated by the fact that the darker part of the bar increases quite substantially in the first and second half of December 2014, when compared to November, and to January 2015. A closer look at the data reveals that the biggest increases in state violence at this time are to be found in Aleppo. At the end of 2014 Aleppo, located in the northwest of Syria, was an area that witnessed some of the most intense fighting in the entire country (The Carter Center, 2015). On the events in December, The Carter Center reports:

> In mid-December, government and pro-government forces broke through opposition lines and engaged opposition positions in Handarat Camp. The push placed government forces within 3 km (2 mi) of the last opposition-controlled highway into Aleppo city, and approximately 6 km (4 mi) from government positions on the eastern side of Aleppo city.
> (The Carter Center, 2015: 7)

The spike in violence visible in the data suggests that the breaking of opposition lines was accompanied with substantial increases in untargeted violence, but that due to the intensity of the situation and the number of conflict actors simultaneously present in Aleppo, documentation work was not as able to fully keep up with the level of violence. The difference between documented and estimated violence presented here further supports the need for working with estimated levels of violence. As the intensity of fighting increases, documentation work may not be able to keep up with events on the ground.

A further noteworthy dynamic is the increase in targeted killings in March 2015, a change that is not found in the levels of untargeted violence. The majority of this increase in targeted violence in March 2015 is perpetrated in Damascus, and the region surrounding it (Rural Damascus). According to reports by the Syrian Observatory of Human Rights, a large number of opposition fighters defected to the Syrian Army in southern Damascus in March 2015. Evidently, the surrendering of insurgent fighters was accompanied by increases in targeted violence in Damascus, as well as the area immediately surrounding it (Al-Khalidi, 2015). Overall, a regaining of territory by the government, and an increase in defections by anti-government groups is associated with a significant increase in targeted killings in March 2015.

The patterns presented in Figure 6.2 show how the distinction between state violence that is targeted and violence that is untargeted helps trace changes in the government's repressive activities throughout the period under investigation. It also highlights the importance of accounting for unreported fatalities, as the level of reporting varies both over time and across different forms of violence.

6.4 Subnational evidence

For each of the 14 Syrian governorates and every two-week time period, I establish the number of targeted killings (y_{jt}), and the number of untargeted killings (z_{jt}), which together form the overall number of killings per observation ($N_{jt} = y_{it} + z_{it}$). Table 6.1 presents a number of regression models investigating the relationship between Internet accessibility, measured as third generation (3G) of wireless mobile Internet, and the violent state repression.

Models 1 and 2 measure targeted violence as proportion of the total number of killings. Model 1 only includes temporal fixed effects and governorate-clustered standard errors. Whether the government is predominately using targeted or untargeted repression at a given time in a given area is likely to also be dependent on their overall conflict engagement. To account for conflict intensity, I include the overall logged *number of killings* perpetrated by the government in Model 2. In both models, Internet accessibility is positively and significantly correlated with an increase in the proportion

106 REPRESSION IN THE DIGITAL AGE

Table 6.1 Internet accessibility (3G) and violent repression. Models I and II estimate the proportion of targeted killings (generalized linear regression, binomial with logit link). Model III estimates the number of targeted killings, and Model IV estimates the number of untargeted killings (negative binomial model).

	I: prop. targ.	II: prop. targ.	III: number targ.	IV: number untarg.
Intercept	−2.309***	−1.370***	2.917***	5.212***
	(0.176)	(0.304)	(0.253)	(0.206)
Internet Access (3G)	0.223***	0.186***	0.086**	−0.135***
	(0.046)	(0.045)	(0.031)	(0.027)
Number of Killings (log)		−0.161***		
		(0.044)		
Temporal Fixed Effects	yes	yes	yes	yes
AIC	10592.525	10418.524	5285.576	7405.673
BIC	10802.507	10632.974	5500.026	7620.123
Log Likelihood	−5249.262	−5161.262	−2594.788	−3654.837
Deviance	8080.874	7904.873	768.678	742.398
Num. obs.	640	640	644	644

***$p < 0.001$, **$p < 0.01$, *$p < 0.05$. Governorate-clustered SEs. Temporal fixed-effects not shown.

of targeted state violence, offering preliminary support for the relationship proposed in this chapter. Model 3 estimates the number of targeted killings, and Model 4 estimates the number of untargeted killings. The results of these two models demonstrate that Internet accessibility is not only associated with a relative increase in targeted violence, it is also associated with an increase in the *number* of targeted killings, and with a decrease in the number of untargeted killings.

These baseline results do not account for important drivers of violent dynamics, which I turn to next.

6.4.1 Regional armed group control

Figure 6.3 shows the different factions controlling territory for January 2014 and January 2015, respectively. The data was collected by the Syria Conflict Mapping Project (SCMP) that is part of the Carter Center to construct an indicator of individual armed group presence and territorial control.[6] The project tracked more than 5,000 local communities and determines

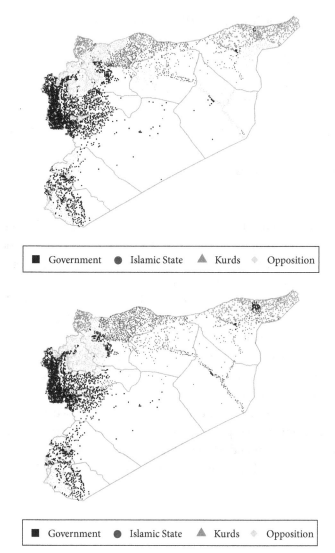

Fig. 6.3 Armed group presence in Syria—community level, January 2014 and 2015.

which conflict party is in control. I follow their aggregate categorization of four main conflict lines: opposition forces, so-called 'Islamic State' forces, government forces, and Kurdish forces.

Square-shaped communities are controlled by Government forces, diamond-shaped by the Opposition, circle-shaped by 'Islamic State' forces and triangle-shaped areas are controlled by Kurdish forces, most notably the YPG. In Figure 6.3, the progression of Islamic State forces in both

Al-Hasakah (the North-East) as well as Aleppo and Ar-Raqqah governorates are clearly visible. By January 2015 (Figure 6.3b), Islamic State forces have pushed out Kurdish forces from even larger parts of Aleppo, Ar-Raqqah, and Al-Hasakah. The top right corner of the map shows that the Islamic State forces were not the only group to gain ground in the Kurdish North Eastern territory, regime forces also made territorial gains during this time.

For the time period under investigation here I create a number of governorate-level measures from the community-level control data that reflect armed group presence, control, and temporal changes in control at the governorate level to match the information on regime violence and Internet accessibility.

The main measure of control is a categorical variable which takes on the name of the group that has more than 60% of all communities in a governorate under its control. When and where none of the groups hold more than 60% (such as in Aleppo in January and July 2014), the variable is coded as *contested control*.[7] To account for the changing role of Internet controls in different local contexts, I interact armed group presence with levels of Internet accessibility.

Figure 6.4 shows the average proportion of targeted killings, depending on territorial control. Unsurprisingly, the proportion is highest in areas under government control. In areas controlled by opposition forces, areas where control is contested, and in those areas controlled by Kurdish or 'Islamic State' forces, the proportion is significantly lower. This confirms established theoretical and empirical findings on the relationship between territorial control and the nature of violence (see Kalyvas, 2006), which

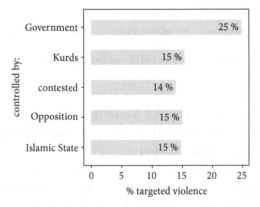

Fig. 6.4 Percentage of violence that is targeted, by type of control.

INTERNET ACCESSIBILITY AND TARGETED VIOLENCE   109

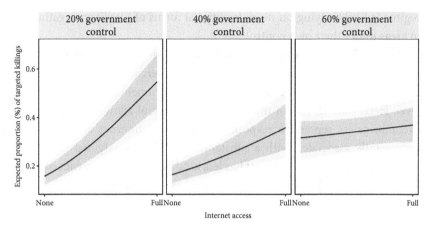

Fig. 6.5 Expected proportion (83% and 95% confidence intervals) of targeted killings, given Internet accessibility and different levels of government control.

predict that in zones where armed actors control the territory, they will also be more likely to use a targeted repressive tactic.

Figure 6.5 simulates the expected proportion of targeted killings, given different levels of Internet accessibility and different degrees of government control. The left panel shows the relationship between Internet accessibility and targeted repression, where all other variables are held constant, and the government is in control of only 20% of the territory. An example of this would be Idlib governorate in northwestern Syria in early 2014.

The expected proportion of targeted killings in areas where the government has little control and where there is no Internet access is around 15%, which is corroborated by the numbers presented in Figure 6.4. However, holding government control constant, the left panel shows that with increasing Internet accessibility, the proportion of targeted killings increases significantly and substantially. The middle panel shows the same relationship between Internet access and targeted repression for a scenario where the government controls 40% of the territory. The proportion of targeted repression starts out at a similar level, but the increase, while still substantial, is not as pronounced as in the previous panel. The right panel simulates areas where the government controls the majority of the territory. The proportion of targeted violence starts out at a significantly higher level, indicating that the government uses more targeted violence in areas it controls, regardless of Internet accessibility. But here, increasing Internet accessibility is not associated with a significant increase in targeted killings, indicating that the

REPRESSION IN THE DIGITAL AGE

regime is likely relying on more traditional forms of intelligence gathering in areas under their own control.

Figure 6.5 shows that the relationship between Internet accessibility and state repression is mediated by levels of local territorial control. Internet control loses its importance with increasing government strength at the local level. Here, other forms of more traditional control allow the government to calibrate its repressive response. In contrast, Internet accessibility is significantly associated with a substantive increase in targeted repression when and where the government has less local power. Here, Internet controls constitute a crucial tool in the regime's repressive strategy.

6.4.2 Regional ethnic group presence

Politically relevant ethnic groups have made up an important part of the ongoing Syrian conflict. In addition to the predominant Sunni Muslims, the Alawi, Druze, Kurdish, and Christian Syrians form politically ethnic groups. To measure ethnic group presence, I make use of the GeoEPR Dataset (Wucherpfennig et al., 2011) which codes the geographic location and time period of *politically relevant groups* for the entire world, starting in 1946. As the Assad regime belongs to, and has historically predominantly recruited its inner circle from the Syrian Alawite community, I interact Alawi presence with Internet accessibility to account for other forms of control that may be at play in traditional government strongholds.

Figure 6.6 simulates the expected proportion of targeted killings, given no or full Internet accessibility, in both Alawi and non-Alawi regions, using governorate-clustered standard errors.[8] It shows that the association between Internet access and state violence is mediated by the presence of Alawi citizens, who are traditionally known for their loyalty towards the Assad regime. While Internet access remains significant in this model, the interaction term between accessibility and Alawi presence is both negative and significant. In non-Alawi regions, all else equal, the proportion of targeted killings perpetrated by the government is significantly and substantially higher when the Internet is fully accessible than when the Internet is shut down. In areas that are traditionally known to be inhabited by large amounts of regime supporters, Internet accessibility, if anything, indicates a negative relationship between access and targeted violence.

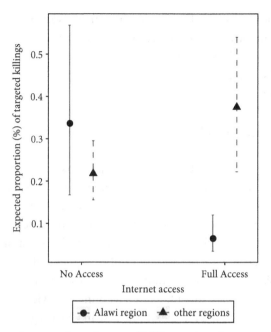

Fig. 6.6 Expected proportion of targeted killings, given Internet accessibility and whether a region is inhabited by the Alawi minority.

The results offer support for the empirical expectations: Internet control, through the provision or limiting of accessibility, will be a useful tool for governments to enhance their repressive capabilities, in particular when and where they cannot rely on other forms of more traditional control mechanisms.

Discussion

The evidence presented here offers a number of interesting findings. Across a range of model specifications it shows that higher levels of Internet accessibility granted by the government are significantly and substantially associated with a more targeted strategy of regime violence. In contrast, where Internet access is limited or shut down, the Syrian government employs a significantly more indiscriminate campaign of violence. However, this relationship is mediated by local conditions that determine whether the regime is able to rely on more traditional forms of intelligence, or whether digital surveillance will enhance their ability to target those deemed threatening to their political survival. The results show that Internet controls become increasingly important with decreasing levels of government control. In contrast, in areas inhabited by the Alawi minority, traditionally known to support the Assad regime, Internet accessibility is not associated with higher levels of targeted violence. In such areas the government is more likely to rely on conventional forms of obtaining information. Similar dynamics are observable in regions and at times when the government controls most of the territory.

This chapter has offered the most comprehensive test for the overall theoretical argument. It also provides a number of solutions for common challenges to measuring both state control of the Internet and variations in the strategies of state repression. Survey data on the level of accessibility of the Internet was used to gauge the state's implementation of network controls. But there are also important limits to its generalizability.

The analysis presented here studies a large-scale civil conflict involving a highly repressive government, as well as numerous violent, armed, non-state actors. It represents a more extreme case in which a government makes use of coercive measures against challenges to its political stability. The logic of where states will prioritize access to high-quality online intelligence, however, is likely to be relevant in other contexts where governments are prepared to use repressive tools against a real or perceived threat. While the scale at which states will use violence will differ, mass uprisings or even smaller-scale protests perceived to be of particular danger to the government's stability may trigger similar choices.

This chapter concludes the analysis of cyber controls and repression in Syria. In the next chapter I turn to digital politics and repression in Iran.

7

Online controls and the protest-repression nexus in Iran

During the early 2000s, Iran was known for its flourishing blogosphere that enabled the country's youth to find its voice (Sreberny and Khiabany, 2012) and by mid-2005, Iran had one of the fastest growing online communities worldwide (OpenNet Initiative, 2007: 2). In 2005, the populist hardliner Mahmoud Ahmadinejad won the presidential elections and ushered in a new era of ramped-up digital censorship. While bloggers and other online activitists continued to challenge the regime's authority, Ahmadinejad's presidency brought with it a tightening of digital screws that would come to define the coming decades of digital politics. As Rahimi (2008: 37) contended in 2008: "[i]n a country where 70 percent of its 70 million population remains under the age of 30, [the rapid development of the Internet] poses one of the most important threats against authoritarian hegemony in Iran."

Control of the online sphere had already picked up speed prior to Ahmadinejad taking office. In 2004, the regime began using the Secure Computing's SmartFilter software designed to filter and block content deemed inappropriate or dangerous by the authorities (OpenNet Initiative, 2006). A study by the OpenNet Initiative published in 2007 showed the pervasive breadth and depth of filtering related to political and social content, as well as blogging platforms and circumvention tools (OpenNet Initiative, 2007). A number of new laws were implemented to further restrict online content in 2006. A few months later, domain owners in Iran were required to formally register their personal information with the Ministry of Islamic Culture and Guidance. Websites without official registration would become illegal, and bloggers were required to abstain from posting politically or socially sensitive content (OpenNet Initiative, 2007: 3). The implementation of this new order turned out to be challenging, and by 2009 only a small number of websites had officially registered (OpenNet Initiative, 2009a). This led the regime to instead move towards improving

Repression in the Digital Age: Surveillance, Censorship, and the Dynamics of State Violence. Anita R. Gohdes, Oxford University Press. © Oxford University Press 2024. DOI: 10.1093/oso/9780197743577.003.0007

114 REPRESSION IN THE DIGITAL AGE

its domestic surveillance and filtering capabilities by developing its own software that would make them less dependent on foreign companies. Rerouting Internet traffic through proxy servers meant that the authorities could monitor unencrypted data and keep tabs on unwanted content and potentially threatening users. In spring 2009, a few months before the contested presidential election that would trigger the largest protest movement since the 1979 revolution, reports emerged that the authorities had purchased surveillance equipment from the German-Finnish Nokia Siemens Networks. Human rights defenders had already raised awareness in 2009 about the link between surveillance capabilities and the targeting of activists. When a prominent dissident was arrested in 2009, his lawyer told a reporter "he had received a call from the Ministry of Intelligence, [and during his interrogation], they put in front of him printed copies of his chats with me. He said he was dumbfounded, and he was sent to prison" (Lake, 2009).

7.1 Elections and protest in 2009

Amidst growing investments in digital technology to monitor and filter Internet traffic, President Ahmadinejad was re-elected in June 2009. The result of more than 62% of all cast votes seemingly in favor of the incumbent was accompanied by reports of widespread irregularities and provoked mass protest that spread across the country, with diaspora and foreign sympathizers following suit and taking to the streets around the world (Milani, 2010). Mass demonstrations decrying election fraud continued for weeks. Being a young and tech-savvy country that had learned to use the Internet to circumvent much of the traditional news censorship, the protesters made use of social media and messaging services from the start of the protests (Memarian and Nesvaderani, 2010; Golkar, 2011; Sreberny and Khiabany, 2012). One week into the protests, the philosophy student and musician Neda Agha Soltan was shot by a paramilitary sniper while on the sidelines of a protest. Her murder was filmed by bystanders using their cell phones, and uploaded to social media. The videos quickly went viral, creating international outrage and further igniting the Green Movement. The amateur footage of her death demonstrated the brutality of the pro-government forces, while also highlighting how digital documentation shared in real-time on social media could spark solidarity with protest movements and

ONLINE CONTROLS AND THE PROTEST-REPRESSION NEXUS IN IRAN 115

garner support for accountability and political change. In many ways, the footage of her killing came to symbolize the resistance building against the regime (Mortensen, 2011). And as the movement matured into the fall of 2009, the focus slowly shifted from solely protesting election fraud to calling into question the legitimacy of the entire political system.

Analyses of the Green Movement have highlighted the ways in which the forceful turnout and decentralized organization took the regime by surprise (Milani, 2010). The government's security forces, including its paramilitary forces, were quick to respond with widespread beatings, arrests, and sniper fire. One day after the elections, as thousands were taking to the streets, the Internet was briefly shut down all across the country. When it came back on, connectivity had been throttled further, and more domains and circumvention tools had been blocked (Article 19, 2013; Anderson, 2013: 19). As the movement became more organized, the government targeted 100 of the most prominent organizers of the protests and put them on show trial. Some of them were tortured to death before even making it to trial (Milani, 2010: 4). At the height of the protests, an estimated three million people were on the streets calling for fair elections and changes to the system, the largest protests since the revolution of 1979. Tweets, pictures, and videos of the protests and the ensuing repression were shared all across the Internet, garnerning worldwide media attention. The killing of Neda Agha Soltan exemplified how the government was not able to control the narrative of the protests due to the rapid spread of information online. As thousands of Iranian protesters shared footage of her death online, the incident was quickly picked up by international media, including CNN. By the time Iranian state-run media reacted to her killing with a number of conspiracies aimed at deflecting blame, it was too late. The story had already spread.

7.2 Ramping up online controls after 2009

The unanticipated size, duration, and intensity of the 2009 protests had a long-lasting impact on the digital security approach of the regime. In the following section I describe how digital controls were scaled up and expanded in the aftermath of the Green Movement's uprising. The manifold innovations made in the area of Internet infrastructure, software, laws and policies, institutions, and practice showcase the ways in which the regime aimed to expand its control of Internet traffic, while at the same time working towards minimizing political pushback and economic repercussions of an over-blocked Internet.

In the immediate aftermath of the protests, harassment, intimidation, interrogations, arrests, and executions of bloggers and other digitally active people were significantly ramped up (Article 19, 2013: 16). Many Iranian dissidents who had previously been vocal about political and social issues fled the country and continued their work abroad. Many reported being hacked, digitally surveiled and harassed, and their family and friends targeted in the process, as well (Michaelsen, 2018). Activists in- and outside of Iran were repeatedly targeted by hackers with a variety of phishing attacks (Center for Human Rights in Iran, 2018). Within Iran, domestic controls were further expanded, for example by requiring cybercafés to keep a record of their users' personal identification as well as their browsing histories (Article 19, 2013: 15).

While the start of the new decade in Egypt, Syria, Tunisia, and other Arab countries was marked by widespread civilian upheavals, the Iranian regime established new institutions to deal with digital threats and prevent another Green Movement. In November 2009, it launched an Internet crime unit, a team that worked with the chief prosecutor to investigate "illegal" content online, including political material that was categorized as lies or insults (Trait, 2009). In 2012, the Supreme Council of Cyberspace, chaired by the president, was established; it would become the highest policy-making body for all cyber-related activities in Iran (Robertson and Marchant, 2015: 20). The SCC was put in charge of both domestic and international cyber issues. Below the SCC, the Committee Charged with Determining Offensive Content (CCDOC) is the executive body in charge of creating lists of websites and online content that should be censored for religious, political, or social reasons. Together, the SCC and CCDOC, who share seven members, are at the core of the country's monitoring and filtering activities (Article 19, 2013: 17; Robertson and Marchant, 2015).

Immediately following the 2009 protests, the government pushed along its plan for a national Internet infrastructure. First discussions of Iran's National Information Network (NIN) dated back to the mid-2000s, but investments in this large and expensive project picked up speed in 2010 (Kargar, 2018). Building a national Internet infrastructure fully controlled by the government and independent of the World Wide Web would allow the country to exercise more control over its digital space and the content produced within it. Early on, the discussions surrounding the NIN stressed the importance of

ONLINE CONTROLS AND THE PROTEST-REPRESSION NEXUS IN IRAN   117

being independent from the West and having in place a functioning system in case the country were to be cut off from the World Wide Web. After the Stuxnet cyber attack on the Iranian nuclear enrichment site became publicly known in 2010, the motivation to develop cyber capabilities and become independent from Western technology and infrastructure shifted to an ever greater priority (Anderson and Sadjadpour, 2018).

While the narrative was aimed towards a possible shutdown instituted by the US, the NIN would also bring with it a series of advantages if Iran's leadership were to initiate a shutdown themselves. In the event of shutting down access to the World Wide Web but keeping open access to the domestic network, it would avoid interrupting business and financial transactions, thereby reducing the economic costs and possibly the pushback from local businesses and organizations dependent on it. The second advantage for the government would be that users who normally relied on foreign applications for their work and private communications, such as Telegram or WhatsApp, would be motivated to use domestic applications if access to the Internet were suddenly cut. For a long time, the Iranian regime had done its best to discourage the use of foreign social media and messaging and had repeatedly blocked them, with varying levels of success. Apps like Telegram were not only used by dissidents and activists, but also by large sections of the population for everyday communication and for conducting business. Blocking them without having an attractive alternative therefore had the consequence that people quickly became extremely savvy at getting around the block through the use of VPNs and other circumvention tools. In tandem with trying to prevent the usage of Telegram and other apps, the regime now also started to pursue the Chinese model of offering domestic alternatives to its people. Applications that were built by Iranian companies with servers located in the country could be more readily monitored and facilitated the filtering of unwanted communication. Domestically controlled apps might help the regime prevent another Green Movement from spreading its ideas digitally.

Next to domestic infrastructure developments, Iran's ICT sector heavily invested in building and refining their interception and monitoring hardware and software. In 2010, Iran's largest telecommunications provider reportedly signed a 100 million Euro deal to buy Chinese interception software that would allow the government to monitor landlines, voice and text communication on mobile phones, and general Internet traffic (Stecklow, 2012). The software principally relies on deep packet inspection, a type of interception mechanism that was reportedly already purchased and used by the Iranian regime in 2009 (Fuchs, 2013: 1343). While Western technology companies were becoming increasingly wary of dealing with Iran in the face of sanctions, the regime extended its economic relationship with China. Investment in new technology also came into play during the 2013 and 2016 elections and showcases how the government continuously worked on refining its censorship approach with an eye towards effectively curtailing political protest, while avoiding backlash. Research by Deibert, Oliver, and Senft (2019) demonstrates how censorship surrounding the 2013 elections involved intense throttling and blocking more content than was actually needed from the perspective of the regime, while doing so for longer periods of time and thereby provoking condemnation from the broader population and from the international community. Three years later, when President Rouhani was re-elected, the censorship strategy was far more targeted in both content and timing, focusing on time periods that were particularly contentious (Deibert, Oliver, and Senft, 2019: 351).

The regime's long-standing effort at prohibiting fast Internet access for the broader population showcases its fear of stimulating access to independent political and social multimedia content online. As early as 2006, the Ministry of Communications and Information Technology (MICT) ordered an explicit limit on the permitted speed of Internet access for Iranian households. This order was seen by many as a way to stifle access to alternative media content by non-state media sources (OpenNet Initiative, 2009a: 3). As citizens took to the streets in June 2009, reports of even further slowed Internet access were manifold (Article 19, 2013). As discussed in Chapter 2, throttling allows governments to plausibly deny intentionally tampering with Internet access, although researchers have worked on detecting specific patterns associated with throttling (Anderson, 2013). Slowed down Internet access provoked less international attention, while also allowing general communications to continue, albeit at a slower pace. But for dissidents and other users trying to access blocked content through circumvention tools that in and of themselves slow down access, the combination of a VPN or Tor with throttled access would make it almost impossible to swiftly consume multimedia content online. In stark contrast to the snail-paced access to foreign apps and websites, the regime therefore heavily advertised the fact that the national intranet NIN would enable high-speed content consumption. The choice would therefore be between frustratingly slow uncensored access to the World Wide Web or fast and smooth access to a monitored and censored domestic network.

In August 2016, the regime announced that it had made significant progress in building its own intranet infrastructure that would allow Iranians to access all essential services and domestic programs in a low cost, fast manner (Vasilogambros, 2016). The NIN already covered e-government and banking services and was set to add multimedia content and further business services the following year (BBC News, 2016). Launching the NIN allowed the government to usher in a new era of digital control. From the perspective of the regime, the best-case scenario would see all Iranian Internet users substitute their current online tools and habits with options provided by the NIN. And even though the uptake turned out to be sluggish, particularly when it came to leaving essential messaging apps such as Telegram, the presence of the NIN meant that shutting down access to the World Wide Web would no longer be associated with a grinding halt of the country's economy that was increasingly dependent on the web. Therefore, it was not surprising that in the face of protests in December 2017 and January 2018, access to the international Internet was repeatedly shut down, and Telegram repeatedly blocked and access to the app throttled (Article 19, 2018).

At first glance, the breadth and depth of digital controls introduced and expanded after the events of 2009 may suggest a highly principled and effective government response to the challenges posed by information and communication technology. Yet on closer inspection, the workings of the SCC, the CCDOC, and the rollout of the national Internet project reveal a more complex picture that more accurately reflects the challenges and pushback to online controls experienced by repressive regimes (Article 19, 2017, 2020b). Since 2009, the SCC and CCDOC have repeatedly clashed when it comes to the decision-making and implementation of domain blocking. For example, when Facebook announced its acquisition of WhatsApp in 2014, the CCDOC motioned to block the messaging app within Iran. The motion was opposed by both the president and the Minister of Information and Communications Technology, Mahmoud Vaezi. Because the CCDOC is an executive body that is subordinate to the SCC, and the SCC is chaired by Iran's president, President Rouhani's opposition to the CCDOC nominally meant that the WhatsApp block would be overturned. Yet members of the CCDOC have been extremely outspoken against the president's approach towards enforcing his cabinet's own agenda, thereby diminishing the mandate of

120 REPRESSION IN THE DIGITAL AGE

the Committee. Ultimately, the app was not permanently banned, but the discussions surrounding the country's censorship strategy highlight how inconsistencies can and do arise. Besides internal tensions, the regime's goal of motivating users to migrate their messaging activities to domestic apps has also been comparatively unsuccessful (Akbari and Gabdulhakov, 2019). Despite attempts to block the app and impose restrictions on bandwidth, Telegram remains the most popular messaging app in the country, and users have largely chosen circumvention tools to continue using it. The regime has repeatedly advertised a number of approved apps, such as Soroush, boasting that users "can benefit from over 1,000 gigabits per second of added bandwidth, which is double the total bandwidth of foreign social networks in the country" (Hamid Fattahi, managing director of Telecommunication Infrastructure Company, quoted in Tehran Times, 2018). Thus far, these campaigns have showed little success.

In the following section, I investigate the dynamics of online controls and repression in the context of the widespread protests that swept across the country in November 2019. In the decade leading up to these protests, citizens had repeatedly and loudly protested the regime's economic, religious, and social policies, oftentimes calling into question the very foundations of theocratic rule. Yet the events in 2019 exceeded all of them in size, constituting the largest protests since the 1979 revolution.

7.3 Protests and Internet shutdown, November 2019

On Thursday, the 14th of November, 2019, President Hassan Rouhani announced a 200% increase in the price of petrol, saying that the proceeds of the increase were to be redistributed to the poorest (BBC Middle East, 2019). The announcement was immediately met with widespread outrage, and by the following day the first mass protests erupted in the southwest of Iran, including cities close to the border with Iraq, such as Khorramshahr. Within the first 24 hours, the protests spread across the country to the eastern border with Afghanistan. People all across Iran shared their frustration, anger, and protest strategies on both social media and location-based apps, for example calling on others to block the streets with their cars and create traffic jams on major motorways. Videos of large groups of protesters emerged on Twitter, Telegram, and other channels, clearly showing the response by the security services. According to human rights organizations the protesters were largely peaceful, practicing civil disobedience, except for a small number that threw stones and damaged property (Amnesty International, 2019a; Justice for Iran, 2020). By Sunday, the demonstrations had spread across the country, moving beyond fuel prices, towards decrying overall economic distress and dissatisfaction with the government.

On the early evening of the 16th, the second day of the protests, Iranians were suddenly cut off from the World Wide Web. Access to the Internet was shut down. The national intranet (NIN, or SHOMA) remained intact (Article 19, 2020b: 18). Protesters were not able to access many of the social media, mapping, and messenger applications they had been using to coordinate protests. With turn-out ramping up across the country, including Teheran, those organizing themselves online therefore had to find other ways of coordinating their activities. As described above, the shutdown essentially left protesters with two problematic options: either resort to non-digital communication or migrate towards using government-supported (and surveilled) apps available via the national infrastructure. The latter would immediately allow authorities to monitor and locate the planned activities, all while keeping track of those engaged in them.

The Internet remained offline for a week, and only slowly returned in some parts of the country starting on November 23, but some regions in the southwest and east remained offline for a few more weeks (Article 19, 2020b: 20). Figure 7.1 traces the shutdown through network measurement data collected by the Center for Applied Internet Data Analysis' Internet Outage Detection and Analysis (IODA) Project (IODA, 2021). IODA provides network measurements from three different data sources, which include their own active probing, Internet routing announcements (BGP), and Internet background radiation (denoted as "Darknet" in the figure). All three measurements display a sharp drop on the evening of the 16th. By all comparisons, this shutdown was an extraordinarily long and pervasive blackout. Recall that the nationwide shutdowns in Syria seldom lasted longer than two or three days, and even the prominent shutdown in Egypt in January of 2011 lasted just under six days.

7.3.1 Mass repression and intimidation

The regime's response to the protests was immediate and unmistakably strong. Demonstrators were subjected to tear gas, live ammunition shot

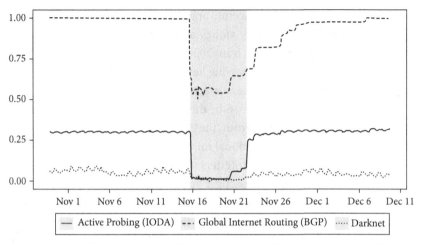

Fig. 7.1 Normalized Internet traffic in Iran, November 15–25, 2019. Light gray area denotes the commonly understood nationwide Internet shutdown from the evening of November 16 until the early afternoon of November 23. IODA recorded the very first signs of traffic on November 21, while Netblocks observed signs of access being restored on November 23 (NetBocks, 2019). Some ISPs and regions remained offline until November 27. Data source in graph: IODA.

at short distance, and water cannons, while thousands were detained and arrested in cities and towns all across the country. Security forces involved in the repression included, among others, the country's police, the Revolutionary Guards, and the paramilitary Basij force. One human rights organization documented the use of unlawful lethal force in 39 cities across 15 provinces (Justice for Iran, 2020: 13). State-run media reported that within the first three days more than 1,000 protesters were arrested. Within the first week, human rights defenders claimed that at least 2,700 people were arrested, some suggesting the number might be as high as 4,000 (Center for Human Rights in Iran, 2019a). In addition, reports of overcrowded prisons mounted. Recorded visual footage as well as eyewitness accounts confirm that a large proportion of killings by security forces occurred as a result of targeting the head, the heart, and other vital organs which is compatible with a shoot-to-kill strategy (Amnesty International, 2019b). On November 17, with no end of the upheaval in sight, the country's supreme leader himself, Ayatollah Khomeini, gathered his inner circle of government and security officials together and told them, "The Islamic Republic is in danger. Do whatever it takes to end it. You have my order" (reported in

Reuters, 2019). Reports of this direct order by the supreme leader to use excessive and lethal force against the protesters underlines the coordinated and systematic use of indiscriminate violence against unarmed citizens across Iran.

Security forces employed high levels of indiscriminate violence from the first day of the protests. Yet, despite harsh repression, the protests diffused in ever greater numbers across the country. The supreme leader's words demonstrate how quickly the regime realized that the situation would require a concerted response that went beyond the regular type of repression used against those who dared to take to the streets. On the day the Internet was shut down, the interior minster is reported to have instructed the security forces to no longer show "tolerance" or "self control" when dealing with the demonstrators (Amnesty International, 2019a), suggesting an escalation in both rhetoric and action. Preventing protesters' from using their favorite online tools meant that they could not coordinate their tactics across cities and neighborhoods, and it also introduced significant hurdles in reaching out to others to encourage them to join and support the protests. But shutting down the web was more than just a way to curtail further mobilization, it directly supported a repressive response that capitalized on secrecy, intimidation, and covert violence, as would slowly become clear in the weeks following the blackout.

While security forces continued to target protesters and those suspected of participating in the demonstrations, repressive efforts were widened to include the friends and relatives of those directly involved in public dissent. Families of children who had been killed in the context of the protests were placed under particularly strong pressure to remain silent about the loss (Amnesty International, 2020b). The victims' relatives were intimidated by security forces to discourage them from publicly decrying the death or disappearance of their loved ones. Families further reported to have been placed under surveillance, repeatedly harassed, and in some instances made to sign papers assuring the security forces that they would refrain from talking to journalists about the plight of those killed and disappeared by the regime (Amnesty International, 2019b; Center for Human Rights in Iran, 2019a; Justice for Iran, 2020). Eyewitnesses recounted that they had seen members of the authorities involved in removing dead and injured people from medical facilities and from the side of the road during protests, and taking them to locations to conceal their whereabouts (Amnesty International, 2019a). In some cases, the victim's remains were only returned under the condition of secrecy (Justice for Iran, 2020: 16). Where families were allowed to bury their loved ones, they were pressured into keeping the funerals small so as not to draw public attention to them.

In the context of a nationwide Internet shutdown, the employment of intimidation tactics aimed at pressuring those who had a credible story to tell about the disappearance, detention, and death of their family members suggests that the concerted repressive strategy not only stifled mobilization through the absence of digital coordination tools, but was aimed at forcefully limiting the flow of information about the scale of violent repression. Security forces killed hundreds and arrested thousands of individuals, including children. The concerted effort made to intimidate, monitor, and threaten the relatives and friends of the deceased and arrested shows that the authorities intended to crush dissent in a way that would deter backlash. Having observed the outcry surrounding the death of Neda Agha Soltan in 2009, security forces were likely well aware of the backlash mass repression may trigger. In this instance, violent repression was not intended to be an overt example of what punishment the security forces would inflict on those who protested regime policy. Amidst the nationwide Internet shutdown, and with thousands of protesters already having taken to the streets, the regime's repressive response was geared towards a mass punishment of protesters and silencing of witnesses. This strategy also supported the regime's intention of molding a narrative about the size, goals, and agressiveness of the protesters.

7.3.2 Controlling the narrative

The shutdown made the documentation of violent events significantly harder. Without access to social media and other platforms not regulated by the Iranian regime, images and videos recording both the size of the protests and the disproportionately violent response of the authorities had to either remain on individuals' devices or could only be shared via domestic apps. Both of these options exposed those who had recorded or were saving the content to the risk of becoming known to the regime. Possessing visual evidence of state repression was highly dangerous and in the general climate of fear and intimidation some felt pressured to delete or bury evidence for fear of being targeted and arrested. That fear was not unfounded, as reports demonstrated that in some cases the security service refused to return the devices of deceased victims to their families. This led the families to believe that the devices contained incriminating evidence of coercion (Amnesty International, 2020*b*). In the aftermath of the protests, and after the Internet came back on, security forces continued to arrest individuals and search their homes.

The effects of the shutdown on the framing and scale of both the protests and the ensuing government response was profound. Diaspora, rights groups, and international media decried their inability to accurately report events in real-time. A few days into the protests, a London-based digital rights group estimated that because of the shutdown "there is currently around a 24-hour [delay] in the transmission of video footage out of Iran, and this delay is reflected in our reporting" (Filterwatch, 2019). Rana Rahimpour, a reporter with BBC Persia worried that the shutdown was making it "very difficult to get a real sense of how widespread the protests are" for journalists based outside of Iran (BBC Middle East, 2019). On November 19, four days after the protests started, Amnesty International reported it had verified at least 106 killings in 21 cities (Amnesty International, 2019*a*). By the beginning of December, Amnesty increased its confirmed death toll to 304 (Amnesty International, 2019*b*), with at least 23 of those killed being children (Amnesty International, 2020*b*). By the end of December, three Iranian interior ministry officials reportedly told Reuters that about 1,500 people had been killed in the last two weeks of November 2019 (Reuters, 2019).

With the Internet unavailable and the authorities refusing to publicize the numbers of arrested and killed people, the true scale of repression remained opaque (Center for Human Rights in Iran, 2019*a*). Instead, the government used state TV to paint the protesters as rioters and foreign conspirateurs, and justified the arrests due to their involvement in violence and property destruction (Center for Human Rights in Iran, 2019*a*). An investigation by the Center for Human Rights in Iran (2019*b*) revealed that the government had anticipated public protests following the price increases and had summoned local journalists in an effort to dictate how they were to cover the protests. The authorities also tried to downplay the extent of public outcry, reporting that approximately 200,000 people had taken to the streets across Iran, but independent sources suggest the numbers were three times higher (Justice for Iran, 2020: 9). When, despite shutdown and intimidation, reports on mass violence gained traction, President Rouhani attempted to deny regime involvement, stating that "the bullets and the kind of weapons from which they were fired [...] are not of the kinds

126 REPRESSION IN THE DIGITAL AGE

used by the Iranian police or Basij forces" (quoted in Justice for Iran, 2020: 12). Evidently, the efforts to push the narrative of foreign-funded rioters being responsible for the majority of unrest were disproven by independent sources in the months following the protests. Likewise, Iranians based inside and outside of the country tirelessly worked to uncover and document the extent of violence perpetrated by the regime during the course of and in the aftermath of the protests. Yet the regime's decision to shut down virtually all access to the World Wide Web during the most intense turmoil stalled people's ability to share stories, images, and videos of the injustice they were being subjected to. In the aftermath of the protests, a number of citizens attempted to obtain information on the regime's justification for the Internet shutdown through Iran's Freedom of Information Act, but the responses were largely inadequate (Article 19, 2020a).

7.3.3 Evading censorship after the shutdown

Due to Iran's long history of censoring websites, social media apps, and messengers, Iranians have actively used circumvention tools for years. Many popular circumvention tools exists, such as Lantern and Psiphon, and users often switch between different programs to optimize effectiveness (Deibert, Oliver, and Senft, 2019: 344). Many circumvention tools are focused on providing uncensored access to online content, but still leave users vulnerable to regime surveillance. For this reason the Tor software, which allows users to anonymously browse the web, is also very popular in Iran. Access to Tor has also been blocked in the context of protests in the past (Xynou and Filastò, 2018). Figure 7.2 displays the average number of daily concurrent Tor users connecting from Iran, with the light gray area mirroring the time period identified in Figure 7.1 as the commonly understood nationwide shutdown.

During the first two days of the protest, Tor user connections remained relatively unchanged. But with the shutdown of the Internet on November 16, they dropped to a few hundred users, confirming the patterns of the network measurements presented above. With no means of accessing websites outside of Iran, the requests by Tor users within Iran virtually stopped. The numbers presented show that prior to the shutdown, Tor users within Iran were active and manifold. In the month before the shutdown an average of 89,000 users from Iran used the Tor circumvention software. That number increased quite substantially in the aftermath of the shutdown. In the ten

ONLINE CONTROLS AND THE PROTEST-REPRESSION NEXUS IN IRAN 127

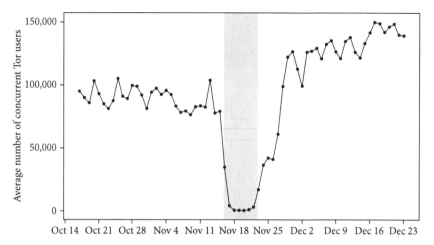

Fig. 7.2 Average number of daily concurrent Tor users. Light gray area denotes the commonly understood nationwide Internet shutdown from November 16–23.

days *after* the Internet came back on more than 119,000 users on average turned to Tor on a daily basis. In light of the fact that Internet access was still geographically restricted in the days following the full shutdown, this number is particularly impressive because it suggests that even though fewer people were able to go online, many users were interested in either accessing websites that were blocked in Iran or in generally accessing the Internet anonymously for fear of being monitored.

Figure 7.3 shows boxplots of the number of daily concurrent Tor users in the month prior to and following the nationwide shutdown in November 2019. In the month before the Internet shutdown, almost ninety thousand people connected to Tor from Iran on a daily basis. In the month after the shutdown, that number jumped to almost 120,000 average daily users (median of approx. 127,000). In the aftermath of the shutdown, many more people were motivated to browse the web freely and anonymously. Interest in using circumvention tools to access the Internet freely and anonymously remained high in the month following the shutdown, in fact slightly increasing towards the end of December 2019. The pattern observed here is in line with other work that has shown how sudden censorship can increase citizen demand for unrestricted access to information. Hobbs and Roberts (2018) studied an instance when Instagram was blocked in China, which triggered significantly heightened interest in censorship circumvention tools in the days immediately following the block. Tor usage in Iran before and

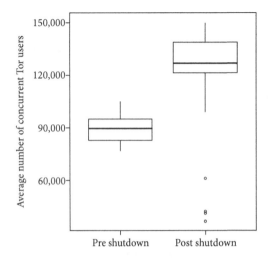

Fig. 7.3 Boxplots showing the number of daily concurrent Tor users, one month before and one month after the November 2019 Internet shutdown.

after the nationwide shutdown in November 2019 follows a similar pattern, but one which persisted for a longer period of time.

Conclusion

Cyber controls constitute a core part of Iran's repressive strategy aimed at maintaining political stability and suppressing dissent from Iranians at home and abroad. Over the years, the regime has overhauled its surveillance and censorship infrastructure and refined its approach of instrumentalizing digital communications to its own advantage. During this time, dissidents, activists, and civil society more generally have adapted and innovated to circumvent and challenge the digital grip the regime keeps on the domestic Internet. Citizens have resisted the banning of popular apps, and the use of circumvention software, such as Tor, Lantern, and Psiphon is widespread (Deibert, Oliver, and Senft, 2019). Yet with every wave of protest, the regime has responded by further developing its capabilities to control Iranian cyberspace (Hall and Ambrosio, 2017), with the ultimate goal of creating what they have called a "halal" Internet that is under full domestic control (Salamatian et al., 2021: 12). This also includes strategies aimed at incentivizing users to migrate to national apps and search engines (Akbari and Gabdulhakov, 2019).

In this chapter, I focused on a major instance of domestic popular unrest in Iran, but the continuous development of censorship and surveillance approaches has also heavily been influenced by lessons learned in neighboring countries (Heydemann and Leenders, 2011). Regimes and their security forces have traditionally weighed the benefits of employing violent mass repression against the potential of sparking popular backlash or risking costly international condemnation. The Iranian regime's inclusion of cyber controls in their repressive toolkit indicates that similar trade-offs are considered when it comes to censoring content or fully blocking access to the Internet. The type of near total shutdown ordered in November 2019 is rare, and demonstrates that the regime was willing to take into account widespread domestic and international outrage if, in turn, it could keep mobilization and the spread of images of the crackdown against protesters at bay. The timing of the shutdown, well into the protests, and Khomeini's instructions calling for security forces to do whatever it takes suggests the regime had underestimated the level of discontent and readiness to protest. Since the nationwide shutdown in 2019, there have been regional shutdowns, such as the shutdowns in Khuzestan in July 2020 and in Sistan and Baluchistan in February 2021. While digital rights groups issued a joint statement expressing their concern over these shutdowns (Access Now et al., 2021), regional cuts to the Internet have received significantly less international attention. Autocrats have learned that cutting off their entire population from the Internet will lead to mass outrage and international condemnation, while more localized shutdowns will receive far less attention. These developments suggest that authoritarian countries will only implement nationwide shutdowns when their perception of the political threat they face calls for desparate measures, which are then paired with mass repression, intimidation, and serious efforts to control the narrative.

8

Global evidence

Internet outages and repression

Are countries that frequently experience disruptions to their regular Internet access also more likely to have governments that make use of state-sanctioned violence against their own citizens? The results presented up to now have focused on evidence from individual cases. In this chapter, I focus on a type of cyber control that can be systematically and comparatively evaluated across countries and time: the occurrence of Internet outages. To test the external validity of a key argument set out in this book, I present evidence from a global analysis of the relationship between Internet outages and state repression.

Based on the theoretical argument formulated in Chapter 3, I expect that all else equal, state actors are likely to abuse citizens' physical integrity rights at a higher level in countries with Internet outages than in countries where no Internet outages are implemented. Although my theoretical argument is based on scenarios where and when state actors intentionally implement shutdowns, I take into account all occurrences of Internet outages, which include intentional shutdowns and technical outages. As I discuss in the next section, relying solely on collected reports of government-directed shutdowns runs the risk of overestimating the relationship between shutdowns and repression. To address this issue, I construct two indicators based on network measurement data that globally monitor the Internet for instances of outages in near real-time (IODA, 2021). The multivariate analysis of the relationship between Internet shutdowns and physical integrity violations across 168 countries between 2017 and 2020 suggests that Internet outages are significantly associated with an increase in violations of citizens' physical integrity rights, when compared to years and countries where uninterrupted Internet access was available. The relationship is significant, even when taking into account important confounders known to influence state respect for human rights.

Repression in the Digital Age: Surveillance, Censorship, and the Dynamics of State Violence. Anita R. Gohdes, Oxford University Press. © Oxford University Press 2024. DOI: 10.1093/oso/9780197743577.003.0008

8.1 How to measure Internet outages

Early studies on the blocking of individual websites leveraged direct technical testing to probe accessibility (e.g. Deibert et al., 2008), but first efforts to comprehensively identify Internet shutdowns largely relied on media sources. For example, Howard, Agarwal, and Hussain (2011) collected data based on international and domestic news reports, as well as information from security blogs and specialized Internet fora to construct a catalogue of reported major disruptions and shutdowns of national digital networks between 1995 and 2010 (see *Howard, Agarwal, and Hussain*, 2011).

Since then, a variety of projects, including the Open Observatory of Network Interference (OONI)[1] and Netblocks,[2] have started to publicly share detailed technical information on individual instances of shutdowns.[3] Digital rights organizations, such as Access Now, have also started collecting information on censorship events, relying on local civil society, technology companies, and other members of the digital rights community. In addition, a number of regional projects have started collecting event data on government-led shutdowns.[4] Network operators and security providers have shared details on individual outages over the past years, but none of them publish comprehensive, publicly available data on global outage patterns. Lastly, technology companies such as Google have published information on traffic disruptions to their own products, as was used in Chapter 5.[5]

The diversity of sources that have recently become available reflect an improved understanding of the dire repercussions Internet shutdowns can bring with them. For the purpose of studying the relationship between outages and state repression, the sources just mentioned present a number of challenges that may affect our ability to draw correct inferences. The probing-based and technical measurement sources described provide useful and highly contextual insight into individual instances of shutdowns, but do not offer the temporal or geographic coverage needed for a global comparison.

To globally compare the relationship between Internet outages and repression, we would ideally have full information on every shutdown that was implemented purposefully by state actors. When relying on media sources, we risk only collecting information on shutdowns that were accompanied by heightened political contention, as these are the cases media houses will most likely report on. Internet outage data based on the aggregation of prominent cases or on an exhaustive study of news reports is more likely to include information on outages that occurred in the

132 REPRESSION IN THE DIGITAL AGE

context of political unrest or other significant events, such as elections. It will also be *less* likely to report on shutdowns that were *not* directly associated with political changes. Consequently, if we fail to account for government-directed shutdowns that were not widely reported on during contentious political events, then we are likely to overestimate the relationship between shutdowns and state repression. I therefore opt for a combined, global network measurement of Internet outages.

A combined network measure

To assess the global prevalence of Internet disruptions, I construct two different indicators that are based on network measurements by the Internet Outage Detection and Analysis (IODA) project, which was started by a team of researchers at the Center for Applied Internet Data Analysis (CAIDA) at the University of California, San Diego, and is now based at the Georgia Institute of Technology (IODA, 2021). IODA combines three types of data sources that can be used to detect outages (Dainotti et al., 2011). The first, referred to as Global Internet Routing, or BGP (Border Gateway Protocol) data, builds on updates with roughly 500 monitors that record at regular intervals which network blocks are reachable.[6] The second source, referred to as "Darknet" traffic, measures the Internet background radiation (IRB), also known as unproductive traffic on the Internet (Beneduce et al., 2006). IODA monitors this unsolicited traffic through the UCSD Network Telescope which probes a sizeable portion of the entire IPv4 address space (Dainotti et al., 2011: 5). The third source is called "Active Probing," which describes the process of continuously probing a large fraction of the IPv4 address space using methodology developed by Quan, Heidemann, and Pradkin (2013). Each of the three sources form the basis of a separate indicator for a possible network outage.

IODA provides access to an Event API that can be queried for outage events as they are detected through these three sources. The project defines an outage event as "an instance of a macroscopic Internet outage affecting the edge of the network":[7]

Detection is performed by comparing the current value for each data-source/aggregation (e.g. the number of networks visible on BGP and geolocated to Italy) to an historical value that is computed by finding the median of a sliding window of recent values. If the current value is lower than a given fraction of the history value, an alert is generated.

The Event API was queried to obtain information on all outages that occurred across the globe at the country-level between 2017 and 2020. The API returns a number of variables for every event, including the start time and duration of the outage, as well as the data source reporting the outage. I then aggregate the outage information in the following way: First, I exclude countries that had a population below 500,000 between 2017 and 2020, to avoid measurement errors that may arise in locations where the number of active Internet users is quite small.[8] Second, for each of the three datasources, I exclude outage events that were shorter than one day (24 hours). I only include outage events that are at least a day long in order to avoid picking up shorter technical failures. Third, I construct my yearly measure of Internet outages in a two-step process. I build a daily dataset that reports whether an outage was recorded by one of the three datasources for every country and every day between 2017 and 2020. I then create a new variable outage that takes on a 1 if at least two of the sources recorded an outage on any given day, and a 0 otherwise. Relying on at least two sources to confirm an outage helps to further reduce the impact of possible technical failures related to only one of the data sources picking up a radical change in availability. In a final step, I aggregate the daily information to a yearly level, creating a binary variable outage_binary that takes on the value 1 when there was at least one day where at least two data sources reported an outage that was at least one day long. The second measure outage_30 takes on the value 1 when there were at least 30 days where at least two data sources reported an outage that was at least one day long.

An advantage of operationalizing Internet outages on the basis of this combined network measurement is that it allows me to address the previously discussed problem of potentially biased reporting. Outages that were implemented but not reported in the media or other outlets will still be included in this database, thereby offering a harder test of their relationship with other state behavior. Although this process helps filter out many of the technical outages, we cannot completely rule out that some of the events included in the analysis are in fact network outages that were not explicitly ordered by government actors.[9] We can describe such outages, for example technical failures or misconfigurations, as measurement error that is less likely to be correlated with state repression.[10]

8.2 Internet outages and political institutions

Figure 8.1 shows the percentage of countries where at least one day-long nationwide Internet outage event was measured. The percentages are disaggregated by year and the type of regime a country is classified as according to the V-Dem regimes of the world measure (Coppedge et al., 2021: 283). The most rapid increase in outages are recorded in countries classified as electoral autocracies, defined as countries that hold multi-party elections, but where conventional indicators of free and fair elections fail to be met (Coppedge et al., 2021: 283). Examples of countries that have increasingly experienced

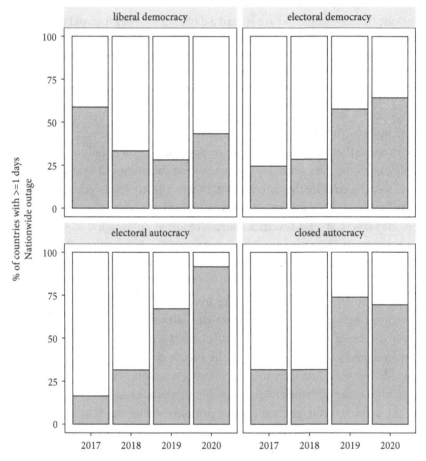

Fig. 8.1 Percent of countries where at least one nationwide Internet outage was measured, by year and regimes of the world (V-Dem).

outages are Cameroon and Venezuela. In electoral democracies (such as Tunisia) and closed autocracies (such as Jordan or Uzbekistan), the occurrence of Internet outages also rapidly increased between 2018 and 2019. Liberal democracies are the only countries that saw a reduction in the occurrence of outages throughout this time period.

In 2017, liberal democracies had the highest prevalence of Internet outages. Four years later, they had the lowest prevalence when compared to other regime types. The changes visible here are unlikely to be due to changes in the underlying sample of countries. The number of closed autocracies fluctuated between 22 and 23 cases, electoral autocracies were between 55 and 61 cases, electoral democracies between 52 and 57, and liberal democracies between 30 and 34.

The proportions shown here indicate that countries that permit fewer (or no forms) of institutional political participation for the masses have experienced an increase in Internet outages in the past years. Interestingly, the strongest increase is visible in countries that display some characteristics related to democratic institutions, but fall short of actually being an electoral democracy. The rapid increase in Internet outages in the countries that— in terms of democratic performance—fall in the "middle," i.e. are neither fully democratic nor fully autocratic, is compatible with findings that show these are the countries most likely to employ more overt forms of non-violent and violent repression to maintain political control and stability (Fein, 1995; Carey, 2010). There might, however, be a number of confounding factors that account for this observed difference. I address this question in the next section, where I investigate the relationship between Internet outages and violent repression, controlling for the most common explanations for a country's failure to respect physical integrity rights.

8.3 Internet outages and state repression

To compare the respect for physical integrity rights across countries and time I make use of the Political Terror Scales (Wood and Gibney, 2010), a five-point ordinal scale that is based on human rights reports published annually by the US State Department, Amnesty International, and Human Rights Watch. I rely on the indicator based on US State Department reports because they offer the most complete coding.[11] Separate indicators are coded for each source and the following coding scheme is used (Haschke, 2020: 4):

Level 1 Countries under a secure rule of law, people are not imprisoned for their views, and torture is rare or exceptional. Political murders are extremely rare.

Level 2 There is a limited amount of imprisonment for non-violent political activity. However, few persons are affected, torture and beatings are exceptional. Political murder is rare.

Level 3 There is extensive political imprisonment, or a recent history of such imprisonment. Execution or other political murders and brutality may be common. Unlimited detention, with or without a trial, for political views is accepted.

Level 4 Civil and political rights violations have expanded to large numbers of the population. Murders, disappearances, and torture are a common part of life. In spite of its generality, on this level terror affects primarily those who interest themselves in politics or ideas.

Level 5 The terrors of Level 4 have been extended to the whole population. The leaders of these societies place no limits on the means or thoroughness with which they pursue personal or ideological goals.

Classifying repression cross-nationally and temporally is a challenging exercise, as reporting practices vary substantially on both of these dimensions. I opt for the Political Terror Scales in an effort to capture broad dynamics. PTS only records changes when large qualitative increases or decreases in the intensity of state repression occur. Using PTS as a measure of repression thus puts my research question to a hard empirical test, because minor changes in repression are not picked up by the scale.

I include a number of standard variables that have been found to affect a government's willingness to enforce state-sanctioned violence (see, e.g. Poe and Tate, 1994; Poe, Tate, and Keith, 1999; Hill and Jones, 2014). The presence of organized internal dissent (armed conflict) is the most consistent and robust predictor for increases in state repression and is measured using the UCDP/PRIO measure of armed internal conflict (Pettersson and Eck, 2018). An armed internal conflict is defined as a contested incompatibility that "concerns government and/or territory where the use of armed force between two parties, of which at least one is the government of a state, results in at least 25 battle-related deaths in a calendar year" (Pettersson, 2020: 1). Governments that marginalize ethnic groups from politics may be more likely to use more repression. For this reason I include a measure for the percentage of the population that belongs to politically excluded ethnic groups, using the Ethnic Power Relations Data (Wucherpfennig et al., 2011).

Political institutions are measured using the electoral democracy index (Electoral Democracy Index) by the Varieties of Democracy Project, which asks "To what extent is the ideal of electoral democracy in its fullest sense achieved?" (Coppedge et al., 2021: 43). The electoral democracy index offers a more fine grained measurement than the categorical data used in Figure 8.1. To account for size and wealth of a country, the population size (log) as well as the gross domestic product (GDP) per capita (log) are lagged by one year and included as control variables.

Table 8.1 presents the results from an ordered probit model that accounts for armed conflict, electoral democracy, ethnic exclusion, population size, and wealth, as well as yearly fixed effects. Models 1 and 2 specify outages as a binary indicator where at least one day-long outage event was reported (with Model 2 also including a lagged dependent variable), whereas Models 3 and 4 include a variable that measures whether at least 30 day-long outages events were recorded or not. The results demonstrate that Internet outages, across both measurements, are significantly associated with higher levels of basic human rights respect. In years where states purposefully disrupted their Internet, they were also significantly more likely to use state-sanctioned violence against their own population. The control variables included provide support to established findings that countries involved in armed conflict, more populous countries, and countries with higher levels of past repression have a higher likelihood of being more repressive in any given year. Faced with credible challenges to their political authority, states will be highly motivated to increase coercive violence against their citizens in an attempt to regain their previous status quo. Furthermore, the regime type of a government significantly affects a government's inclination to employ violence domestically: the higher countries rank on the democracy scale, the more likely they are to respect and protect citizens' human rights. The more people who belong to ethnic groups that are excluded from politics (as a fraction of the overall population), the more likely a government will use repression, but only when not taking into account past levels of repression. Lastly, higher levels of economic wealth are positively correlated with improved rights protection.

Figure 8.2 shows the marginal effect of nationwide Internet outages on a government's likelihood to repress its people. All else equal, governments in countries with at least one day-long Internet outage event had a significantly lower likelihood of using rare (Level 1) or limited forms of repression

138 REPRESSION IN THE DIGITAL AGE

Table 8.1 Network disruptions and state repression. Ordered probit regression.

	I	II	III	IV
Internet Outage (>= 1 day)	0.26*	0.31*		
	(0.12)	(0.14)		
Internet Outage (>= 30 days)			0.37**	0.44**
			(0.13)	(0.16)
Electoral Democracy Index	−2.84***	−1.35***	−2.89***	−1.40***
	(0.27)	(0.34)	(0.27)	(0.35)
Log Pop (lag)	0.37***	0.16**	0.36***	0.15**
	(0.04)	(0.05)	(0.04)	(0.05)
Log GDP pc (lag)	−0.41***	−0.21***	−0.43***	−0.23***
	(0.05)	(0.06)	(0.05)	(0.06)
Armed Conflict (0/1)	1.35***	0.77***	1.37***	0.80***
	(0.18)	(0.22)	(0.18)	(0.23)
PTS (lag)		2.12***		2.12***
		(0.13)		(0.13)
% Excluded ethnic pop. (EPR)	1.19***	0.64	1.22***	0.66
	(0.33)	(0.41)	(0.33)	(0.41)
1|2	−0.08	3.07***	−0.40	2.69**
	(0.68)	(0.86)	(0.70)	(0.87)
2|3	1.33+	5.59***	1.01	5.21***
	(0.68)	(0.87)	(0.70)	(0.89)
3|4	3.31***	8.69***	3.01***	8.36***
	(0.71)	(0.95)	(0.72)	(0.96)
4|5	4.87***	11.53***	4.57***	11.20***
	(0.74)	(1.04)	(0.75)	(1.05)
AIC	873.17	512.28	870.42	509.85
BIC	923.18	566.46	920.43	564.03
Log Likelihood	−424.58	−243.14	−423.21	−241.92
Num. obs.	477	477	477	477

***$p < 0.001$, **$p < 0.01$, *$p < 0.05$, +$p < 0.1$. Country-clustered standard errors. Year fixed effects not shown.

(Level 2) when compared to countries that did not experience Internet outages. Instead, governments were significantly more likely to use extensive (Level 3) and expansive (Level 4) repression and in years with Internet outages. The marginal effect is negligible for governments that employ full state terror (Level 5). The results suggest that Internet outages are significantly and substantively associated with higher levels of violent state repression. When countries implement Internet outages, they are much less likely to moderately or fully respect physical integrity rights, even when controlling

GLOBAL EVIDENCE: INTERNET OUTAGES AND REPRESSION 139

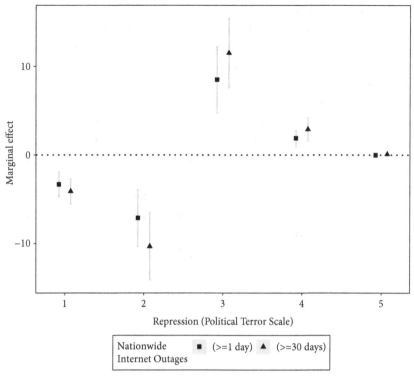

Fig. 8.2 Marginal effect of nationwide Internet outages and repression, global analysis. Effects calculated using Models I and III from Table 8.1.

for important factors such as economic wealth, population size, and other forms of political violence.

Summary

This chapter has presented a global analysis for the argument that governments integrate varying forms of network control into their repressive strategies. To systematically investigate the generalizability of my argument, I study the prevalence and relevance of network outages when it comes to explaining state repression across the globe. The global analysis does not capture the trade-off states make when choosing between different repressive strategies, but it does offer substantial support for the relationship between Internet disruptions and heightened state violence. State-implemented Internet disruptions have increased over time, and this increase has largely been driven by countries whose governments fail to provide democratic forms of participation for their citizens. The cross-national analysis of 168 countries showed that even when controlling for the most important factors that affect human rights respect, governments that disrupt their domestic Internet are significantly more likely to abuse human rights. The positive relationship between shutdowns and conventional forms of violent coercion cast significant doubt on the justification that has been used by governments implementing them. Sometimes implicitly and other times explicitly, governments have claimed that limits to social media or the entire Internet are implemented to reduce tensions and limit social unrest (see e.g. Gohdes, 2016). While this chapter has not directly tested whether shutdowns have a demobilizing effect, other work on responses to outages has shown that, if anything, shutdowns lead to increased collective mobilization (Hassanpour, 2014; Rydzak, 2019). The findings in this chapter contribute to this discussion by showing that shutdowns do not act as a substitute for conventional repression, but rather as a supportive tool.

9

Conclusion

In 2013, as people were reeling from the global surveillance disclosures leaked by Edward Snowden, a former head-of-department at the *Stasi* told a reporter that the United States National Security Agency's capabilities would have been a "dream come true" for the secret service of the German Democratic Republic (Schofield, 2013). A decade later it is still hard to overstate the degree to which online surveillance and censorship have affected the politics of information control for state actors. This book contributes to our understanding of state repression and authoritarian methods of political control in the information age.

9.1 Summary of findings

The in-depth investigation of online control in Syria in Chapters 4 to 6 provided detailed and disaggregated evidence for the instrumental value governments ascribe to controlling online accessibility in times of civil conflict. The results discussed in Chapter 5 suggest that the Syrian government implemented full-blown blackouts of the Internet in conjunction with larger military offensives against the opposition and civilians supporting the opposition. Chapter 6 provides evidence for the differential value of online information, which is dependent on the regime's ability to obtain high-quality intelligence through more traditional modes of surveillance. It further shows that not only the *scale*, but also the *type* of repression is linked to variations in online control, when comparing the level of targeted and untargeted lethal violence used by the Syrian regime in different regions of the country. Syria represents the first conflict that has been meticulously followed and fueled by a vast online audience: by the opposition fighters and supporters, by regime forces and their supporters, and by the outside world at large. The increasing importance of establishing control over online content and access to the Internet is likely to exert a growing appeal for regimes

Repression in the Digital Age: Surveillance, Censorship, and the Dynamics of State Violence. Anita R. Gohdes, Oxford University Press. © Oxford University Press 2024. DOI: 10.1093/oso/9780197743577.003.0009

eager to adjust their repertoire of repressive tools in dealing with new digital threats to the status quo.

Chapter 7 studies the evolution of domestic cyber control and infrastructure in Iran, an authoritarian country with a young, connected, and digitally informed population. The lead-up to the protests, Internet shutdown, and massive repression in November 2019 suggests that Iranian regime forces integrated the nationwide shutdown into their repressive strategy aimed at crushing the opposition and silencing relatives of those who suffered at the hands of the security forces. More so than in the Syrian case, the Iranian authorities placed an emphasis on deflecting blame, spreading the narrative of violent rioters instigated by foreign powers, and covering up their repressive activities.

In both Iran and Syria, nationwide shutdowns of the Internet are clearly associated with heightened mass repression. In the Syrian case I find little evidence for incentives to use shutdowns as a means of covering up repressive actions, whereas in Iran, the 2019 shutdown was accompanied by a shift in repressive strategy aimed at obfuscation and intimidation of the victims and their relatives. In both cases, the shutdown helped disrupt non-state online coordination, but the type of opposition they were facing was very different. Syria's shutdowns came at a time when significant opposition had already formed and organized, and many of the blackouts occurred in the contexts of military offensives against an armed insurgency. The Iranian shutdown in 2019 occurred within the first 48 hours of largely spontaneous mass demonstrations in response to a policy change. These differences showcase that, while shutdowns are likely to coincide with mass repression, additional incentives are likely to vary based on the level on political contention, the type of non-state organizing, and the degree to which the state forces are fearful of international involvement and attention.

The global analysis of network disruptions and states' abuse of physical integrity rights presented in Chapter 8 shows that even when taking into account the main predictors of state repression, disruptive Internet controls are significantly and positively associated with increased state terror.

Measuring Internet control and state violence are both highly challenging undertakings. Both phenomena, by the nature of their subject, are not intended to be fully observable. Sometimes, states want their citizens to know they are controlling the Internet, and sometimes they do not. Furthermore, some online controls are more readily observable than others. State actors sometimes want, or cannot prevent, their citizens from witnessing coercive violence, while in other circumstances they will do their best to hide their actions from the public. Due to its covert nature, it is considerably harder to obtain systematic evidence on surveillance than it is to study the occurrence of censorship. It is therefore not surprising that much of the evidence presented in this book has built on fine-grained data on Internet shutdowns, while piecing together the occurrence of online monitoring from a multitude of sources that provide information on the existence and employment of monitoring technology. To study the ways in which cyber controls support violent repression, I make use of a variety of techniques to analyze large-scale data on human rights violations, including supervised machine learning and statistical methods to correct for incomplete data on violence. Overall, I attempt to establish evidence of the supportive role of cyber controls at different levels of geographic and temporal aggregation.

9.2 The implications of tech-supported repression

The rapid shift in the nature, access to, and producers of information in an online world call for theoretical approaches that account for these changes. The availability of intelligence and the manipulation of information access have featured prominently in research on political violence (Davenport, 2010; Frantz and Kendall-Taylor, 2014; Gehlbach, Luo, and Shirikov, 2022). In her study of the design of states' coercive institutions and the effects this has on the nature of repression used, Greitens (2016) finds that more fragmented security apparatuses that are oriented towards managing elite-based threats are more likely to use higher levels of untargeted repression. Greitens' work shows that the lack of restraint in using mass violence is linked to the inability and low interest in collecting intelligence that would enable selective repression. The evidence presented in this book supports the notion that access to actionable intelligence is likely to lead to more targeted forms of repression, and when state authorities cut themselves off from such information, violence is likely to increase and become more indiscriminate. The argument and evidence I present here expands our understanding of state coercion by studying how the control of digital infrastructure is supercharging states' abilities to engage in information management. Online monitoring has facilitated state access to previously hard-to-reach sectors of society, as it bypasses the need for local in-person intelligence gathering that necessitates long-term investment in trustworthy personnel (Eck, 2015;

144 REPRESSION IN THE DIGITAL AGE

Blaydes, 2019). Online censorship has accelerated states' abilities to flexibly stifle or even shut down popular coordination and information exchange for short periods of time, thereby avoiding long-term information vacuums that could prove dangerous for regime stability (Kuran, 1989; Cairns and Plantan, 2016).

This book has focused on repression perpetrated by state actors within the confines of their own national borders. But cyber-enabled repression has expanded states' spheres of influence in important new ways. Hacking, surveillance technology, and online harassment have facilitated states' abilities to target and threaten individuals based in other countries. So while the Internet has allowed exiled activists and dissidents to stay connected to their home country, digitally enabled transnational repression is transforming their lives, communities, and personal safety (Michaelsen, 2017; Moss, 2018; Tsourapas, 2021).

Implications of domestic cyber capabilities

The last decade has seen governments across the world integrate cyber controls into their standard toolbox of responding to dissent. Denial of service attacks against human rights defenders' websites (Zuckerman et al., 2010) and in the context of contested elections (OpenNet Initiative, 2005) have been used since the early 2000s. As social media networks have become central exchange points for activists, states have turned their attention towards controlling them. When protests erupted in Hong Kong in 2014, Chinese authorities quickly blocked access to the picture-sharing service Instagram. Four years later, the Ethiopian authorities shut down mobile and broadband networks in the Oromia region for 40 days (Taye, 2019: 13). The interest in using brute force censorship has evidently not diminished.

Although domestic applications of states' cyber capabilities are not new, much of the discourse around the dynamics and risks of cyber tools has focused on the interstate context. Only recently have scholars turned to studying the role of cyber attacks in intrastate warfare (Kostyuk and Zhukov, 2019). Egloff and Shires (2021) provide a useful framework to help us think about the integration of offensive cyber capabilities in the politics of state violence. The authors discuss three logics of integration, where offensive cyber capabilities may either substitute, support, or complement

CONCLUSION 145

states' use of violence. Their approach expands the realm of influence of cyber tools from interstate analyses to also include violence directed against a state's own people. This conceptualization is important because it helps link cyber capabilities to the realm of contentious domestic politics, two areas of research that have largely operated in separate communities (Valeriano and Maness, 2014; Liu and Sullivan, 2021).

The evidence presented in this book suggests that cyber capabilities in the form of online surveillance and censorship have taken a *supportive role* in a state's repressive apparatus. Neither surveillance nor censorship have replaced the use of violent repression. Instead, we see that online surveillance can support security forces in obtaining better intelligence on potential targets of repression. Conversely, online censorship has the potential to constitute a supportive role, both within protest management strategies and military offensives. The analyses of Internet shutdowns and state killings suggest that regimes use large-scale disruptions selectively and purposely in conjunction with concerted repressive offensives against perceived threats. Not all military offensives and repressive responses to protests are accompanied by mass censorship, but when access is denied, there is a significant rise in the number of lives lost. As such, the findings contribute to the study of armed conflict in the twenty-first century (Buhaug and Gates, 2002; Kalyvas, 2006; Dafoe and Lyall, 2015).

In sum, this book suggests that cyber controls are, at this point in time, tipping the balance of power between repressive state forces and non-state challengers in favor of the state. Having access to infrastructure control, powerful spying tools, and increasingly expansive online propaganda ecosystems is helping governments manage their masses more effectively, both preemptively and reactively (see Guriev and Treisman, 2022). However, the implications are more nuanced than saying that state forces everywhere are winning the tech race. Many governments are grappling with the effective use of technology and with the exception of a few outliers, remain overwhelmingly dependent on imported soft- and hardware, placing them at the whims of their international partners. With the exception of China, they also remain at the behest of foreign social media companies (Pan, 2017). Policy discussions in DC and Brussels have a tendency to ignore how social media regulation—or the absence thereof—will play out in countries where civil society is largely dependent on Western social media sites for organizing and coordinating. This neglect can have disastrous consequences for vulnerable populations; abuse of social media by repressive government

146 REPRESSION IN THE DIGITAL AGE

therefore necessarily needs to feature prominently in discussions on technology and human rights (Stevenson, 2018).

The battle for digital infrastructure

This book has focused on the supportive role of cyber controls within domestic contentious politics, but the implications extend beyond intra-state affairs. The ability to control the enemy's digital infrastructure is likely to only gain importance in the future of interstate warfare. The current Russian military invasion of Ukraine already showcases this dynamic. Throughout its kinetic offensives, Russia has repeatedly engaged in the digital annexation of Ukrainian Internet traffic. When Russian forces captured the Ukrainian city of Kherson in the spring of 2022, they worked on rerouting local Internet traffic through Russian state-owned telecommunications networks in Crimea, even before they had fully occupied the city (Burgess, 2022). The speed with which this rerouting occurred suggests it was a priority, highlighting the strategic importance the Russian forces see in maintaining control of the digital infrastructure in the territories they physically occupy.

Control of digital infrastructure is also dependent on its configuration and ownership. Regarding the ease with which governments can censor the Internet, research has shown how state ownership and centralization of the telecommunications sector are important predictors of Internet disruptions (Cowie, 2014; Freyburg and Garbe, 2018; Salamatian et al., 2021). Policy-makers should therefore actively encourage the diversification of the telecommunications market in countries with a known history of state terror. Foreign governments and the international community should begin to understand state-led disruptions of Internet accessibility as a serious signal; they should strongly and swiftly condemn any such occurrence. Shutdowns should not only be viewed as a means of stifling the opposition's ability to communicate. They should also be understood as a clear signal of repressive intent by a government set on maintaining its political power at all costs.

With the increase of surveillance software being used by governments to spy on their citizens, the opportunities for identifying dissidents and willingness to eliminate them has risen dramatically. The cases described in this book highlight the fact that much of the surveillance software used by autocratic governments is exported from companies located in the European Union and the United States (see e.g. Raoof, 2011; Wagner

CONCLUSION 147

and Guarnieri, 2014). State abuse of digital surveillance software should give policy-makers in democratic countries serious reason to consider the careful regulation of exports on these types of software. Analogous to policies restricting the export of arms to governments known to turn these weapons against their own population, policy reform is needed to address the proliferation of digital spyware and malware. Thanks to the work done by journalists and by organizations such as Amnesty International, the Citizen Lab, and Article 19, policy makers are starting to take note of the detrimental impact this industry is having on individuals and entire communities (Sanger et al., 2021).

9.3 Resistance to online repression

The Internet has facilitated collective mobilization, by reducing both the costs of entry into movements and the costs of organizing, and by improving protesters' abilities to adapt and respond to state repression (Earl and Kimport, 2011; Steinert-Threlkeld, 2017). As digital communication has become a bedrock of modern opposition and protest movements, answers to the question of how states digitally inform their strategies of violence provide a crucial contribution to understanding the challenges and providing solutions for contemporary and future social movements.

The evidence presented here has implications for citizens and activists engaged in challenging the political status quo in the face of repressive state power. Few social movements today do not have a public facing online presence, and many are dependent on it for coordination, campaigning, and garnering financial and non-material support. At the time of writing, a feminist movement led by women in Iran is fighting for freedom and an end to the repressive Iranian regime. Risking their lives, activists are not only voicing their demands on the streets but also online, in an effort to raise awareness and spur international solidarity. Iranians at home and abroad have emphasized the importance of consistent international attention and pressure in supporting the protesters in their efforts. The international spotlight created through online information would be significantly harder to uphold over many months without the savvy use of online media by the feminist movement (Basmechi, 2022).

Yet the same technology that is responsible for supporting activists in their work is also being harnessed by the Iranian authorities. Since the outbreak of the demonstrations in the aftermath of the killing of the young Kurdish-Iranian woman Mahsa Zhina Amini, the regime has cracked down on protesters both online and in the streets. Full and partial shutdowns of the Internet have been complemented with close monitoring of online spaces (Akbari, 2022) and the alleged use of facial recognition technology to identify those women who resist the strict hijab laws (Strzyżyńska, 2022). Thus, digital fingerprints—from emails to video footage, or mere *likes* and *follows*—mean that activists and others who are at risk of being repressed are liable to be placed under close surveillance. Online monitoring means that they can be identified long before their activities are public knowledge, and can be retrospectively identified with the help of digital forensics.

Learning to securely communicate, work, live, and travel without leaving a digital paper-trail is thus no longer simply recommendable to a select number of clandestine dissidents. It may well become a matter of survival for all members of an opposition, because the findings of this study suggest that where repressive governments do allow the free exchange of information, they will also be more likely to be engaged in selective targeting and killing of its citizens.

But how do social movements fare in the face of near-total surveillance? Research from past resistance movements can be instructive here. In his study of anti-Nazi Jewish resistance groups during the Holocaust, Finkel (2015) shows that when these groups were faced with intense monitoring and targeting by security services, they were actually better equipped to develop what he calls the "resister's toolkit" (Finkel, 2015: 340–341). This toolkit would include the ability to establish secure communication channels, procure weapons without being detected by government agents, maintain well-hidden meeting places and munitions caches, produce high-quality forged identification documents, and the ability to identify and neutralize informers and government agents trying to infiltrate the organization (paraphrased from Finkel, 2015: 341). Some of these tools can directly be translated into the digital age, and digital rights groups working with human rights defenders and opposition groups to strengthen their practical and operational security are helping forge this digital resister's toolkit. Movements that manage to incorporate these tools into the design of their organizations will likely have an advantage over those that do not.

While repressive governments are adapting their tactics to the new digital reality of conflicts, resistance movements are likely to adapt and learn new tools that help them survive and operate in this new environment (see

CONCLUSION 149

Sullivan and Davenport, 2018). The rise in alternative means of obtaining Internet accessibility, for example by using satellite connections or connections from neighboring countries, means that it has become increasingly difficult for governments to impose true isolation on a whole population. Between 2010 and 2012, across Syria, there was a marked uptick in the interest of censorship circumvention technology that would allow people to access individually blocked pages and social media sites (Al-Saqaf, 2016). And as the conflict in Syria progressed, forces opposing the government became increasingly savvy in circumventing digital controls, for example by making use of encrypted software, switching to conventional walkie-talkies when planning military offensives, and listening in on the regime's military communications (Hanna, 2015). More generally, civil society, journalists, and digital rights activists have made the exposing of surveillance infrastructures an important part of resistance itself (e.g. Greenberg, 2011; Gohdes, 2018a; Marczak et al., 2018; Nyst and Monaco, 2018).

Consistent use of censorship methods is also likely to make censorship circumvention technology more attractive for broader sectors of the population. Recent work on the consequences of online repression questions whether online controls themselves are, in fact, working effectively as a deterrent against online dissent (Beyer and Earl, 2018; Pan and Siegel, 2020; Roberts, 2020). Evidence presented in Chapter 7 showed that in the aftermath of the nationwide Internet shutdown in 2019, more people in Iran made regular use of Tor, a censorship circumvention tool that has the added benefit of allowing users to surf the web anonymously. What this tells us is that overly zealous censorship can backfire in the long-term by alerting large swaths of the population to the advantages of evading censorship *and* surveillance, thus triggering a higher demand for uncensored access to information, instead of dampening it.

9.4 Beyond state control: the role of private companies

This book has focused on online controls carried out by the government or directly ordered by the government and implemented by Internet Service Providers (ISPs) or other organizations. It has only paid passing attention to the choices and incentives of private companies tasked with implementing state-ordered cyber controls. Market dominance, domestic and international dependencies, and shareholder interests all play an important role in understanding ongoing power struggles between public and private actors. And it is also clear that states are not the only actors interested in reaping the benefits of online surveillance and censorship. Big technology companies such as Google and Facebook provide the infrastructure for large parts of the Internet, and consequently can access individualized data about their users in ways that many governments can only dream of (Zuboff, 2019; Nothias, 2020). But it is not only user-facing companies that engage in the politics of information management. We are also witnessing the increased politicization of companies that provide security and fast content delivery (van Geuns and Cath-Speth, 2020), such as when Cloudfare came under fire for hosting a website where users were inciting online hate and offline violence, primarily against women and members of the LGBTQ+ community (Menn and Lorenz, 2022). The complex interactions and at times competing interests between states and companies affect censorship dynamics in myriad ways that call for more interdisciplinary research (York and Stender, 2016; Pan, 2017; Gohdes, 2018b).

Algorithmic choices, data privacy concerns and content moderation policies of technology companies are currently among the most pertinent topics debated by policy-makers and civil society. The market for surveillance and filtering technology has exploded in the last decade, and ground-breaking work by researchers, journalists, and activists has documented the complex linkages between vendors and government clients (Amnesty International, 2015; Marczak et al., 2018; Srivastava, 2020). The complex dynamics that characterize the relationship between governments and companies need to be the subject of future research.

Notes

Chapter 1

1. Renesys was a US-based Internet intelligence company that now belongs to Oracle.
2. HRDAG is a non-profit organization that has provided scientific support to the human rights community for many decades, including NGOs, UN bodies, Truth Commissions, and civil society groups across the world. I have been involved with HRDAG in various capacities since 2009.

Chapter 2

1. Their computer is connected to the Internet, and like all devices that are connected to the Internet, it also has its own unique IP address.
2. Note that larger organizations such as Facebook or Google will usually have many thousands of servers and therefore have many IP addresses that lead users to the same website.
3. If they do not have the address in their own database they may forward the request to a different server.
4. Other scholars have focused on distinguishing Internet controls by network layers, which is useful for understanding the technical level at which controls are injected by governments (see e.g. Keremoğlu and Weidmann, 2020). The conceptualization I present overlaps with this layers approach but focuses specifically on which users and what content are affected.
5. Because Internet traffic that traveled through the same cables that connect Egypt to the rest of the world was still functioning throughout the shutdown in Egypt, it is highly unlikely that the Egyptian government physically damaged network access as this would have affected more of the dependent surrounding countries (Van Beijnum, 2011).
6. Roberts's conception of friction goes beyond bandwidth throttling by describing it as the processes whereby "[t]he citizen will simply experience more difficulty in accessing or spreading information" (p. 59).
7. Attackers can also inject malicious code into the defaced or redirected webpage, so that visitors risk infecting their machines with malware.
8. The group *RosKomSvoboda* maintains a registry of banned sites and IP addresses: https://reestr.rublacklist.net/.
9. As an example, under the right to be forgotten, European citizens may request to have content referring to themselves removed from Google search results. This process is also known as "delisting."

152 NOTES

10. See https://transparency.twitter.com/en/removal-requests.html.
11. Making posts "invisible" is different from deleting posts. When a post becomes invisible, it can be viewed only by the person who wrote it, leaving the user unaware that his or her post has, in effect, been taken down (Wang, 2016).
12. See: https://ssd.eff.org/en/module/how-avoid-phishing-attacks.

Chapter 3

1. Kalyvas's argument extends to non-state armed groups, but here I focus on the implications for state-sanctioned violence.
2. Like any new technology, online surveillance tools require training and education, and mass monitoring often raises complex data management questions (see e.g. Chen and Greitens, 2021).

Chapter 4

1. As Mazur (2021: 60) has highlighted, cross-ethnic ties between the predominately Alawite regime and representatives of local ethnic communities was central to the regime's ability to maintain political stability.
2. In the context of this book the focus is on repressive tactics, but much has been written on the strategies of co-optation employed by both Assad regimes (e.g. Hinnebusch, 2001; Perthes, 2006).
3. Note that the data for Syria's share of Internet users published by the ITU has largely been based on estimates by the ITU itself. Only in 2008, 2009, 2010, and 2011 does the ITU report the Syrian Telecommunication Establishment as the source to their numbers.
4. Our data sharing agreements allow me to publish work based on our findings, while not sharing any identifying information on the victims included in the data. Work on establishing the number of documented killings in the Syrian conflict was originally commissioned by the United Nations Office of the High Commissioner (Price, Gohdes, and Ball, 2014). Since then, we have published a series of reports and articles investigating the dynamics of wartime documentation and violence in Syria (Price, Gohdes, and Ball, 2015, 2016; Price and Gohdes, 2020).
5. The model is implemented in the **dga** R package (Johndrow, Lum, and Ball, 2015).
6. Over the course of the conflict, citizens and opposition groups have increasingly attempted to access the Internet through the Turkish and Iraqi wireless networks, in particular in the border regions (Al-Khatieb, 2015).

Chapter 5

1. Ann Harrison, Middle East and North Africa Programme, Deputy Director Amnesty USA (Amnesty International, 2012).

NOTES 153

2. http://www.google.com/transparencyreport/traffic/.
3. The model estimates a hyperparameter ω that accounts for dependence between event counts across time, where values close to 0 indicate more dependence, and values approaching 1 indicate few dynamics, and a data structure that could potentially be modeled with a conventional Poisson model. I make use of the estimation code provided by Brandt et al. (2000): http://www.utdallas.edu/~pbrandt/pests/pests.htm.
4. The placebo dates created were at t $[-30, -25, -20, -15, -10, -5, +5, +10, +15, +20, +25, +30]$.

Chapter 6

1. https://secdev-foundation.org/.
2. The survey asks respondents to separately rate their ability to use the Internet (distinguishing between DSL, 2G, and 3G) as well as mobile phones on a four-point scale, where 1 = general availability, 2 = available often, 3 = intermittent availability, and 4 = no availability. To ensure comparability, SDSM attempts to survey the same set of respondents in every wave, but also makes use of social media sources. To obtain a standardized unit of analysis, the accessibility measures are aggregated to an average continuous measure of accessibility at the governorate level, measured in two-week intervals. To ease interpretation, the scale is reversed, so that lower values indicate lower levels of accessibility and higher values indicate higher levels of accessibility. Note that for a select few months, only one survey is available, not two.
3. Researchers at Cloudflare explained that "[w]hile we cannot know for sure, our network team estimates that Syria likely has a small number of edge routers. All the edge routers are controlled by Syrian Telecommunications. The systematic way in which routes were withdrawn suggests that this was done through updates in router configurations, not through a physical failure or cable cut" (Prince, 2012).
4. The coding of targeted and untargeted killings is highly conflict and actor specific. For example, armed actors, such as the provisional IRA in Northern Ireland (Heger, 2015), may use small-scale bombings to target their enemies. In the Syrian conflict, the use of barrel bombs and indiscriminate bombardment by the government as a means of indiscriminately killing civilians has been extensively documented (Pinheiro, 2015).
5. A variety of different algorithms were tested, including support vector machine-learning and random forest models, however, the results based on the extreme gradient booster provided the highest overall algorithm performance.
6. See https://www.cartercenter.org/syria-conflict-map/. The SCMP collected the most accurate and detailed open source information on conflict events occurring across the country to date, including information on changing relationships between the main conflict actors.
7. I specify alternative models where I alter the 60% threshold to 70% and find consistent results. In order to measure the government's local presence more precisely, I also run alternative models with the actual *percentage of control* for the government.

154 NOTES

8. Next to the just discussed measures of ethnic group presence, the model accounts for interactions between armed group control and Internet accessibility, as described in the previous section.

Chapter 8

1. https://ooni.org/.
2. https://netblocks.org/.
3. The OONI project provides a free software that allows volunteers to participate in probing access to websites, and the Internet more generally, all across the world. Both OONI and Netblocks collect information on Internet censorship, which includes Internet outages, but also includes the blocking of individual domains.
4. For example, Internetshutdowns.in collects information on regional shutdowns in India. See: https://internetshutdowns.in.
5. https://transparencyreport.google.com/traffic/overview.
6. IODA also includes full snapshots of the entire control pane, which each of the monitors regularly publish and which contain all known routing information that is reachable at the moment (Dainotti et al., 2011: 4).
7. https://ioda.caida.org/ioda/api/event.
8. I thank the team at IODA for their guidance on these decisions.
9. Note that such technical failures may also mistakenly be reported on as intentional government action when and where such failures occur in the context of political unrest. Because governments have an incentive to deny or obfuscate their involvement, it is not always clear whether such denials are trustworthy, or not.
10. The multivariate analysis will take into account economic development and armed challenges to the political status quo, two factors that could potentially be correlated with the occurrence of technical failures.
11. I impute values for the US from the Amnesty International indicator. Scholars have raised important concerns that the PTS indicators based on the US Department Reports may be impacted by changes in domestic US politics (Poe, Carey, and Vazquez, 2001). For example, Berry and Hendrix (2018) show that under the Trump administration, the US State Department reduced their reporting on women's and LBGTI rights violations. As the period under investigation here only falls within the Trump administration I don't expect structural breaks in the reporting but do expect issues regarding the repression of women and the LBGTI community to be underrepresented.

Bibliography

Abadpour, Arash and Collin Anderson. 2013. *Fights, Adapts, Accepts: Archetypes of Iranian Internet Use*. Iran Media Program, Annenberg School for Communication, University of Pennsylvania.

Access Now, Amnesty International, Article 19, and Group Miaan. 2021. "Iran: Internet shutdowns curb protests and conceal human rights violations in Sistan and Baluchistan." https://www.article19.org/resources/iran-internet- shutdowns-curb-protests-and-conceal-human-rights-violations-in-sistan-and-baluchistan/.

Akbari, Azadeh. 2022. "Shutting down the internet is another brutal blow against women by the Iranian regime." *The Guardian*, September 26. https://www.theguardian.com/commentisfree/2022/sep/26/elon-musk-iran-women-mahsa-amini-feminists-morality-police.

Akbari, Azadeh and Rashid Gabdulhakov. 2019. "Platform surveillance and resistance in Iran and Russia: the case of Telegram." *Surveillance and Society* 17(1–2):223–231.

Al-Assad, Bashar. 2011. "Speech by Bashar al-Assad." Speech by Bashar al-Assad at Damascus University, June 20, 2011. https://al-bab.com/albab-orig/albab/arab/docs/syria/bashar_assad_speech_110620.htm.

Al-Hussien, Obada. 2017. "Internet is back in Raqqa countryside areas." *Northern Syria Observer*. https://www.nso-sy.com/Details/752/Internet-is-back-in-Raqqa-countryside-areas/en January 15.

Al-Jazeera. 2012. "Tanks roll on Damascus as violence reigns." July 19. https://www.aljazeera.com/news/2012/7/19/tanks-roll-on-damascus-as-violence-reigns.

Al-Khalidi, Suleiman. 2013. "Assad's forces capture strategic town in southern Syria." Reuters, May 8. https://www.reuters.com/article/amp/idUKBRE94703J20130508.

Al-Khalidi, Suleiman. 2015. "Seventy insurgents defect to Syrian army in Damascus suburb." *Reuters World News*. 11 March. https://www.reuters.com/article/us-mideast-crisis-defections-idUSKBN0M722D20150311.

Al-Khatieb, Mohammed. 2015. "Seeking Internet access, Syrians turn to Turkey's wireless network." *Al-Monitor*, April 14. https://www.al-monitor.com/originals/2015/04/aleppo-rebel-control-internet-networks-syria- turkey.html.

Al-Rawi, Ahmed K. 2014. "Cyber warriors in the middle east: the case of the syrian electronic army." *Public Relations Review* 40(3):420–428.

Al-Saqaf, Walid. 2016. "Internet censorship circumvention tools: escaping the control of the syrian regime." *Media and Communication* 4(1):39–50.

Alrababa'h, Ala' and Lisa Blaydes. 2021. "Authoritarian media and diversionary threats: lessons from 30 years of Syrian state discourse." *Political Science Research and Methods* 9(4):693–708.

Amnesty International. 2012. "{S}yria: Shutting down of internet and mobile networks alarming development." Amnesty International Press Release November 29. http://www.amnestyusa.org/news/press-releases/syria-shutting-down-of-internet-and-mobile-networks-alarming-development.

156 BIBLIOGRAPHY

Amnesty International. 2015. "How governments are using spyware to attack free speech—Amnesty International." August 20. https://www.amnesty.org/en/latest/campaigns/2015/08/how-governments-are-using-spyware-to-attack-free-speech/.

Amnesty International. 2019a. "Iran: more than 100 protesters believed to be killed as top officials give green light to crush protests." November 19. https://www.amnesty.org/en/latest/press-release/2019/11/iran-more-than-100-protesters-believed-to-be-killed-as-top-officials-give-green-light-to-crush-protests/.

Amnesty International. 2019b. "Iran: thousands arbitrarily detained and at risk of torture in chilling post-protest crackdown." December 16. https://www.amnesty.org/en/latest/news/2019/12/iran-thousands-arbitrarily-detained-and-at-risk-of-torture-in-chilling-post-protest-crackdown/.

Amnesty International. 2020a. "A web of impunity: the killings Iran's internet shutdown hid." November 16. https://iran-shutdown.amnesty.org/.

Amnesty International. 2020b. "Iran: at least 23 children killed by security forces in November protests—new evidence." March 4. https://www.amnesty.org/en/latest/news/2020/03/iran-at-least-23-children-killed-by-security-forces-in-november-protests-new-evidence/.

Anderson, Collin. 2013. "Dimming the Internet: detecting throttling as a mechanism of censorship in Iran." Working Paper. http://arxiv.org/abs/1306.4361.

Anderson, Collin and Karim Sadjadpour. 2018. *Iran's Cyber Threat: Espionage, Sabotage, and Revenge*. Washington, DC: Carnegie Endowment for International Peace.

Andrejevic, Mark and Kelly Gates. 2014. "Editorial. Big Data Surveillance: Introduction." *Surveillance & Society* 12(2):185–196.

Anthony, Sebastian. 2015. "GitHub battles 'largest DDoS' in site's history, targeted at anti-censorship tools." *ArsTechnica*, March 30. https://arstechnica.com/information-technology/2015/03/github-battles-largest-ddos-in-sites-history-targeted-at-anti-censorship-tools/.

Arreguin-Toft, Ivan. 2001. "How the weak win wars: a theory of asymmetric conflict." *International Security* 26(1):93–128.

Arrington, Michael. 2009. "Twitter hacked, defaced by 'Iranian Cyber Army'." *TechCrunch*, December 17. https://techcrunch.com/2009/12/17/twitter-reportedly-hacked-by-iranian-cyber-army/?guccounter=1.

Arsenault, Amelia, Sheldon Himelfarb, and Susan Abbott. 2011. "Evaluating media interventions in conflict countries." *United States Institute of Peace.*

Article 19. 2013. "Computer crimes in Iran: online repression in practice." *Article 19*, March 15. Technical report. https://www.article19.org/data/files/medialibrary/37385/Computer-Crimes-in-Iran-.pdf.

Article 19. 2017. "Tightening the net Part 3: a new cabinet and new attempts at control." *Article 19*, September 18. https://www.article19.org/resources/tightening-the-net-a-new-cabinet-and-new-attempts-at-control/.

Article 19. 2018. "Tightening the net: Internet controls during and after Iran's protests." *Article 19*, March 8. https://www.article19.org/resources/tightening-net-internet-controls-irans-protests/.

Article 19. 2020a. "Iran: citizens exercise their right to know, to demand a response to illegal Internet shutdowns." *Article 19* https://www.article19.org/resources/iran-citizens-illegal-internet-shutdowns/.

Article 19. 2020b. "Iran: tightening the net 2020 after blood and shutdowns." *Article 19*, September. https://www.article19.org/wp-content/uploads/2020/09/TTN-report-2020.pdf.

BIBLIOGRAPHY   157

Aryan, Simurgh, Homa Aryan, and J. Alex Halderman. 2013. "Internet censorship in Iran: A first look." *3rd USENIX Workshop on Free and Open Communications on the Internet (FOCI 13)*. 2013. https://www.usenix.org/conference/foci13/workshop-program/presentation/aryan.

Atassi, Basma. 2012. "Breaking the silence over Hama atrocities." *Al Jazeera*, February 2. http://www.aljazeera.com/indepth/features/2012/02/20122232155715210.html.

Baczko, Adam, Gilles Dorronsoro, and Arthur Quesnay. 2018. *Civil War in Syria: Mobilization and Competing Social Orders*. New York: Cambridge University Press.

Bagozzi, Benjamin E., Daniel Berliner, and Ryan M. Welch. 2021. "The diversity of repression: measuring state repressive repertoires with events data." *Journal of Peace Research* 58(5):1126–1136.

Baiazy, Amjad. 2012. "Syria's cyber operations." *Jadaliyya*, February 15. https://www.jadaliyya.com/Details/25272/Syria%60s-Cyber-Operations.

Bak, Daehee, Surachanee Sriyai, and Stephen A. Meserve. 2018. "The Internet and state repression: a cross-national analysis of the limits of digital constraint." *Journal of Human Rights* 17(5):1–38.

Ball, Kirstie and Frank Webster. 2003. *The Intensification of Surveillance: Crime, Terrorism and Warfare in the Information Age*. London: Pluto Press.

Ball, Kirstie, Kevin D. Haggerty, and David Lyon. 2012. *Handbook of Surveillance Studies*. New York: Routledge.

Barberá, Pablo, Ning Wang, Richard Bonneau, John T. Jost, Jonathan Nagler, Joshua Tucker, and Sandra González-Bailón. 2015. "The critical periphery in the growth of social protests." *PLOS ONE* 10(11):1–15.

Basmechi, Farinaz. 2022. "How Gen Z is using social media in Iran's Women, Life, Freedom movement." *The Conversation*, December 19. https://theconversation.com/how-gen-z-is-using-social-media-in-irans-women-life-freedom-movement-195783.

BBC Middle East. 2019. "Iran protests: at least 12 killed at unrest over petrol price rise— BBC News." November 18. https://www.bbc.com/news/world-middle-east-50459971.

BBC News. 2011a. "Egypt severs internet connection amid growing unrest." January 28. https://www.bbc.com/news/technology-12306041.

BBC News. 2011b. "Syria: 'dozens killed' as thousands protest in Hama." June 4. https://www.bbc.com/news/world-middle-east-13642917.

BBC News. 2012a. "Syria crisis: profiles of security and defence chiefs killed in Damascus blast." July 20. https://www.bbc.com/news/world-middle-east-18889030.

BBC News. 2012b. "Syria: Internet and mobile communication 'cut off'." November 29. https://www.bbc.com/news/technology-20546302.

BBC News. 2013. "Russia and US agree to hold Syria conference." May 7. https://www.bbc.com/news/world-middle-east-22430063.

BBC News. 2016. "Iran rolls out domestic internet." August 29. https://www.bbc.com/news/technology-37212456.

Beiser, Elana. 2013. "Syria, Iraq, Egypt most deadly nations for journalists." Committee to Protect Journalist Special Report, December 30. https://cpj.org/reports/2013/12/syria-iraq-egypt-most-deadly-nations-for-journalis/.

Bell-Martin, Rebecca V. and Jerome F. Marston. 2019. "Confronting selection bias: the normative and empirical risks of data collection in violent contexts." *Geopolitics* 26(1):159–192.

Beneduce, R., L. Jourdan, T. Raeymaekers, and K. Vlassenroot. 2006. "Violence with a purpose: exploring the functions and meaning of violence in the Democratic Republic of Congo." *Intervention* 4(1):32.

158 BIBLIOGRAPHY

Benkler, Yochai, Robert Faris, and Hal Roberts. 2018. *Network Propaganda*. Oxford: Oxford University Press.

Bentham, Jeremy. 1995. "Panopticon". In *The Panopticon Writings*, ed. Miran Bozovic. London: Verso, pp. 29–95.

Berry, Marie E. and Cullen Hendrix. 2018. "Sins of omission: women's and LGBTI rights reporting under the Trump administration." https://webassets.oxfamamerica.org/media/documentsSins_of_Omission_April_2019.pdf.

Beyer, Jessica L. and Jennifer Earl. 2018. "Backfire online: studying reactions to the repression of Internet activism". In *The Paradox of Repression and Nonviolent Movements*, ed. Lester R. Kurtz and Lee A. Smithey. Syracuse: Syracuse University Press, pp. 102–142.

Blaydes, Lisa. 2010. *Elections and Distributive Politics in Mubarak's Egypt*. Cambridge: Cambridge University Press.

Blaydes, Lisa. 2019. *State of Repression: Iraq under Saddam Hussein*. Princeton, NJ: Princeton University Press.

Boas, Taylor C. 2006. "Weaving the authoritarian web: the control of Internet use in nondemocratic regimes". In *How Revolutionary Was the Digital Revolution? National Responses, Market Transitions, and Global Technology*, ed. John Zysman and Abraham Newman. Stanford, CA: Stanford Business Books.

Bond, Kanisha D. 2018. "Reflexivity and revelation." *Qualitative & Multi-Method Research* 16(1):45–47.

Borger, Julian and Nick Hopkins. 2013. "West training Syrian rebels in Jordan." *The Guardian*, March 8. https://www.theguardian.com/world/2013/mar/08/west-training-syrian-rebels-jordan.

Boswell, Alan. 2011. "How Sudan used the Internet to crush protest movement." McClatchy Newspapers. https://www.mcclatchydc.com/news/nation-world/world/article24619936.html.

Brandt, Patrick T., John T. Williams, Benjamin O. Fordham, and Brain Pollins. 2000. "Dynamic modeling for persistent event-count time series." *American Journal of Political Science* 44(4):823–843.

Brewster, Thomas. 2019. "Moroccan activist says NSO's elite spy tools hacked his iPhone." *Forbes*, October 9. https://www.forbes.com/sites/thomasbrewster/2019/10/09/moroccan-activist-says-nsos-elite-spy-tools-hacked-his-iphone/.

Brigden, Noelle K. and Anita R. Gohdes. 2020. "The politics of data access in studying violence across methodological boundaries: what we can learn from each other?" *International Studies Review* 22(2):250–267.

Brownlee, Billie Jeanne. 2018. "Mediating the Syrian revolt: how new media technologies change the development of social movements and conflicts". In *The Syrian Uprising: Domestic Factors and Early Trajectory*, ed. Raymond Hinnebusch and Omar Imady. London: Routledge, pp. 188–206.

Brownstone, Andy. 2011. "Meet the Libyan rebels on the front line." *BBC*, May 24. http://www.bbc.co.uk/newsbeat/13505340.

Buhaug, Halvard and Scott Gates. 2002. "The geography of civil war." *Journal of Peace Research* 39(4):417–433.

Burgess, Matt. 2022. "Russia is taking over Ukraine's Internet." *WIRED*, June 15. https://www.wired.com/story/ukraine-russia-internet-takeover/.

Cairns, Christopher and Elizabeth Plantan. 2016. "Why autocrats sometimes relax online censorship of sensitive issues: a case study of microblog discussion of air pollution in China." In *Midwest Political Science Association Annual Conference, Chicago, IL, April*. Vol. 8.

BIBLIOGRAPHY 159

Carey, Sabine C. 2010. "The use of repression as a response to domestic dissent." *Political Studies* 58(1):167–186.

Carey, Sabine C. and Anita R. Gohdes. 2021. "Understanding journalist killings." *Journal of Politics* 83(4):1216–1228.

Carey, Sabine C. and Neil J. Mitchell. 2017. "Progovernment militias." *Annual Review of Political Science* 20(1):127–147.

Center for Human Rights in Iran. 2018. "Hackers with ties to security agencies launch phishing attacks on well known Iranians and dual nationals." May 4. https://iranhumanrights.org/2018/05/hackers-with-ties-to-security-agencies-launch-phishing-attacks-on-well-known-iranians-and-dual-nationals/.

Center for Human Rights in Iran. 2019*a*. "Initial reports show thousands arrested in Iran's crackdown on November protests." November 22. https://www.iranhumanrights.org/2019/11/initial-reports-show-thousands-arrested-in-irans-crackdown-on-november-protests/.

Center for Human Rights in Iran. 2019*b*. "Iranian government dictated to local media how to cover protests, new documents reveal." November 25. https://iranhumanrights.org/2019/11/iranian-government-dictated-to-local-media-how-to-cover-protests-new-documents-reveal/.

Chaabane, Abdelberi, Terence Chen, Mathieu Cunche, Emiliano De Cristofaro, Arik Friedman, and Mohamed Ali Kaafar. 2014. "Censorship in the wild: analyzing Internet filtering in Syria." In *Proceedings of the 2014 Conference on Internet Measurement Conference*. New York: ACM, pp. 285–298.

Chen, Huirong and Sheena Chestnut Greitens. 2021. "Information capacity and social order: the local politics of information integration in China." *Governance* 35(2): 497–523.

Chen, Jidong and Yiqing Xu. 2017. "Why do authoritarian regimes allow citizens to voice opinions publicly?" *Journal of Politics* 79(3):792–803.

Chen, Tianqi, Tong He, Michael Benesty, Vadim Khotilovich, and Yuan Tang. 2017. "xgboost: extreme gradient boosting." https://cran.r-project.org/package=xgboost.

Chenoweth, Erica, Evan Perkoski, and Sooyeon Kang. 2017. "State repression and non-violent resistance." *Journal of Conflict Resolution* 61(9):1950–1969.

Cherribi, Sam. 2017. *Fridays of Rage*. Oxford: Oxford University Press.

Choudry, Aziz. 2019. *Activists and the Surveillance State: Learning from Repression*. London: Pluto Press.

Chowdhury, Mridul. 2008. The role of the Internet in Burma's Saffron Revolution." Berkman Center Research Publication no. 2008–8.

CIPESA. 2014. "State of Internet freedoms in Ethiopia 2014." OpenNet Africa. https://www.opennetafrica.org/?wpfb_dl=16.

Committee to Protect Journalists. 2014. *Attacks on the Press: Journalism on the World's Front Lines, 2014 Edition*. New York: John Wiley & Sons.

Committee to Protect Journalists. 2021. "CPJ database of attacks on the press." https://cpj.org/data/.

Conrad, Courtenay R., Daniel W. Hill, and Will H. Moore. 2018. "Torture and the limits of democratic institutions." *Journal of Peace Research* 55(1):3–17.

Coppedge, Michael et al. 2021. "V-Dem Dataset v11.1." Varieties of Democracy (V-Dem) Project.

Cowie, James. 2012. "Could an Internet blackout happen in your country?" Renesys Blog, November 30. https://bit.ly/3wD61bN.

160 BIBLIOGRAPHY

Cowie, Jim. 2011*a*. "Egypt leaves the Internet | Internet intelligence." https://web.archive.org/web/20210901100830/https://blogs.oracle.com/internetintelligence/egypt-leaves-the-internet-v3.

Cowie, Jim. 2011*b*. "Syrian Internet shutdown." Renesys Blog, June 3. https://bit.ly/3Y7Zy49.

Cowie, Jim. 2014. "Syria, Venezuela, Ukraine: Internet under fire." Renesys Blog, February 26. https://bit.ly/3jjWKCj.

Dafoe, Allan and Jason Lyall. 2015. "From cell phones to conflict? Reflections on the emerging ICT–political conflict research agenda." *Journal of Peace Research* 52(3): 401–413.

Dahl, Robert A. 1971. *Polyarchy; Participation and Opposition.* New Haven: Yale University Press.

Dainotti, Alberto, Claudio Squarcella, Emile Aben, Kimberly C. Claffy, Marco Chiesa, Michele Russo, and Antonio Pescapé. 2011. "Analysis of country-wide Internet outages caused by censorship". In *ACM Internet Measurement Conference (IMC).* New York: ACM, pp. 1–18.

Danitz, Tiffany and Warren P. Strobel. 1999. "The Internet's impact on activism: the case of Burma." *Studies in Conflict & Terrorism* 22(3):257–269.

Davenport, Christian. 2007*a*. "State repression and political order." *Annual Review of Political Science* 10:1–23.

Davenport, Christian. 2007*b*. *State Repression and the Domestic Democratic Peace.* Cambridge: Cambridge University Press.

Davenport, Christian. 2010. *Media Bias, Perspective, and State Repression: The Black Panther Party.* New York: Cambridge University Press.

Dawkins, Sophia. 2020. "The problem of the missing dead." *Journal of Peace Research* 58(5):1098–1116.

Deibert, Ronald J. 2003. "Black code: censorship, surveillance, and the militarisation of cyberspace." *Millennium* 32(3):501–530.

Deibert, Ronald, John Palfrey, Rafal Rohozinski, and Jonathan Zittrain. 2011. *Access Contested: Security, Identity, and Resistance in Asian Cyberspace.* Cambridge, MA: MIT Press.

Deibert, Ronald, John Palfrey, Rafal Rohozinski, Jonathan Zittrain, and Janice Gross Stein. 2008. *Access Denied: The Practice and Policy of Global Internet Filtering.* Cambridge, MA: MIT Press.

Deibert, Ronald, John Palfrey, Rafal Rohozinski, Jonathan Zittrain, and Miklos Haraszti. 2010. *Access Controlled: The Shaping of Power, Rights, and Rule in Cyberspace.* Cambridge, MA: MIT Press.

Deibert, Ronald, Joshua Oliver, and Adam Senft. 2019. "Censors get smart: evidence from Psiphon in Iran." *Review of Policy Research* 36(3):341–356.

Deutch, Jeff and Hadi Habal. 2018. "The Syrian archive: a methodological case study of open-source investigation of state crime using video evidence from social media platforms." *State Crime Journal* 7(1):46–76.

Dimitrov, Martin K. and Joseph Sassoon. 2014. "State security, information, and repression: a comparison of Communist Bulgaria and Ba'thist Iraq." *Journal of Cold War Studies* 16(2):3–31.

Driessen, Benedikt, Ralf Hund, Carsten Willems, Christof Paar, and Thorsten Holz. 2012. "Don't trust satellite phones: a security analysis of two satphone standards." In *2012 IEEE Symposium on Security and Privacy*, IEEE, pp. 128–142.

BIBLIOGRAPHY   161

Earl, Jennifer, Andrew Martin, John D. McCarthy, and Sarah A. Soule. 2004. "The use of newspaper data in the study of collective action." *Annual Review of Sociology* 30:65–80.

Earl, Jennifer and Katrina Kimport. 2011. *Digitally Enabled Social Change: Activism in the Internet Age*. Cambridge, MA: MIT Press.

Eck, Kristine. 2012. "In data we trust? A comparison of UCDP GED and ACLED conflict events datasets." *Cooperation and Conflict* 47(1):124–141.

Eck, Kristine. 2015. "Repression by proxy: how military purges and insurgency impact the delegation of coercion." *Journal of Conflict Resolution* 59(5):924–946.

Edmond, Chris. 2013. "Information manipulation, coordination, and regime change." *Review of Economic Studies* 80(4):1422.

Egloff, Florian J. and James Shires. 2021. "Offensive cyber capabilities and state violence: three logics of integration." *Journal of Global Security Studies* 7(1):ogab028.

Elmer, Greg. 2012. "Panopticon—discipline—control." In *Handbook of Surveillance Studies*, ed. Kirstie Ball, Kevin D. Haggerty, and David Lyon. New York: Routledge, pp. 21–29.

Else, Liz. 2012. "The revolution will be tweeted." *New Scientist*, February 6. http://www.newscientist.com/article/mg21328500.400-the-revolution-will-be-tweeted.html.

Fein, Helen. 1995. "More murder in the middle: life-integrity violations and democracy in the world, 1987." *Human Rights Quarterly* 17(1):170–191.

Feldstein, Steven. 2021. *The Rise of Digital Repression: How Technology Is Reshaping Power, Politics, and Resistance*. Oxford: Oxford University Press.

Filterwatch. 2019. "Iran shutdown monitor." Technical report Small Media. https://filter.watch/en/2019/11/19/iran-shutdown-monitor/.

Finkel, Evgeny. 2015. "The phoenix effect of state repression: Jewish resistance during the holocaust." *American Political Science Review* 109(2):339–353.

Fisher, Max. 2013. "Web monitor: 'Syria has largely disappeared from the Internet.'" *Washington Post*, May 7. https://www.washingtonpost.com/news/worldviews/wp/2013/05/07/web-monitor-syria-has-largely-disappeared-from-the-internet/.

Flock, Elizabeth. 2011. "Syria internet services shut down as protesters fill streets." *Washington Post*, June 3. https://www.washingtonpost.com/blogs/blogpost/post/syria-internet-services-shut-down-as-protesters-fill-streets/2011/06/03/AGtLwxHH_blog.html.

Frantz, Erica and Andrea Kendall-Taylor. 2014. "A dictator's toolkit: understanding how co-optation affects repression in autocracies." *Journal of Peace Research* 51(3):332–346.

Freedom House. 2015. "Syria." Freedom on the Net 2015. https://www.refworld.org/cgi-bin/texis/vtx/rwmain?page=search&docid=563217a43&skip=0&query=Freedom%20on%20the%20Net%202015%20syria

Freyburg, Tina and Lisa Garbe. 2018. "Blocking the bottleneck: Internet shutdowns and ownership at election times in Sub-Saharan Africa." *International Journal of Communication* 12:3896–3916.

Friberg, Michael. 2016. "Forget Apple vs. the FBI: WhatsApp just switched on encryption for a billion people." *Wired*, April 5. https://www.wired.com/2016/04/forget-apple-vs-fbi-whatsapp-just-switched-encryption-billion-people/.

Friedman, Uri. 2011. "How Syrian activists name their Friday protests." *The Atlantic*, September 16. https://www.theatlantic.com/international/archive/2011/09/how-syrian-activists-name-their-friday-protests/337848/.

162 BIBLIOGRAPHY

Fuchs, Christian. 2013. "Societal and ideological impacts of deep packet inspection Internet surveillance." *Information Communication and Society* 16(8):1328–1359.

Fujii, Lee Ann. 2015. "Five stories of accidental ethnography: turning unplanned moments in the field into data." *Qualitative Research* 15(4):525–539.

Gallagher, Sean. 2012. "Updated: paint it black—how Syria methodically erased itself from the 'Net." *Ars Technica*, December 1. http://arstechnica.com/information-technology/2012/12/paint-it-black-how-syria-methodically-erased-itself-from-the-net/.

Galperin, Eva, Morgan Marquis-Boire, and John Scott-Railton. 2013. "Quantum of surveillance: familiar actors and possible false flags in Syrian malware campaigns." Technical report Citizen Lab and Electronic Frontier Foundation. https://www.eff.org/document/quantum-surveillance-familiar-actors-and-possible-false-flags-syrian-malware-campaigns.

Gandhi, Jennifer and Ellen Lust-Okar. 2009. "Elections under authoritarianism." *Annual Review of Political Science* 12(1):403–422.

Gehlbach, Scott, Zhaotian Luo, Anton Shirikov, and D. Vorobyev. 2022. *A Model of Censorship, Propaganda, and Repression*. Working Paper.

Gill, Tony. 2008. "Metadata and the web." In *Introduction to metadata*, ed. Murtha Baca, 2nd Edition. Getty Publications, pp. 20–38.

Gläßel, Christian and Katrin Paula. 2019. "Sometimes less is more: censorship, news falsification, and disapproval in 1989 East Germany." *American Journal of Political Science* 64(3):682–698.

Gohdes, Anita R. 2016. "Internet shutdowns during political unrest are becoming normal—and it should worry us." *Political Violence at a Glance*. https://politicalviolenceataglance.org/2016/09/16/internet-shutdowns-during-political-unrest-are-becoming-normal-and-it-should-worry-us/.

Gohdes, Anita R. 2018*a*. "Reflections on digital technologies, repression, and resistance: epilogue." *State Crime Journal* 7(1):141–144.

Gohdes, Anita R. 2018*b*. "Studying the Internet and violent conflict." *Conflict Management and Peace Science* 35(1):89–106.

Gohdes, Anita R. 2018*c*. "The relationship between state and corporate censorship." *Comparative Politics Newsletter* 28(2):31–37.

Goldstein, Joshua. 2007. "The role of digital networked technologies in the Ukrainian Orange Revolution." *Berkman Center Research Publication* 14.

Goldstein, Robert Justin. 1978. *Political Repression in Modern America from 1870 to the Present*. Cambridge, MA: Schenkman.

Golkar, Saeid. 2011. "Liberation or suppression technologies? The internet, the green movement and the regime in Iran." *Australian Journal of Emerging Technologies and Society* 9(1):50–70.

González-Bailón, Sandra, Javier Borge-Holthoefer, Alejandro Rivero, and Yamir Moreno. 2011. "The dynamics of protest recruitment through an online network." *Nature* 1:1–7.

González-Bailón, Sandra, Javier Borge-Holthoefer, and Yamir Moreno. 2013. "Broadcasters and hidden influentials in online protest diffusion." *American Behavioral Scientist* 57(7):943–965.

Goodin, Dan. 2015. "Massive denial-of-service attack on GitHub tied to Chinese government." *Ars Technica*. https://arstechnica.com/information-technology/2015/03/massive-denial-of-service-attack-on-github-tied-to-chinese-government/.

Greenberg, Andy. 2011. "Meet Telecomix, the hackers bent on exposing those who censor and surveil the Internet." *Forbes*, December 26. https://www.forbes.com/sites/

andygreenberg/2011/12/26/meet-telecomix-the-hackers-bent-on-exposing-those-who-censor-and-surveil-the-internet/.

Greitens, Sheena Chestnut. 2016. *Dictators and Their Secret Police: Coercive Institutions and State Violence*. New York: Cambridge University Press.

Greitens, Sheena Chestnut, Myunghee Lee, and Emir Yazici. 2020. "Counterterrorism and preventive repression." *International Security* 44(3):9–47.

Gunitsky, Seva. 2015. "Corrupting the cyber-commons: social media as a tool of autocratic stability." *Perspectives on Politics* 13(1):42–54.

Guriev, Sergei and Daniel Treisman. 2022. *Spin Dictators: The Changing Face of Tyranny in the 21st Century*. Princeton, NJ: Princeton University Press.

Hall, Stephen G. F. and Thomas Ambrosio. 2017. "Authoritarian learning: a conceptual overview." *East European Politics* 33(2):143–161.

Hanna, Asaad. 2015. "How Syrian opposition bypasses Assad's communication blocks." *Al-Monitor*, December 15. www.al-monitor.com/pulse/originals/2015/12/syria-opposition-means-of-communication-regime.html.

Harms, Florian. 2004. "Syrien im Wandel: Mit Internet und Handy gegen die Diktatur." *Der Spiegel*, October 28. https://www.spiegel.de/politik/ausland/syrien-im-wandel-mit-internet-und-handy-gegen-die-diktatur-a-322990.html.

Haschke, Peter. 2020. "The political terror scale (PTS) codebook Version 1.40." University Of North Carolina, Asheville.

Hashem, Mohamed. 2015. "Q&A: in Syria the 'internet has become a weapon' of war." *Al-Jazeera*, June 20. http://www.aljazeera.com/indepth/features/2015/06/qa-syria-internet-weapon-war-150619215453906.html.

Hassanpour, Navid. 2014. "Media disruption and revolutionary unrest: evidence from Mubarak's quasi-experiment." *Political Communication* 31(1):1–24.

Heger, Lindsay L. 2015. "Votes and violence: pursuing terrorism while navigating politics." *Journal of Peace Research* 52(1):32–45.

Hegghammer, Thomas. 2021. "How the War on Terror supercharged state power." *Foreign Affairs*, September/October. https://www.foreignaffairs.com/articles/middle-east/2021-08-24/resistance-futile.

Hellmeier, Sebastian. 2016. "The dictator's digital toolkit: explaining variation in Internet filtering in authoritarian regimes." *Politics & Policy* 44(6): 1158–1191.

Hendrix, Cullen S. and Idean Salehyan. 2015. "No news is good news: mark and recapture for event data when reporting probabilities are less than one." *International Interactions* 41(2):392–406.

Heydemann, Steven and Reinoud Leenders. 2011. "Authoritarian learning and authoritarian resilience: regime responses to the 'Arab Awakening'." *Globalizations* 8(5): 647–653.

Hill, Daniel W. and Zachary M. Jones. 2014. "An empirical evaluation of explanations for state repression." *American Political Science Review* 108(3):661–687.

Hinnebusch, Raymond A. 1993. "State and civil society in Syria." *Middle East Journal* 47(2):243–257.

Hinnebusch, Raymond A. 2001. *Syria: Revolution from Above*. London: Routledge.

Hinnebusch, Raymond A. 2012. "Syria: from 'authoritarian upgrading' to revolution?" *International Affairs* 88(1):95–113.

Hobbs, William R. and Margaret E. Roberts. 2018. "How sudden censorship can increase access to information." *American Political Science Review* 112(3):621–636.

Holliday, Joseph. 2013. *The Assad Regime: From Counterinsurgency To Civil War*. Washington, DC: Institute for the Study of War.

164   BIBLIOGRAPHY

Hoover Green, Amelia. 2019. *The Commander's Dilemma*. Ithaca: Cornell University Press.

Hounshell, Blake. 2011. "The revolution will be tweeted." *Foreign Policy*, June 20. http://www.foreignpolicy.com/articles/2011/06/20/the_revolution_will_be_tweeted.

Howard, Philip N., Sheetal D. Agarwal, and Muzammil M. Hussain. 2011. "When do states disconnect their digital networks? Regime responses to the political uses of social media." *Communication Review* 14(3):216–232.

Hu, Margaret. 2022. "Kazakhstan's internet shutdown is the latest episode in an ominous trend: digital authoritarianism." *The Conversation*, January 24. https://theconversation.com/kazakhstans-internet-shutdown-is-the-latest-episode-in-an-ominous-trend-digital-authoritarianism-174651.

Human Rights Watch. 2011. "'We live as in war': crackdown on protesters in the governorate of Homs." https://www.hrw.org/report/2011/11/11/we-live-war/crackdown-protesters-governorate-homs-syria.

Human Rights Watch. 2014. "'They know everything we do': telecom and Internet surveillance in Ethiopia." http://elibrary.worldbank.org/doi/book/10.1596/978-0-8213-9531-8.

International Crisis Group. 2013. "Syria's metastasising conflicts." Middle East Report nr. 143, June 27.

International Telecommunication Union (ITU). 2022. "Individuals using the Internet (% of population)." https://data.worldbank.org/indicator/IT.NET.USER.ZS.

IODA. 2021. "Internet Outage Detection and Analysis IODA." https://ioda.caida.org/.

Johndrow, James, Kristian Lum, and Patrick Ball. 2015. "dga: capture-recapture estimation using Bayesian model averaging." *R Package*. https://cran.r-project.org/web/packages/dga/index.html.

Justice for Iran. 2020. "Shoot to kill: preliminary findings of justice for Iran's investigation into the November 2019 protests." Report, February 28. https://justice4iran.org/15229/.

Kalathil, Shanthi and Taylor C. Boas. 2003. *Open Networks, Closed Regimes: The Impact of the Internet on Authoritarian Rule*. Washington, DC: Carnegie Endowment for International Peace.

Kalyvas, Stathis. 2006. *The Logic of Violence in Civil War*. New York: Cambridge Univeristy Press.

Kalyvas, Stathis and Laia Balcells. 2010. "International system and technologies of rebellion: how the end of the Cold War shaped internal conflict." *American Political Science Review* 104(3):415–429.

Kargar, Simin. 2018. "Iran's national information network faster speeds but at what cost." *Internet Monitor Research Bulletin*. https://thenetmonitor.org/bulletins/irans-national-information-network-faster-speeds-but-at-what-cost.

Kargar, Simin and Adrian Rauchfleisch. 2019. "State-aligned trolling in Iran and the double-edged affordances of Instagram." *New Media and Society* 21(7):1506–1527.

Kathuria, Rajat, Mansi Kedia, Gangesh Varma, Kaushambi Bagchi, and Richa Sekhani. 2018. "The anatomy of an internet blackout: measuring the economic impact of Internet shutdowns in India." https://tile.loc.gov/storage-services/service/gdc/gdcovop/2018305075/2018305075.pdf.

Keating, Joshua. 2013. "Firing mortars? There's an app for that." *Slate*, September 18.

Keck, Margaret E. and Kathryn Sikkink. 1998. *Activists beyond Borders: Advocacy Networks in International Politics*. New York: Cambridge Univeristy Press.

BIBLIOGRAPHY 165

Keremoğlu, Eda and Nils B. Weidmann. 2020. "How dictators control the Internet: A review essay." *Comparative Political Studies* 53(10–11):1690–1703.

Kerr, Jaclyn A. 2016. "Rewiring authoritarianism: the evolution of Internet policy in Putin's Russia." Working Paper.

King, Gary, Jennifer Pan, and Margaret E. Roberts. 2013. "How censorship in China allows government criticism but silences collective expression." *American Political Science Review* 107:1–18.

Kirchgaessner, Stephanie, Paul Lewis, David Pegg, Sam Cutler, Nina Lakhani, and Michael Safi. 2021. "Revealed: leak uncovers global abuse of cyber-surveillance weapon." *The Guardian*, July 18. https://www.theguardian.com/world/2021/jul/18/revealed-leak-uncovers-global-abuse-of-cyber-surveillance-weapon-nso-group-pegasus.

Kostyuk, Nadiya and Yuri M. Zhukov. 2019. "Invisible digital front: can cyber attacks shape battlefield events?" *Journal of Conflict Resolution* 63(2):317–347.

Kuran, Timur. 1989. "Sparks and prairie fires: a theory of unanticipated political revolution." *Public Choice* 61(1):41–74.

Kuran, Timur. 1997. *Private Truths, Public Lies: The Social Consequences of Preference Falsification.* Cambridge, MA: Harvard University Press.

Lake, Eli. 2009. "Fed contractor, cell phone maker sold spy system to Iran." *Washington Times*, April 13. https://www.washingtontimes.com/news/2009/apr/13/europe39s-telecoms-aid-with-spy-tech/.

Landler, Mark and Brian Stelter. 2009. "Washington taps into a potent new force in diplomacy." *New York Times*, June 16. http://www.nytimes.com/2009/06/17/world/middleeast/17media.html.

Larson, Jennifer M., Jonathan Nagler, Jonathan Ronen, and Joshua A. Tucker. 2019. "Social networks and protest participation: evidence from 130 million Twitter users." *American Journal of Political Science* 63(3):690–705.

Leenders, Reinoud. 2013. "Social movement theory and the onset of the popular uprising in Syria." *Arab Studies Quarterly* 35(3):273.

Leenders, Reinoud. 2015. "Repression is not 'a stupid thing': regime responses to the Syrian uprising and insurgency". In *The Alawis of Syria: War, Faith and Politics in the Levant*, ed. Michael Kerr and Craig Larkin. Oxford: Oxford University Press, pp. 245–273.

Leverett, Flynt. 2005. *Inheriting Syria: Bashar's Trial by Fire.* Washington, DC: The Brookings Institution Press.

Little, Andrew T. 2016. "Communication technology and protest." *Journal of Politics* 78(1):152–166.

Liu, Howard and Christopher M. Sullivan. 2021. "And the heat goes on: police repression and the modalities of power." *Journal of Conflict Resolution* 65(10):1657–1679.

Lohmann, Susanne. 1994. "The dynamics of informational cascades: the Monday demonstrations in Leipzig, East Germany, 1989–91." *World Politics* 47(1):42–101.

Lorentzen, Peter L. 2013. "Regularizing rioting: permitting public protest in an authoritarian regime." *Quarterly Journal of Political Science* 8(2):127–158.

Lorentzen, Peter L. 2014. "China's strategic censorship." *American Journal of Political Science* 58(2):402–414.

Lotan, Gilad, Erhardt Graeff, Mike Ananny, Devin Gaffney, Ian Pearce, and Danah Boyd. 2011. "The Arab Spring: the revolutions were tweeted: information flows during the 2011 Tunisian and Egyptian revolutions." *International Journal of Communication* 5(0):1375–1405.

Lowe, David. 2016. "Surveillance and international terrorism intelligence exchange: balancing the interests of national security and individual liberty." *Terrorism and Political Violence* 28(4):653–673.

Lu, Yingdan and Jennifer Pan. 2021. "Capturing clicks: how the Chinese government uses clickbait to compete for visibility." *Political Communication* 38(1–2):23–54.

Lum, Kristian, Megan Emily Price, and David Banks. 2013. "Applications of multiple systems estimation in human rights research." *American Statistician* 67(4):191–200.

Lutscher, Philipp M. 2021. "Hot topics: denial-of-service attacks on news websites in autocracies." *Political Science Research and Methods*, 1–16.

Lutscher, Philipp M., Nils B. Weidmann, Margaret E. Roberts, Mattijs Jonker, Alistair King, and Alberto Dainotti. 2019. "At home and abroad: the use of denial-of-service attacks during elections in nondemocratic regimes." *Journal of Conflict Resolution* 64(2–3):373–401.

Lynch, Marc, Deen Freelon, and Sean Aday. 2014. "Blogs and bullets III: Syria's social mediated war." *United States Institute of Peace, Peaceworks* 91(5).

Lyon, David. 2001. *Surveillance Society: Monitoring Everyday Life*. McGraw-Hill Education (UK).

Lyon, David, ed. 2006. *Theorizing surveillance*. Routledge.

MacFarquhar, Neil and Hwaida Saad. 2012. "Rebel groups in Syria make framework for military." *New York Times*, December 7.

Macías-Medellín, Martín and Laura H. Atuesta. 2021. "Constraints and military coordination: how ICTs shape the intensity of rebel violence." *International Interactions* 47(4):692–719.

Mackenzie, Laura. 2021. "Surveillance: how Gulf states keep watch on us." *Wired*, January 21. https://wired.me/technology/privacy/surveillance-gulf-states/.

MacKinnon, Rebecca. 2011. "China's 'networked authoritarianism.'" *Journal of Democracy* 22(2):32–46.

MacKinnon, Rebecca. 2012. *Consent of the Networked: The Worldwide Struggle for Internet Freedom*. New York: Basic Books.

Madigan, David and Jeremy C. York. 1997. "Bayesian methods for estimation of the size of a closed population." *Biometrika* 84(1):19–31.

Madory, Doug. 2019. "Historic Internet blackout in Iran." https://blogs.oracle.com/cloudsecurity/post/historic-internet-blackout-in-iran.

Magaloni, Beatriz. 2006. *Voting for Autocracy*. Cambridge: Cambridge University Press.

Malejacq, Romain and Dipali Mukhopadhyay. 2016. "The 'tribal politics' of field research: a reflection on power and partiality in 21st-century warzones." *Perspectives on Politics* 14(4):1011–1028.

Marchant, Eleanor and Nicole Stremlau. 2020. "The changing landscape of Internet shutdown in Africa: a Spectrum of shutdowns: reframing Internet shutdowns from Africa." *International Journal of Communication* 14:4327–4342.

Marczak, Bill, John Scott-Railton, Sarah Mckune, Abdul Razzak, and Ron Deibert. 2018. "HIDE AND SEEK: tracking NSO group's Pegasus spyware to operations in 45 countries." Citizen Lab Research Report September(113). https://citizenlab.ca/2018/09/hide-and-seek-tracking-nso-groups-pegasus-spyware-to-operations-in-45-countries/.

Marczak, William Russell. 2016. *Defending Dissidents from Targeted Digital Surveillance*. Berkeley: University of California.

BIBLIOGRAPHY 167

Marczak, William R., John Scott-Railton, Morgan Marquis-Boire, and Vern Paxson. 2014. "When governments hack opponents: a look at actors and technology." In *23rd USENIX Security Symposium (USENIX Security 14)*, pp. 511–525. https://www.usenix.org/node/184470.

Mare, Admire. 2020. "State-ordered Internet shutdowns and digital authoritarianism in Zimbabwe." *International Journal of Communication* 14:4244–4263.

Mason, T. David and Dale A. Krane. 1989. "The political economy of death squads: toward a theory of the impact of state-sanctioned terror." *International Studies Quarterly* 33(2):175–198.

Mazur, Kevin. 2021. *Revolution in Syria*. Cambridge: Cambridge University Press.

Memarian, Omid and Tara Nesvaderani. 2010. "The youth." In *The Iran Primer: Power, Politics, and US Policy*, ed. Robin B. Wright. US Institute of Peace Press. https://iranprimer.usip.org/sites/default/files/PDF%20Youth_Memarian_Opposition.pdf.

Menn, Joseph and Taylor Lorenz. 2022. "Cloudflare drops KiwiFarms." *Washington Post*, September 3. https://www.washingtonpost.com/technology/2022/09/03/cloudflare-drops-kiwifarms/.

Michaelsen, Marcus. 2017. "Far away, so close: transnational activism, digital surveillance and authoritarian control in Iran." *Surveillance and Society* 15(3–4):465–470.

Michaelsen, Marcus. 2018. "Exit and voice in a digital age: Iran's exiled activists and the authoritarian state." *Globalizations* 15(2):248–264.

Milani, Abbas. 2010. "The Green movement." In *The Iran Primer: Power, Politics, and US Policy*, ed. Robin B. Wright. US Institute of Peace Press. http://www.iranprimer.com/sites/default/files/The%20Green%20Movement.pdf.

Miller, Elhanan. 2012. "Syrian opposition uses home-made rockets and Google technology, video reveals." *The Times of Israel*, August 20.

Miller, James and Matt Sienkiewicz. 2012. "Straight news from the citizens of Syria: how reporters sort, organize—and verify—a flood of information from a chaotic civil war." *Columbia Journalism Review*. https://archives.cjr.org/behind_the_news/straight_news_from_the_citizen.php.

Mitchell, Neil J. 2004. *Agents of Atrocity. Leaders, Followers, and the Violation of Human Rights in Civil War*. New York: Palgrave Macmillan.

Moore-Gilbert, Kylie and Zainab Abdul-Nabi. 2021. "Authoritarian downgrading, (self)censorship and new media activism after the Arab Spring." *New Media & Society* 23(5):875–893.

Morgenbesser, Lee. 2020. "The menu of autocratic innovation." *Democratization* 27(6):1053–1072.

Mortensen, Mette. 2011. "When citizen photojournalism sets the news agenda: Neda Agha Soltan as a Web 2.0 icon of post-election unrest in Iran." *Global Media and Communication* 7(1):4–16.

Moss, Dana M. 2018. "The ties that bind: Internet communication technologies, networked authoritarianism, and 'voice' in the Syrian diaspora." *Globalizations* 15(2):265–282.

Mountz, Alison. 2007. "Smoke and mirrors: an ethnography of the state". In *Politics and Practice in Economic Geography*, ed. Adam Tickell, Eric Sheppard, Jamie Peck, and Trevor Barnes. New York: Sage, pp. 38–48.

Müller-Crepon, Carl, Philipp Hunziker, and Lars-Erik Cederman. 2021. "Roads to rule, roads to rebel: relational state capacity and conflict in Africa." *Journal of Conflict Resolution* 65(2–3):563–590.

168 BIBLIOGRAPHY

Munger, Kevin, Richard Bonneau, Jonathan Nagler, and Joshua A. Tucker. 2019. "Elites tweet to get feet off the streets: measuring regime social media strategies during protest." *Political Science Research and Methods* 7(4):815–834.

Murphy, Heather. 2014. "Ominous text message sent to protesters in Kiev sends chills around the internet." *New York Times*, January 22. http://thelede.blogs.nytimes.com/ 2014/01/22/ominous-text-message-sent-to-protesters-in-kiev-sends-chills-around-the-internet/.

Musiani, Francesca, Derrick L. Cogburn, Laura DeNardis, and Nanette S. Levinson. 2016. *The Turn to Infrastructure in Internet Governance.* New York: Palgrave Macmillan.

Neistat, Anna and Ole Solvang. 2011. " 'By all means necessary!': individual and command responsibility for crimes against humanity in Syria." *Human Rights Watch*, December. http://www.hrw.org/sites/default/files/reports/syria1211webwcover_0.pdf.

Neo, Ric. 2020. "A cudgel of repression: analysing state instrumentalisation of the 'fake news' label in Southeast Asia." *Journalism* 23(9): 1919–1938.

NetBlocks. 2019. "Internet being restored in Iran after week-long shutdown." November 23. https://netblocks.org/reports/internet-restored-in-iran-after-protest-shutdown-dAmqddA9.

Ng, Jason. 2013. *Blocked on Weibo: What Gets Suppressed on China's Version of Twitter (And Why).* New York: New Press.

Nothias, Toussaint. 2020. "Access granted: Facebook's free basics in Africa." *Media, Culture & Society* 42(3):329–348.

Nyst, Carly and Nick Monaco. 2018. "State-sponsored trolling: how governments are deploying disinformation as part of broader digital harassment campaigns." Report, Institute for the Future (IFTF), July.

OECD. 2011. "The economic impact of shutting down Internet and mobile phone services in Egypt." *OECD Report Egypt*, February 4. http://bit.ly/1ehhDmB.

O'Flaherty, Kate. 2018. "YouTube keeps deleting evidence of Syrian chemical weapon attacks." *Wired UK.* June 6. https://www.wired.co.uk/article/chemical-weapons-in-syria-youtube-algorithm-delete-video.

OHCHR. 2011. "1st report of the Commission of Inquiry on the Syrian Arab Republic." Technical report, Office of the United Nations High Commissioner for Human Rights Geneva. https://digitallibrary.un.org/record/720796?ln=en https://documents-dds-ny.un.org/doc/UNDOC/GEN/G11/170/97/PDF/G1117097.pdf?.

OHCHR. 2014. "The right to privacy in the digital age." Technical report, Report of the Office of the United Nations High Commissioner for Human Rights, June 30. https://www.ohchr.org/en/calls-for-input/report-right-privacy-digital-age-focus-surveillance.

OpenNet Initiative. 2005. "Special report: election monitoring in Kyrgyzstan." Technical report, OpenNet Initiative. https://opennet.net/special/kg/.

OpenNet Initiative. 2006. "Internet filtering in Iran in 2004–2005." OpenNet Initiative. https://cyber.harvard.edu/publications/2005/Internet_Filtering_ in_Iran_in_ 2004_2005.

OpenNet Initiative. 2007. "Internet filtering in Iran." OpenNet Initiative. https:// opennet.net/studies/iran2007.

OpenNet Initiative. 2009*a*. "Internet filtering in Iran." OpenNet Initiative. https:// opennet.net/sites/opennet.net/files/ONI_Iran_2009.pdf.

OpenNet Initiative. 2009*b*. "Internet filtering in Syria." June 16. https://opennet.net/ research/profiles/syria.

BIBLIOGRAPHY 169

Osborn, Andrew. 2012. "How 'Damascus Volcano' erupted in Assad's stronghold." July 20. https://www.reuters.com/article/us-syria-crisis-damascus-idUSBRE86J17E20120720.

Dalek, Jakub, Nica Dumlao, Miles Kenyon, Irene Poetranto, Adam Senft, Caroline Wesley, Arturo Filastó, Maria Xynou, and Amie Bishop. 2021. *No Access: LGBTIQ Website Censorship in Six Countries*. No. 142. Technical Report Citizen Lab Research Report.

Oweis, Khaled Yacoub. 2008. "Syria expands iron censorship over Internet." *Reuters Internet News*, March 13. https://www.reuters.com/article/us-syria-internet/syria-expands-iron-censorship-over-internet-idUSL138353620080313.

Padmanabhan, Ramakrishna, Arturo Filastò, Maria Xynou, Ram Sundara Raman, Kennedy Middleton, Mingwei Zhang, Doug Madory, Molly Roberts, and Alberto Dainotti. 2021. A multi-perspective view of Internet censorship in Myanmar. In *Proceedings of the ACM SIGCOMM 2021 Workshop on Free and Open Communications on the Internet (FOCI '21)*. Association for Computing Machinery, New York, NY, USA, pp. 27–36.

Pan, Jennifer. 2017. "How market dynamics of domestic and foreign social media firms shape strategies of Internet censorship." *Problems of Post-Communism* 64(3–4): 167–188.

Pan, Jennifer and Alexandra Siegel. 2020. "How Saudi crackdowns fail to silence online dissent." *American Political Science Review* 114(1):109–125.

Parkinson, Sarah Elizabeth. 2013. "Organizing rebellion: rethinking high-risk mobilization and social networks in war." *American Political Science Review* 107(3):418–432.

Parks, Lisa and Rachel Thompson. 2020. "The slow shutdown: information and Internet regulation in Tanzania from 2010 to 2018 and impacts on online content creators." *International Journal of Communication* 14:4288–4308.

Pearce, Katy E. 2015. "Democratizing kompromat: the affordances of social media for state-sponsored harassment." *Information, Communication & Society* 18(10): 1158–1174.:1–17.

Pearlman, Wendy. 2020. "Mobilizing from scratch: large-scale collective action without preexisting organization in the Syrian uprising." *Comparative Political Studies* 54(10):1786–1817.

Perlroth, Nicole. 2013a. "Syria, and pro-government hackers, are back on the Internet." *New York Times*, May 8. http://nyti.ms/L8zhO7.

Perlroth, Nicole. 2013b. "Syria loses access to the Internet." *New York Times Bits Blog*, May 7.

Perthes, Volker. 2006. *Syria under Bashar al-Asad : Modernisation and the Limits of Change*. London: Routledge.

Peterson, Scott. 2012. "Syria's iPhone insurgency makes for smarter rebellion." *Christian Science Monitor*, August 1. http://www.csmonitor.com/World/Middle-East/2012/0801/Syria-s-iPhone-insurgency-makes-for-smarter-rebellion.

Pettersson, Therese. 2020. "UCDP/PRIO armed conflict dataset codebook v 20.1." *Uppsala: Uppsala Conflict Data Program*.

Pettersson, Therése and Kristine Eck. 2018. "Organized violence, 1989–2017." *Journal of Peace Research* 55(4):535–547.

Pinheiro, Paulo Sérgio. 2015. "The Use of Barrel Bombs and Indiscriminate Bombardment in Syria: The Need to Strengthen Compliance with International Humanitarian Law." *Paper presented by Chair of the Independent International Commission of Inquiry on the Syrian Arab Republic (CoI) and hosted by Permanent Mission of Austria to United*

Nations Human Rights, March 12. https://www.ohchr.org/Documents/HRBodies/HRCouncil/CoISyria/CoISyriaIndiscriminateBombardment12032015.pdf.

Poe, Steven C. and C. Neal Tate. 1994. "Repression of human rights to personal integrity in the 1980s: a global analysis." *American Political Science Review* 88(4):853–872.

Poe, Steven C., C. Neal Tate, and Linda C. Keith. 1999. "Repression of the human right to personal integrity revisited: a global cross-national study covering the years 1976–1993." *International Studies Quarterly* 43(2):291–313.

Poe, Steven C., Sabine C. Carey, and Tanya C. Vazquez. 2001. "How are these pictures different? A quantitative comparison of the US State Department and Amnesty International human rights reports, 1976–1995." *Human Rights Quarterly* 23:650–677.

Poetranto, Irene. 2012. "Update on information controls in Ethiopia." Open-Net Africa Update, November 1. https://www.opennetafrica.org/?wpfb_dl=15.

Porcedda, Maria Grazia. 2013. "Lessons from PRISM and Tempora: the self-contradictory nature of the fight against cyberspace crimes. Deep packet inspection as a case study." *Neue Kriminalpolitik* 25(4):373–389.

Poulsen, Kevin. 2013. "In Syria's civil war, Facebook has become a battlefield." *Wired*, December 23. https://www.wired.com/2013/12/syria-report/.

Preston, Jennifer. 2011. "Syria restores access to Facebook and YouTube." *New York Times*, February 9. https://www.nytimes.com/2011/02/10/world/middleeast/10syria.html.

Price, Megan, Anita Gohdes, and Patrick Ball. 2015. "Documents of war: understanding the Syrian conflict." *Significance* 12(2):14–19.

Price, Megan, Anita Gohdes, and Patrick Ball. 2016. "Technical memo for Amnesty International report on deaths in detention." *Human Rights Data Analysis Group*, August 17. https://hrdag.org/wp-content/uploads/2016/08/HRDAG-AI-memo-2.pdf.

Price, Megan, Anita R. Gohdes, and Patrick Ball. 2014. "Updated statistical analysis of documentation of killings in the Syrian Arab republic." Report commissioned by the Office of the UN High Commissioner for Human Rights. August 1.

Price, Megan E. and Anita R. Gohdes. 2020. "The promises and pitfalls of data analysis for accountability and justice." In *Accountability and Transitional Justice in a Postconflict Society*, ed. Radwan Ziadeh. The Rowman & Littlefield Publishing Group, Inc., pp. 109–120.

Prince, Matthew. 2012. "How Syria turned off the Internet." Cloudflare Blog, November 29. http://blog.cloudflare.com/how-syria-turned-off-the-internet.

Prince, Matthew. 2013. "How Syria turned off the Internet (again)." Cloudflare Blog, July 5. https://blog.cloudflare.com/how-syria-turned-off-the-internet-again/.

Privacy International. 2016. "Open season: building Syria's surveillance state." December 12. https://privacyinternational.org/report/1016/open-season- building-syrias-surveillance-state.

Qin, Bei, David Strömberg, and Yanhui Wu. 2017. "Why does China allow freer social media? Protests versus surveillance and propaganda." *Journal of Economic Perspectives* 31(1):117–140.

Qtiesh, Anas and Rainey Reitman. 2013. "Syrian Internet goes dark, leaving questions and uncertainty." Electronic Frontier Foundation, May 7. https://www.eff.org/deeplinks/2013/05/syrian-internet-goes-dark-leaving-questions-and-uncertainty-0.

Quan, Lin, John Heidemann, and Yuri Pradkin. 2013. "Trinocular: understanding internet reliability through adaptive probing." *Computer Communication Review* 43(4):255–266.

BIBLIOGRAPHY 171

Rahimi, Babak. 2008. "The politics of the Internet in Iran." In *Media, Culture and Society in Iran : Living with Globalization and the Islamic State*, ed. Mehdi Semati. London: Routledge.

Raoof, Ramy. 2011. "Egypt: how companies help the government spy on activists." Global Voices, May 7. http://advocacy.globalvoicesonline.org/2011/05/07/egypt-how-companies-help-the-government-spy-on-activists/.

Rathmell, Andrew. 1996. "Syria's intelligence services: origins and development: origins and development." *Journal of Conflict Studies* 16(2):75–96.

Rawlinson, Kevin. 2014. "Turkey blocks use of Twitter after prime minister attacks social media site." *The Guardian*, March 21. https://www.theguardian.com/world/2014/mar/21/turkey-blocks-twitter-prime-minister.

Regalado, Daniel, Nart Villeneuve, and John Scott-Railton. 2015. *Behind the Syrian Conflict's Digital Front Lines. FireEye*, February. https://cryptome.org/2015/02/fireeye-syria-hack.pdf.

Reporters Without Borders. 2007. "Reporters Without Borders annual report 2007—Syria." February 1. https://www.refworld.org/docid/46e692cc23.html.

Reporters Without Borders. 2013. "Syria using 34 Blue Coat servers to spy on Internet users." May 23. https://rsf.org/en/syria-using-34-blue-coat-servers-spy-internet-users.

Reuters. 2019. "Special report: Iran's leader ordered crackdown on unrest—'Do whatever it takes to end it'." *Reuters*, December 23. https://www.reuters.com/article/us-iran-protests-specialreport/special-report-irans-leader-ordered-crackdown-on-unrest-do-whatever-it-takes-to-end-it-idUSKBN1YR0QR.

Roberts, Margaret E. 2018. *Censored: Distraction and Diversion inside China's Great Firewall*. Princeton, NJ: Princeton University Press.

Roberts, Margaret E. 2020. "Resilience to online censorship." *Annual Review of Political Science* 23(1):401–419.

Robertson, Bronwen and James Marchant, eds. 2015. *Revolution Decoded: Iran's Digital Landscape*. Small Media. https://web.archive.org/web/20220320101924/https://smallmedia.org.uk/revolutiondecoded/

Robinson, Darrel and Marcus Tannenberg. 2019. "Self-censorship of regime support in authoritarian states: evidence from list experiments in China." *Research & Politics* 6(3).

Rydzak, Jan. 2019. "Of blackouts and bandhs: the strategy and structure of disconnected protest in India." Technical Report ID 3330413 Social Science Research Network, Rochester, NY.

SalamaTech. 2015. "Facebook prison: testimonies from Syria." Flash Notes, September 23. https://secdev-foundation.org/wp-content/uploads/2015/09/FlashNote-6-Facebook Prison-Salamatech-sept-231.pdf.

Salamatian, Loqman, Frédérick Douzet, Kavé Salamatian, and Kévin Limonier. 2021. "The geopolitics behind the routes data travel: a case study of Iran." *Journal of Cybersecurity* 7(1):1–19.

Sands, Phil. 2008. "Syria tightens control over internet." *The National*, June 26. https://www.thenational.ae/world/mena/syria-tightens-control-over-internet-1.508106.

Sandvig, Christian. 2013. "The Internet as infrastructure". In *The Oxford Handbook of Internet Studies*, ed. William H. Dutton. Oxford: Oxford University Press, pp. 307–362.

Sanger, David E., Nicole Perlroth, Ana Swanson, and Ronen Bergman. 2021. "U.S. blacklists Israeli firm NSO group over spyware." *New York Times*, November 3. https://www.nytimes.com/2021/11/03/business/nso-group-spyware-blacklist.html.

172 BIBLIOGRAPHY

Santos, Marcelo, Magdalena Saldaña, and Andrés Rosenberg. 2020. "From access deprivation to skill acquisition: cluster analysis of user behavior in face of a 12-hour legal blockage of WhatsApp in Brazil." *First Monday* 25(12). https://doi.org/10.5210/fm.v25i12.10401.

Schofield, Matthew. 2013. "Memories of Stasi color Germans' view of U.S. surveillance programs." *McClatchy*, washington DC. https://www.mcclatchydc.com/news/nation-world/national/article24750439.html.

Schrodt, Philip A. 2012. "Precedents, progress, and prospects in political event data." *International Interactions* 38(4):546–569.

Sehegal, Ujala. 2011. "Videos of killings emerge after Syria's Internet shutdown." *The Atlantic*, June 4. https://www.theatlantic.com/international/archive/2011/06/videos-killings-emerge-after-syrian-web-shut-down/351432/.

Sekar, Chandra C. and Edwards W. Deming. 1949. "On a method of estimating birth and death rates and the extent of registration." *Journal of the American Statistical Association* 44(245):101–115.

Sevom, Arseh. 2012. "Breaking and bending censorship with Walid Al-Saqaf." February 14. https://www.arsehsevom.org/en/2012/02/breaking-and-bending-censorship-with-walid-al-saqaf/.

SFLC.in. 2021. "India's shutdown numbers." https://internetshutdowns.in/.

Shapiro, Jacob N. and Nils B. Weidmann. 2015. "Is the phone mightier than the sword? Cell phones and insurgent violence in Iraq." *International Organization* 69(2): 24.

Shehabat, Ahmad. 2012. "The social media cyber-war: the unfolding events in the Syrian revolution 2011." *Global Media Journal: Australian Edition* 6(2). http://www.hca.westernsydney.edu.au/gmjau/archive/v6_2012_2/ahmad_shehabat%20_RA.html.

Sinpeng, Aim. 2020. "Digital media, political authoritarianism, and Internet controls in Southeast Asia." *Media, Culture & Society* 42(1):25–39.

Slim, Hugo. 2007. *Killing Civilians: Method, Madness, and Morality in War*. London: Hurst Publishers Ltd.

Solomon, Daina Beth. 2018. "Cyber attack on Mexico campaign site triggers election nerves." *Reuters*, June 13. https://www.reuters.com/article/uk-mexico-election-cyber/cyber-attack-on-mexico-campaign-site-triggers-election-nerves-idUKKBN1J93C0.

Sreberny, Annabelle and Gholam Khiabany. 2012. *Blogistan: The Internet and Politics in Iran*. London: I. B. Tauris.

Srivastava, Mehul. 2020. "NSO technology implicated in hacking of 36 Al Jazeera phones." *Financial Times*, December 21. https://www.ft.com/content/466b806b-e7cc-4693-9ccc-6d86ae76f008.

Stecklow, Steve. 2012. "Special report: Chinese firm helps Iran spy on citizens." *Reuters*, March 22. https://www.reuters.com/article/us-iran-telecoms/special-report-chinese-firm-helps-iran-spy-on-citizens-idUSBRE82L0B820120322.

Steele, Abbey. 2009. "Seeking safety: avoiding displacement and choosing destinations in civil wars." *Journal of Peace Research* 46(3):419–429.

Steele, Abbey. 2011. "Electing displacement: political cleansing in Apartadó, Colombia." *Journal of Conflict Resolution* 55(3):423–445.

Steinert-Threlkeld, Zachary C. 2017. "Spontaneous collective action: peripheral mobilization during the Arab Spring." *American Political Science Review* 111(2):379–403.

Steinert-Threlkeld, Zachary C., Delia Mocanu, Alessandro Vespignani, and James Fowler. 2015. "Online social networks and offline protest." *EPJ Data Science* 4(1):19.

BIBLIOGRAPHY   173

Stevenson, Alexandra. 2018. "Facebook admits it was used to incite violence in Myanmar." *New York Times*, November 6. https://www.nytimes.com/2018/11/06/technology/myanmar-facebook.html.

Stier, Sebastian. 2015. "Democracy, autocracy and the news: the impact of regime type on media freedom." *Democratization* 22(7):1273–1295.

Strzyżyńska, Weronika. 2022. "Iranian authorities plan to use facial recognition to enforce new hijab law." *The Guardian*, September 5. https://www.theguardian.com/global-development/2022/sep/05/iran-government-facial-recognition-technology-hijab-law-crackdown.

Stukal, Denis, Sergey Sanovich, Richard Bonneau, and Joshua A. Tucker. 2019. "Social media bots for autocrats: how pro-government bots fight opposition in Russia." Working Paper.

Stukal, Denis, Sergey Sanovich, Richard Bonneau, and Joshua A. Tucker. 2022. "Why botter: how pro-government bots fight opposition in Russia." *American Political Science Review* 116(3):843–857.

Sullivan, Christopher M. and Christian Davenport. 2018. "Resistance is mobile: dynamics of repression, challenger adaptation, and surveillance in US 'Red Squad' and black nationalist archives." *Journal of Peace Research* 55(2):175–189.

Sultan, Nabil. 2013. "Al Jazeera: reflections on the Arab Spring." *Journal of Arabian Studies* 3(2):249–264.

Syrian Network for Human Rights. 2013. "Syrian security branches and persons in charge." https://snhr.org/public_html/wp-content/pdf/english/Syrian_security_branches_and_Persons_in_charge_en.pdf.

Taye, Berhan. 2019. "The state of Internet shutdowns around the world." Access Now 2019 Report. https://www.accessnow.org/cms/assets/uploads/2019/07/KeepItOn-2018-Report.pdf.

Taye, Berhan. 2021. "Shattered dreams and lost opportunities: a year in the fight to #KeepItOn." Access Now 2020 Report. https://www.accessnow.org/cms/assets/uploads/2021/03/KeepItOn-report-on-the-2020-data_Mar-2021_3.pdf.

Tehran Times. 2018. "Much more bandwidth for Iranian messaging apps: ICT ministry." December 16. https://www.tehrantimes.com/news/430726/Much-more-bandwidth-for-Iranian-messaging-apps-ICT-ministry.

Telecomix. 2012. "Report of a Syrian spyware." February 21. http://bit.ly/2ydET5T.

The Carter Center. 2015. "Syria countrywide conflict report no. 5." February 28. https://www.cartercenter.org/resources/pdfs/peace/conflict_resolution/syria-conflict/NationwideUpdate-Feb-28-2015.pdf.

The Economist. 2013. "Syria's civil war—The bloody stalemate persists." May 11. https://www.economist.com/middle-east-and-africa/2013/05/11/the-bloody-stalemate-persists.

Theocharis, Yannis, Will Lowe, Jan W. van Deth, and Gema García-Albacete. 2015. "Using Twitter to mobilize protest action: online mobilization patterns and action repertoires in the Occupy Wall Street, Indignados, and Aganaktismenoi movements." *Information, Communication & Society* 18(2):202–220.

Todman, Will. 2017. "Isolating dissent, punishing the masses: siege warfare as counter-insurgency." https://research-repository.st-andrews.ac.uk/bitstream/handle/10023/10931/Todman_2017_SS_9-1_CCBY.pdf?sequence=1.

Trait, Robert. 2009. "Iran moves to silence opposition with internet crime unit." *The Guardian*, November 15. https://www.theguardian.com/world/2009/nov/15/iran-target-mousavi-internet-voice.

174 BIBLIOGRAPHY

Tsourapas, Gerasimos. 2021. "Global autocracies: strategies of transnational repression, l egitimation, and co-optation in world politics." *International Studies Review* 23(3): 616–644.

Tufekci, Zeynep. 2014. "The day the Turkish government banned itself from Twitter." *Medium: Technology and Society,* April 2. https://medium.com/technology-and-society/778b806e38e3.

Valentino, Benjamin A., Paul Huth, and Dylan Balch-Lindsay. 2004. "Draining the sea: mass killing and guerrilla warfare." *International Organization* 58(2):375–407.

Valeriano, Brandon and Ryan C. Maness. 2014. "The dynamics of cyber conflict between rival antagonists, 2001–11." *Journal of Peace Research* 51(3):347–360.

Van Beijnum, Ilijitsch. 2011. "How Egypt did (and your government could) shut down the Internet." *Ars Technica*, January 30. https://arstechnica.com/tech-policy/2011/01/how-egypt-or-how-your-government-could-shut-down-the-internet/.

Van Belle, Douglas A. 1997. "Press freedom and the democratic peace." *Journal of Peace Research* 34(4):405–414.

van Geuns, Suzanne and Corinne Cath-Speth. 2020. "How hate speech reveals the invisible politics of internet infrastructure." *Brookings*, August 20. https://www.brookings.edu/techstream/how-hate-speech-reveals-the-invisible-politics-of-internet-infrastructure/.

Vasilogambros, Matt. 2016. "Iran's own Internet." *The Atlantic*, August 29. https://www.theatlantic.com/news/archive/2016/08/irans-own-internet/497894/.

Wagner, Ben and Claudio Guarnieri. 2014. "German companies are selling unlicensed surveillance technologies to human rights violators—and making millions." *Global Voices Online*, September 5. http://globalvoicesonline.org/2014/09/05/exclusive-german-companies-are-selling-unlicensed-surveillance-technologies-to-human-rights-violators-and-making-millions/.

Walker, Kent. 2017. "Four steps we're taking today to fight terrorism online." Google in Europe, June 18. https://www.blog.google/around-the-globe/google-europe/four-steps-were-taking-today-fight-online-terror/.

Wang, Yaqiu. 2016. "The business of censorship: documents show how Weibo filters sensitive news in China." Committee to Protect Journalists Blog, March 3. https://cpj.org/blog/2016/03/the-business-of-censorship-documents-show-how-weib.php.

Wedeen, Lisa. 1999. *Ambiguities of Domination: Politics, Rhetoric, and Symbols in Contemporary Syria*. Chicago and London: University of Chicago Press.

Wedeen, Lisa. 2019. *Authoritarian Apprehensions: Ideology, Judgement, and Mourning in Syria*. Chicago and London: University of Chicago Press.

Wege, Carl Anthony. 1990. "Assad's legions: the Syrian intelligence services." *International Journal of Intelligence and CounterIntelligence* 4(1):91–100.

Weidmann, Nils B. 2016. "A closer look at reporting bias in conflict event data." *American Journal of Political Science* 60(1):206–218.

Weidmann, Nils B. and Espen Geelmuyden Rød. 2019. *The Internet and Political Protest in Autocracies*. New York: Oxford University Press.

Weidmann, Nils B., Suso Benitez-Baleato, Philipp Hunziker, Eduard Glatz, and Xenofontas Dimitropoulos. 2016. "Digital discrimination: political bias in Internet service provision across ethnic groups." *Science* 353(6304):1151–1155.

Whitten-Woodring, Jenifer. 2009. "Watchdog or lapdog? Media freedom, regime type, and government respect for human rights." *International Studies Quarterly* 53(3): 595–625.

Whitten-Woodring, Jenifer and Douglas A. Van Belle. 2017. "The correlates of media freedom: an introduction of the global media freedom dataset." *Political Science Research and Methods* 5(1):179–188.

Wood, Elisabeth J. 2010. "Sexual violence during war: variation and accountability". In *Collective Violence and International Criminal Justice*, ed. Alette Smeulers. Vol. 8. Antwerp: Intersentia, pp. 297–324.

Wood, Reed M. and Mark Gibney. 2010. "The Political Terror Scale (PTS): a re-introduction and a comparison to CIRI." *Human Rights Quarterly* 32(2):367–400.

World Bank. 2016. *World Development Report 2016: Digital Dividends*. Washington, DC: World Bank. https://elibrary.worldbank.org/doi/epdf/10.1596/978-1-4648-0671-1.

Wucherpfennig, Julian, Nils B. Weidmann, Luc Girardin, Lars-Erik Cederman, and Andreas Wimmer. 2011. "Politically relevant ethnic groups across space and time: introducing the GeoEPR dataset." *Conflict Management and Peace Science* 28(5): 423–437.

Xiao, Qiang. 2019. "The road to digital unfreedom: President Xi's surveillance state." *Journal of Democracy* 30(1):53–67.

Xu, Xu. 2021. "To repress or to co-opt? Authoritarian control in the age of digital surveillance." *American Journal of Political Science* 65(2):309–325.

Xynou, Maria and Arturo Filastò. 2018. "Iran protests: OONI data confirms censorship events (Part 1)." Technical report, January 5. https://ooni.org/post/2018-iran-protests/.

York, Jillian C. and Matthew Stender. 2016. "Facebook must stop pretending to be innocently neutral and start acting more like a media company." *Quartz*, December 5. https://qz.com/848405/can-facebook-ever-really-be-neutral/.

York, Jillian and Trevor Timm. 2012. "Satphones, Syria, and surveillance." Electronic Frontier Foundation, February 23. https://www.eff.org/deeplinks/2012/02/satphones-syria-and-surveillance.

York, Kyle. 2016. "Dyn statement on 10/21/2016 DDoS attack." Dyn Blog, October 21. http://dyn.com/blog/dyn-statement-on-10212016-ddos-attack/.

Youmans, William L. and Jillian C. York. 2012. "Social media and the activist toolkit: user agreements, corporate interests, and the information infrastructure of modern social movements." *Journal of Communication* 62(2):315–329.

Zeitzoff, Thomas. 2011. "Using social media to measure conflict dynamics: an application to the 2008–2009 Gaza conflict." *Journal of Conflict Resolution* 55(6):938–969.

Zuboff, Shoshana. 2019. *The Age of Surveillance Capitalism: The Fight for a Human Future at the New Frontier of Power*. New York: PublicAffairs.

Zuckerman, Ethan. 2010. "Yahoo!, Moniker: why is Mowjcamp.com still offline 6 weeks after hack attack?—Ethan Zuckerman." Technical report, February 2. https://ethanzuckerman.com/2010/02/01/yahoo-moniker-why-is-mowjcamp-com-still-offline-6-weeks-after-hack-attack/.

Zuckerman, Ethan. 2015. "Cute cats to the rescue? Participatory media and political expression." In *From Voice to Influence: Understanding Citizenship in a Digital Age*, ed. Danielle Allen and Jennifer Light. Chicago: University of Chicago Press.

Zuckerman, Ethan, Hal Roberts, Ryan McGrady, Jillian York, and John Palfrey. 2010. "Distributed denial of service attacks against independent media and human rights sites." Technical report, The Berkman Center for Internet & Society at Harvard University, December 20. https://cyber.harvard.edu/sites/cyber.law.harvard.edu/files/2010_DDoS_Attacks_Human_Rights_and_Media.pdf.

Index

Note: Page references followed by a "*t*" indicate table; "*f*" indicate figure.

Access Now 131
accountability
  digital documentation and 115
  violent repression and 8
Active Probing 132
Agha Soltan, Neda 114, 115, 124
Ahmadinejad, Mahmoud 113, 114
Amini, Mahsa Zhina 148
Amnesty International 14, 15, 83, 135,
  147, 154n12
anonymizing software 37
anticipation, online surveillance
  and 47–48
anti-Nazi Jewish resistance groups 148
application blocks 28–30
Arab Spring, Internet shutdowns
  during 23
Arab world, civilian uprisings in 1
armed groups
  as data source 71
  online surveillance of 99
  in Syria 65, 100, 106–10, 107*f*, 109*f*
Article 19 116–21, 147
Assad, Bashar al- 60, 62, 68
Assad, Hafiz al- 61, 65
autocracies
  Internet and 3
  Internet outages and 134*f*, 135
  online censorship and 4

Baidu 26
bandwidth throttling 25
Basij 122, 126
BBC Persia 125
blacklists 29
Blaydes, Lisa 23, 43, 54
blogs 18–20
  Iran and 113
  metadata and 35–36

Blogspot, Syria and 67
Blue Coat Systems 69
BGP. *See* Border Gateway Protocol
Border Gateway Protocol 22, 79, 132
botnets 21
El Bouchattaoui, Abdessadak 38
Branch 225 69
Brigden, Noelle 14
Brownlee, Billie J. 65
Bulgaria 42

CAIDA. *See* Center for Applied Internet
  Data Analysis
Cameroon 135
The Carter Center 104, 106
CCDOC. *See* Committee Charged with
  Determining Offensive Content
censorship
  backfiring 55–56
  constrained choices and 33
  content-level 20, 21*t*, 30–33
  domain-level 20, 21*t*, 25–30
  global 20
  harassment and threats for 31–32
  non-democratic states and 8
  self 31
  state-sanctioned violence and 6–7
  surveillance and lifting 67
  top-level 20, 21–25, 21*t*
  traditional 6, 51
censorship circumvention tools 13, 149
Center for Applied Internet Data Analysis
  (CAIDA) 121, 132
Center for Human Rights in Iran 125
China
  censorship strategies 32–33
  digital controls in 4, 144
  GitHub attack and 26
  hindering collective action in 53

178 INDEX

China (*continued*)
Instagram and 127
interception software from 117
Iran and 117–18
online censorship in 3
online surveillance systems 50
social media platforms in 32–33
Xinjian province 23
circumvention tools 117
citizen journalists 10, 68, 81
Citizen Lab 147
civil conflict 7
intelligence during 43
killing of non-armed citizens in 72
logic of violence in 57
online accessibility in 141
socially mediated 10
civil society
censorship event documentation by 131
digital controls circumvention by 128
digital space use by 64
social media and 145
Syrian conflict documentation by 94
closed autocracies, Internet outages and 134*f*, 135
Cloudflare 150, 153n3
CNN 115
coercive institutions 143
coercive strategy
online censorship implications 56–58
online surveillance implications 49–51
collective organization, online censorship hindering 52–54
commercial DoS protection 26
Committee Charged with Determining Offensive Content (CCDOC) 116, 119–20
Committee to Protect Journalists (CPJ) 81
concerted repression 81–83, 85, 86*t*
content filtering 28, 113
content-level censorship 20, 21*t*, 30–33
content monitoring 34–39
content removal requests or orders 32–33
control plane 154n6

covert surveillance 38
CPJ. *See* Committee to Protect Journalists
CSR-SY. *See* Syrian Center for Statistics and Research
cyber attacks 69
cybercafés, Iran regulation of 116
cyber controls 5, 40, 128, 130, 142
evidence of use 9–15
implications of domestic 144–46
interstate context 144–46
intrastate context 144
methodological approach for 12–15

Damascus, Syria 88, 100, 105
Damascus Center for Human Rights Studies (DCHRS) 72
Daraa, Syria 64–65, 67, 78
siege 64–65, 79, 88
Darknet traffic 132
DCHRS. *See* Damascus Center for Human Rights Studies
DDoS. *See* Distributed Denial of Service attacks
deep packet inspection (DPI) 29, 36, 117–18
Deibert, Ronald 23, 118
delisting 151n9
denial of service (DoS) 26
against human rights group websites 144
plausible deniability and 27
digital annexation 146
digital censorship
evading 126–28
non-democratic states and 8
digital controls 3, 4, 144
public opinion and 13
state-sanctioned violence and 6–7
digital curfews 3
digital development 2
digital documentation 114–15
digital exclusion strategies 23
digital fingerprints 148
digital forensics 148
digital monitoring software 67
digital politics
in Syria, following uprisings 67–70

in Syria, pre-conflict 62–64
digital repression 8
    methodological approach for 12–15
digital rights groups 125, 129, 131
digital surveillance
    exports of software for 146–47
    infrastructure 34
    lifting censorship enabling 67
    metadata and 35–36
    Syria use of 65, 68
Dimitrov, Martin K. 42
distraction 32
Distributed Denial of Service attacks
    (DDoS attacks) 20
    against GitHub 25
    Syria and 70
DNS. *See* Domain Name System
DNS blocking or redirection 29
documented violence 97
    Internet shutdowns and 87–94, 89*f*,
        90*f*, 91*t*, 92*t*
domain blocking
    domestic 28–30
    global 25–28
domain-level censorship 20, 21*t*,
    25–30
domain names 18–19
    Iran and 113
Domain Name System (DNS) 19, 21
    alternative 37
DoS. *See* denial of service
DPI. *See* deep packet inspection
drowning out content 32
Dyn 21

edge routers 153n3
e-government 119
Egloff, Florian J. 144
Egypt
    censorship backfiring in 55, 56
    infrastructure weaponization
        in 23
    Internet shutdowns in 19, 22, 23,
        54–55, 86, 151n5
electoral autocracies, Internet outages
    and 134*f*, 135
electoral democracies, Internet outages
    and 134*f*, 135

electoral processes, information from 41
Ethiopia 144
    Internet shutdowns in 23
Ethnic Power Relations Data 110, 137
Event API 132–33
external threats 8
    Syria and 10

Facebook 10, 25, 60, 150
    malware distribution and 69
    Messenger 24
    Syria and 67
FinFisher 39
Finkel, Evgeny 148
Free Syrian Army (FSA) 65–66, 88

Gabon, Internet curfews in 23
Gamma International Group 39
Galperin, Eva 69
GeoEPR Dataset 110
geolocation 35
German Democratic Republic 42, 141
Germany 39
GitHub 25, 26, 28
global censorship 20
Global Internet Routing 132
Golden Shield Project (GSP) 50
Google 33, 150, 151n9
    traffic disruption information from 131
Google Earth 54, 82
Google Maps 54, 82
Google Transparency Reports 87
greatfire.org 25
Green Movement 114, 115, 117
Greitens, Sheena Chestnut 8, 143
GSP. *See* Golden Shield Project

hacking 67, 144
    delegating 30
    of opposition accounts and
        media 27–28
    social media websites 30
Hama, Syria 78, 88
harassment 31–32, 144
hidden influencers 47
Hinnebusch, Raymond A. 10, 61
Holocaust 148
Hong Kong 144

180 INDEX

Howard, Philip N. 24, 131
HRDAG. *See* Human Rights Data
    Analysis Group
human rights
  non-democratic states and 8
  surveillance of defenders of 38
  Syria and 60
Human Rights Data Analysis Group
    (HRDAG) 14–15, 73, 151n2
Human Rights Watch 135

identification
  coercive strategy and 49
  Internet access and 37, 116
  intimidation and 48
  online surveillance and 46–47
India
  economic impact of Internet
    shutdowns in 56
  Internet restrictions in 3
  Internet shutdowns in 20, 23
informants 42–44
information
  during civil wars 43
  from electoral processes 41
  quality of 49–50, 98
  repression role of 41–45
  restricting exchange of 51–52
  sources of 41
  state security apparatuses and 41–42
information access
  democratization of 6
  Internet and 5–6
information cascade model 52
information control, for regime
    stability 60–62
infrastructure
  control of 146–47
  digital surveillance 34
  Iran 11–12, 11f, 116, 142
  monitoring 117–18
  online surveillance and 44
  of surveillance 5–6
  Syria 11–12, 11f
  Syria weaponization of 9–10
  weaponizing 23
  withholding 54–55
in-person surveillance 5

Instagram 25
  China and 127
interception software 117
internal threats 8
  Syria and 10
International Telecommunications Union
    (ITU) 63, 152n3
Internet
  alternatives for access to 149
  autocracies and 3
  connecting to 18–20
  debates around impact of 1–2
  filtering and blocking access to 6
  identifying information and access
    to 37
  information gathering and 5–6
  mass adoption of 1, 2f, 6
  protocol 18–22, 29
  slowdowns of 118
  state-ordered controls on access to 3
  Syria access to 62, 63, 100, 101f, 102
  Syria civil conflict and 10
Internet background radiation (IRB)
  132
Internet curfews 23
Internet of Things devices 21
Internet Outage Detection and Analysis
    Project (IODA) 121, 122f, 132,
    154n6
Internet outages 130
  measuring 131–33
  political institutions and 134–35, 134f
  state repression and 135–39, 138t, 139f
Internet Service Providers (ISPs) 19, 33
  access throttling 24
  DPI use by 29, 36
  Internet shutdown orders and 22
  mass surveillance and 36–37
  online controls and 149–50
  in Syria 69
  website blocking and 29–30
Internet shutdowns 20–24, 51, 130
  coercive strategy and 57
  concerted repression and 81–83, 85
  data on 87
  documented violence and 87–94, 89f,
    90f, 91t, 92t
  as early-warning systems 84

INDEX

evading censorship after 126–28
infrequency of 84
in Iran 115, 123–24, 129, 142, 148
ISPs and 19
measuring 13
methods for 22
narrative control and 124–26
opposition capability depletion
  with 54
repressive implications of 85–87
reputation saving and 83–84, 86t
slowing access as 24–25
in Syria 22–23, 78–81, 87, 89f, 90f, 91t,
  92t, 142
underreporting during 94–96
understanding full 81–87
violent repression and 85–86, 86t
Internet surveillance 34
intimidation
  mass repression and, in Iran 121–24
  online surveillance and 48–49
IODA. See Internet Outage Detection and
  Analysis Project
IP. See Internet Protocol
IP address 18–19, 21, 151n2
  DNS blocking and 29
  target identification and 46
Iran 9
  blogs in 113
  China and 117–18
  elections and protests of 2009
    114–15
  evading censorship after Internet
    shutdown in 126–28
  feminist movement in 147
  Internet infrastructure in 11–12, 11f,
    116, 142
  Internet shutdowns in 115, 123–24,
    129, 142, 148
  Internet traffic in 121, 122f
  intranet in 121
  journalists in 125
  mass repression and intimidation
    in 121–24
  measuring state repression in 13
  monitoring infrastructure 117–18
  narrative control in 124–26
  online controls after 2009 115–20

phishing attacks and 116
protests and Internet shutdown of
  November 2019 120–28
security forces in 120–23
Tor usage in 118, 126, 127, 127f, 128f
Iranian Cyber Army 28
Iraq 42–43
IRB. See Internet background radiation
Islamic State 107–8, 107f
ISPs. See Internet Service Providers
ITU. See International
  Telecommunications Union

Al-Jazeera 38, 67, 68, 88
Justice for Iran 125–126

Kashmir, Internet shutdowns in 23
Kerr, Jaclyn 29
Kerry, John 79
keyword filtering 29
Khirbet Hazale, Syria 79
Khomeini (Ayatollah) 122, 129
Kurds 107–8, 107f
Kyrgyzstan 27

Lantern 126, 128
Lavrov, Sergei 79
lawful interception management system
  (LIMS) 63
liberal democracies, Internet outages
  and 134f, 135
LIMS. See lawful interception
  management system
location-based services 82
Lohmann, Susanne 52

Maidan Nezaleshnosti protests 48
Makhluf, Rami 62
malicious software
  DPI and injecting 29
  filtering for 19–20
  remote control access through 38
man-in-the-middle attacks 69
mass repression 121–24
mass surveillance 36–39, 46
media
  censorship of 6
  social media and international 68

182 INDEX

media (*continued*)
  state run 68
  Syria regulation of 60
metadata monitoring 35–36
Mexico, DDoS attacks in 27
MICT. *See* Ministry of Communications
  and Information Technology
militias, plausible deniability and use of 30
Ministry of Communications and
  Information Technology
  (MICT) 118, 119
Ministry of Islamic Culture and
  Guidance 113
mobile phone accessibility 100, 101*f*,
  153n2
monitoring content and people 34–39
  metadata and 35–36
Monjib, Maati 38
multi-recapture estimation 13, 94
Muslim Brotherhood 61
Myanmar 20
  Internet restrictions in 3
  Internet shutdowns in 23
  social media platforms and 24

National Action party 27
National Information Network
  (NIN) 116–19, 121
National Security Agency 141
National Security Bureau (NSB) 88
national security laws, mass surveillance
  and 37
Netblocks 131
network analysis 36
network disruptions 142
  data sources on 131
network layers 151n4
NIN. *See* National Information Network
Nokia Siemens Networks 114
Northern Ireland 153n4
NSB. *See* National Security Bureau
NSO group 4, 38–39

offline repression 31–32
online banking services 119
online censorship 6, 144
  autocracies and 4
  backfiring 55–56

coercive strategy implications 56–58
collective organization and 52–54
evading 126–28
forms of 20, 21*t*
logic of 51–58
opposition capability depletion
  with 54
supportive role of 145
withholding infrastructure as 54–55
online controls 3–5
  as double-edged sword 44–45
  Iran and 114
  Iran ramp-up after 2009 of 115–20
  private companies' role in 149–50
  scope conditions 7–9
  state choices in 40
  in Syria 63, 141
  trade-offs in 45
online harassment and threats 31–32
  expanding spheres of influence
    through 144
online information operations 1
  content removal requests or
    orders 32–33
  distraction and drowning out
    content 32
  harassment and threats 31–32
online monitoring 143, 148
online propaganda 145
online repression, resistance to 147–49
online restrictions 3
online surveillance 5, 6, 58
  anticipation and 47–48
  coercive strategy implications of
    49–51
  identification and 46–47
  information quality and 49–50
  infrastructure and 44
  intimidation and 48–49
  logic of 46–51
  observable implications of 99–100
  supportive role of 145
  usefulness of 98–100
OONI. *See* Open Observatory of Network
  Interference
Open Net initiative 26, 113
Open Observatory of Network
  Interference (OONI) 131, 154n3

panopticon 48
Pegasus 4
phishing attacks 69, 116
physical integrity rights 135, 142
physical network attacks 22
plausible deniability
   DoS attacks and 27
   website blocking and 30
political institutions, Internet outages
      and 134–35, 134f
Political Terror Scale (PTS) 13, 135, 136,
      154n12
political violence, challenges to
      studying 71
Privacy International 63
pro-government militias, in Syria 66
propaganda 145
provisional IRA 153n4
proxy servers 114
Psiphon 126, 128
PTS. *See* Political Terror Scale

quantitative text analysis 13

Rahimi, Babak 113
Rahimpour, Rana 125
RATs. *See* Remote Access Tools
regime stability
   external and internal threats to 8
   information control for 60–62
Remote Access Tools (RATs) 69
remote control access 38
Reporters Without Borders 63
repression
   censorship and 6–7
   coding for 135–36
   defining 40–41
   digital 8
   forms of 40–41
   harassment and threats for 31–32
   implications of tech-supported 143–47
   information role in 41–45
   Internet shutdowns and
      concerted 81–83, 85
   Internet shutdowns implications
      for 85–87
   measuring, in Syria 102–5
   online surveillance and 6–7

operationalizing 71–72
resistance to online 147–49
in Syria, data and measurement
   for 70–77
Syria strategy for 10
Syria uprising of 2011 and 64–67
targeted 41
transnational 144
underreporting during Internet
   shutdowns 94–96
repression technology, in Syria 9–11
reputation saving 83–84, 86t
resister's toolkit 148
Revolutionary Guards 122
right to be forgotten 151n9
Roberts, Molly 3, 127
Roskomnadzor 29
Rouhani, Hassan 120, 125
Russia
   digital controls in 4
   digital infrastructure and 146
   website blacklist 29

satellite communications 82–83
Saudi Arabia 39
Sassoon, Joseph 42
SCC. *See* Supreme Council of Cyberspace
SCMP. *See* Syria Conflict Mapping Project
SDSM. *See* Syria Digital Security Monitor
secret service 12, 42, 141
sectarian divides, purposefully
      engineered 65
Secure Computing 113
self-censorship 31, 63
self-defense committees 66
Shabiha 66
Shawkat, Assef 88
Shires, James 144
SHOMA 121
Signal 25
signals intelligence 82
Sina Weibo 32
Skype 11
SmartFilter software 113
SNHR. *See* Syrian Network for Human
      Rights
Snowden, Edward 141
social control 48

184 INDEX

social engineering 38
social media
    anticipation and 47
    civil society and 145
    hidden influencers and 47
    metadata and 35–36
    network analysis and 36
    surveillance through 38, 67, 68
    Syria allowing 67
    Syria civil conflict and 10
social media platforms 1
    in China 32–33
    content-level censorship and 30–31
    content removal requests and 32–33
    Myanmar and 24
    Syria and 60
societal monitoring 48
Soroush 120
spyware 38, 48
State of Emergency Law (Syria)
    60, 62
state repression 7–8
    coding for 135–36
    defining 40
    information role in 41–45
    Internet outages and 135–39, 138t,
        139f
    measuring 13
    operationalizing 71–72
    suppression of evidence of 124–26
state run media 68
state-sanctioned violence 136
state security apparatuses, information
    and 41–42
Stuxnet 117
Supreme Council of Cyberspace
    (SCC) 116, 119
surveillance
    covert 38
    informant networks and 42
    infrastructure of 5–6
    mass 36–39
    modern technologies for 34
    social movements and 148
    state-sanctioned violence and 6–7
    targeted 35, 36–39
surveillance software, exports of 146
surveillance technology 4

Syria
    atrocity cover-ups in 83
    Ba'ath coup in 60
    censorship circumvention technology
        in 149
    cyber controls and repression in 77t
    data and measurement for repression
        in 70–77
    DDoS attacks and 70
    digital politics following
        uprisings 67–70
    digital politics pre-conflict 62–64
    documented violence in 87–94, 89f,
        90f, 91t, 92t, 97
    indiscriminate killings in 153n4
    intelligence services in 61
    Internet access in 62, 63, 152n3
    Internet infrastructure in 11–12, 11f
    Internet shutdowns in 22–23, 78–81,
        87, 89f, 90f, 91t, 92t, 142
    ISPs in 69
    journalists in 81
    measuring repression strategy 102–5
    measuring state repression in 13, 14
    media and telecommunications
        regulation in 60
    military forces 66
    online controls in 63, 141
    opposition group communications in 82
    pro-government militias in 66
    record-linkage for 73–76, 74f
    regional armed group control
        in 106–10, 107f, 109f
    regional ethnic group presence
        in 110–11, 111f
    regional Internet accessibility in 100,
        101f, 102
    repression technology in 9–11
    repressive strategy of 10
    security sector 66, 68, 80
    social media platforms and 60
    state run media in 68
    subnational evidence for 105–11
    underreporting during Internet
        shutdowns in 94–96
    uprising of 2011 and repression 64–67
Syria Conflict Mapping Project
    (SCMP) 106

INDEX   185

Syria Digital Security Monitor (SDSM) 100, 153n2
Syrian Arab Armed Forces 66
Syrian Center for Statistics and Research (CSR-SY) 72
Syrian Electronic Army 10, 27, 68
Syrian Network for Human Rights (SNHR) 72
Syrian Observatory of Human Rights 105
Syrian Telecommunications Establishment (STE) 12, 62, 63, 69, 153n3
Syriatel 62

Tanzania 31–32
targeted killings 102–5, 103*f*
    Internet accessibility and 109, 109*f*
    type of region control and 108–9, 108*f*
targeted repression 41
    subnational evidence of 105–11
targeted surveillance 35, 36–39
telecommunications, Syria regulation of 60
Telegram 11, 20, 25, 56, 117, 119, 120
throttling 24–25
Tigray region 23
Togo 39
top-level censorship 20, 21–25, 21*t*
Tor network 37, 118, 126–28, 128*f*, 149
transnational repression 144
Turkey
    censorship in 55
    Internet restrictions in 3
    Twitter ban in 29–30
Twitter 1, 3, 10, 11, 25, 120
    content removal requests to 32
    Iranian Cyber Army attack on 28
    Turkey ban of 29–30

UCSD Network Telescope 132
Ukraine 146
UN Human Rights Council 66
Uniform Resource Locator (URL) 18, 22
    website blocking and 29
United Arab Emirates 39
United Kingdom 39
UN Office of the High Commissioner for Human Rights 34, 37, 66–67, 152n4

unreported violence, accounting for 75–76
untargeted killings 103–4, 103*f*
URL. *See* Uniform Resource Locator
US State Department 135, 154n12

Vaezi, Mahmoud 119
Varieties of Democracy Project 134, 137
VDC. *See* Violation Documentation Centre
V-Dem. *See* Varieties of Democracy Project
Venezuela 135
Violation Documentation Centre (VDC) 72
violent repression
    democratic states and 8
    Internet accessibility and 106*t*
    Internet shutdowns and 85–86, 86*t*
    in Iran 121–24
    non-democratic states and 8
    subnational evidence of 105–11
virtual private networks 37
Vodafone 19
VPNs 64, 117, 118

war crimes, Internet shutdowns and covering up 85
war on terror 34
website blocking
    domestic 28–30
    global 25–28
    human rights groups targeted by 144
    measuring 131
    plausible deniability and 30
websites 18–20
    Iran and 113
    social movements and 147
WhatsApp 11, 30, 56, 117, 119
World Wide Web
    Iran controls and 116–17, 119
    Iran cut off from 121, 126

Xinjian province 23
Xu, Xu 50

YouTube 10, 60
    Syria and 67
YPG 107

Printed in the USA/Agawam, MA
May 3, 2024

865425.013